AF322718

The Messiah of the Targums

The Messiah of the Targums

Messianic Exegesis of the Hebrew Bible

MICHAEL B. SHEPHERD

WIPF & STOCK · Eugene, Oregon

THE MESSIAH OF THE TARGUMS
Messianic Exegesis of the Hebrew Bible

Wipf & Stock
An Imprint of Wipf and Stock Publishers
199 W. 8th Ave., Suite 3
Eugene, OR 97401

www.wipfandstock.com

PAPERBACK ISBN: 979-8-3852-0425-0
HARDCOVER ISBN: 979-8-3852-0426-7
EBOOK ISBN: 979-8-3852-0427-4

Dedicated to my wife Esther and to my daughters
Abbi, Anna, Audrey, and Ava

Table of Contents

Abbreviations

BDB	The Brown-Driver-Briggs Hebrew and English Lexicon
Frg. Tg.	Fragmentary Targum
GKC	Gesenius' Hebrew Grammar
LXX	Septuagint
MT	Masoretic Text
SP	Samaritan Pentateuch
Syr.	Syriac Peshitta
Tg. Jon.	Targum Jonathan
Tg. Neof.	Targum Neofiti
Tg. Onq.	Targum Onqelos
Tg. Ps.-J.	Targum Pseudo-Jonathan

Introduction

Samson Levey published his work on the messianic exegesis of the Targum entitled *The Messiah: An Aramaic Interpretation* in 1974. Levey's monograph draws eight conclusions from the study.[1] The first is that messianic interpretations in the Targums are somewhat sparse. Levey suggests that this may be either because the official Targums stem from Maccabean times or because they were redacted in Babylon. The second conclusion is that messianic interpretations in the Targums vary in detail, depending upon a variety of factors. Nevertheless, Levey's third conclusion is that it is possible to delineate a portrait of the Messiah in the Targums:

> The Messiah will be the symbol and/or the active agent of the deliverance of Israel. He will be of Davidic lineage, though he may have a non-Davidic predecessor, the Ephraimite Messiah, who will die in battle. Elijah will herald his coming and will serve as his High Priest. A world conflict will rage between Rome, variously identified with Gog, Amalek, Edom, and Armilus, on the one hand, and Assyria or Eber, on the other, indicating that to the Targumist, Assyria and not Babylon was the real enemy of Israel, and this will result in the annihilation of both at the time of the Messianic advent; the enemies of Israel will be shattered either by divine or Messianic intervention. The Messiah will bring an end to the wandering of Israel, and the Jewish people will be gathered in from their Dispersion to their own land. The Northern Kingdom will be re-united with Judah. The drama of the Exodus from Egypt will be re-enacted; in this drama Moses may participate, made possible by a resurrection of the dead. The Messiah will live eternally. He will restore the Temple and rebuild Jerusalem, which will enjoy divine protection for itself and its inhabitants. He will have sovereignty over all the world and make the Torah the universal

1. Levey, *Messiah*, 142–44.

law of mankind, with the ideal of education being realized to the
full. The Messiah will have the gift of prophecy, and may have
intercessory power to seek forgiveness of sin, but he will punish
the unrepenting wicked of his people, as well as of the nations,
and have the power to cast them into Gehenna. There will be a
moral regeneration of Israel and of mankind. The Messiah will be
a righteous judge, dispensing justice and equity, the champion of
the poor and the oppressed, the personification of social justice.
He will reward the righteous, who will surround him and eternally
enjoy the divine effulgence. The essence of the Messiah will be
faith in God; and he will vindicate that faith, and the faithfulness
of Israel, in the eyes of all the world.

The fourth conclusion is that the messianism of the Targums is rabbinic
messianism for the most part, but the Targums can also be remarkably
independent of other rabbinic sources. The fifth is that the Targums have
a varied relationship with other early versions. There is little evidence of direct dependence of the Targums on the Septuagint, although there are areas
of overlap where the two interpret the Hebrew text messianically,[2] but there
is evidence that the Latin Vulgate depends upon messianic interpretations
found in the Targums.[3] Levey's sixth conclusion is that the messianic material of the Targums has been faithfully transmitted, resisting the temptation
to add messianic material where expected or to delete it where it might
not be aligned with mainstream Jewish exegesis. The seventh conclusion
is that the Targum's sensitive rendering of the messianic passages in Isaiah
support the contention that "the architects of Jewish Messianism are the
prophet Isaiah and his disciples, and that the historical event which precipi-
tated it was the Assyrian crisis." Levey's eighth and final conclusion is that
some messianic interpretations in Targum Jonathan indicate that its final
date must be subsequent to the Arab conquest.

The field of Targum studies owes a great debt of gratitude to Levey's
work, and it is upon Levey's work that the present volume seeks to build.
The distinctive contribution of the present study is first and foremost to
show that the sparseness of messianic material in the Targums is not due to
their temporal or geographical setting but to the nature of the material in
the Hebrew Bible itself. The messianism of the Hebrew Bible does not come
in high quantity. Rather, it is qualitative and strategic, and this is reflected

2. The Syriac Peshitta also parallels the Targum occasionally.

3. Levey demonstrates the influence of the Targum on Christian exegesis throughout
his study.

in the Targum renderings.[4] What this means is that the Targums often have good exegetical warrant for their messianic interpretations. If the Targums were simply importing messianism into the Bible, then the reader would expect to find much more of it. The restraint of the Targums in this regard comes from their source text. As noted by William Horbury, the composite portrait of the Messiah that emerges in the Targums is not one created by the Targums but one dictated by the Hebrew Bible:

> Yet although the lengthy development of messianism *from* the Old Testament is obvious, not least when the influence of messianic prototypes is considered, it has also become clear that messianism is important *within* the Old Testament. It flourished especially in the period of the collecting and editing of the books, it deeply influenced the ancient versions, notably the Septuagint and the Targums, but within the corpus of Hebrew scriptures it was integrally linked with the future hopes which form a great theme both of the Pentateuch and of the Prophets, and from the inception of Davidic monarchy and the Israelite capture of Jerusalem it was bound up with the traditions of kingship in Zion.[5]

If this thesis is correct, then messianism does not begin with the book of Isaiah and the Assyrian crisis but with the book of Moses and the sin problem introduced in the opening chapters of Genesis. The messianism of the Pentateuch then finds its way into the Prophets and the Writings via the covenant with David. Such dependence upon the Hebrew Bible explains why the Targums are sometimes independent of other rabbinic sources with which they would normally be expected to agree. Exegetical fidelity, rather than rabbinic tradition, is determining the course of the renderings in many cases. This would also explain why the Targums sometimes

4. It is worth noting here that the word משיח ("anointed one") as the technical term ("Messiah") only occurs twice in the Hebrew Bible (Dan 9:25, 26). Likewise, Μεσσίας ("Messiah") as opposed to Χριστός ("Christ") only appears twice in the Greek New Testament (John 1:41; 4:25). Postbiblical interpretation employs the term "Messiah" much more broadly to cover a range of titles and descriptions.

5. Horbury, *Jewish Messianism*, 35. Even prior to their knowledge of his resurrection, Jesus rebuked his followers for being slow to believe what the prophets spoke about the suffering of the Christ and his entrance into glory. He thus explained to them from Moses and the Prophets all the things about himself in the Scriptures (Luke 24:25–27; see also vv. 44–47). This presupposes that the messianism of the Hebrew Bible was there to be understood without any special hermeneutical key. The evidence of this can be seen both in the innerbiblical readings of messianic passages and in the earliest postbiblical history of interpretation known from the ancient versions, the apocrypha and pseudepigrapha, and the Dead Sea Scrolls.

uniquely agree with messianic interpretations found in the New Testament documents—non-rabbinic texts with which readers might not necessarily expect the Targums to align. While there may be cases where New Testament authors depend upon oral or written Targum renderings or upon exegetical traditions now represented by the Targums, it is also true that these strange bedfellows are in some cases coming to the same conclusions about the meaning of texts in the Hebrew Bible because the Hebrew Bible itself presses them to make those conclusions independently.[6]

The present volume will proceed systematically through the threefold arrangement of the Hebrew canon—Pentateuch, Prophets, and Writings—and discuss each of the messianic renderings of the Targums.[7] In addition to the electronic versions of the Targums provided by the Comprehensive Aramaic Lexicon (Hebrew Union College) in Accordance, the following study will consult Alexander Sperber's edition of Targum Onqelos, Targum Jonathan, and the Targums of the Writings.[8] For Targums Neofiti and Pseudo-Jonathan, the editions by Alejandro Díez Macho (Neofiti) and E. G. Clarke (Pseudo-Jonathan) will also be consulted.[9] The critically annotated translations of the Targums in The Aramaic Bible series published by The Liturgical Press will additionally be important conversation partners.

Each treatment of the messianic interpretations found in the Targums will discuss the Hebrew texts and contexts upon which they are based. This will primarily involve the proto-Masoretic Text (the traditional rabbinic text), but other Hebrew witnesses such as the Dead Sea Scrolls will prove to be valuable resources. The discussion will also include interaction with relevant early versions in Greek, Syriac, and Latin as well as early Christian literature and rabbinic literature. The final chapter will explore the reception

6. "It is highly unlikely that Judaism after the first century AD produced such a rash of messianic renderings that coincided with the very texts that formed the heart of Christian exegesis. Perhaps the NT authors were influenced in some way by targumic renderings, but some measure of independence has to be allowed. The solution probably lies somewhere between these two options. In any case, the exegetical work of these separate corpora highlights the messianic theology of the Hebrew Bible itself" (Shepherd, "Targums, the New Testament," 57). See also Shepherd, "Targums," 931–34.

7. This volume does not pretend to be a general introduction to the literature of the Targums. There is neither the need nor the space for such. Good introductions may be found in Alexander, "Jewish Aramaic Translations," 217–53; Flesher, "Targumim," 611–29; Levine, "Targums," 323–31; Flesher and Chilton, *Targums*. See also Samely, *Interpretation of Speech*.

8. Sperber, *Bible in Aramaic*.

9. Macho, *Neophyti 1*; Clarke, *Targum Pseudo-Jonathan of the Pentateuch*.

of the Messiah of the Targums by two prominent medieval rabbis, Rabbi Solomon ben Isaac ("Rashi") and Rabbi David Kimchi ("Redak"), whose views about messianism and eschatology are considerably different from one another. Their influence via the early Christian Hebraists is still felt today.

The precise origins and interrelationships of the Targums are still largely unknown. Targums Onqelos, Neofiti, and Jonathan were likely completed during the first half of the first millennium CE, but the exegetical tradition that they represent reaches back to a much earlier time than the date of their final form, thus requiring a case-by-case assessment of individual renderings. Likewise, Pseudo-Jonathan and the Targums of the Writings were not finalized until the early medieval period, but the oral and written traditions that went into their making were developed over centuries. The Targums were not translations of the Bible for Aramaic-speaking people who no longer understood Hebrew. Rather, they were guides to the interpretation of the Hebrew text for those who could read the Hebrew text.[10] In contrast to other early forms of biblical commentary, the Targums present their interpretation of the Hebrew text in the form and sequence of the Bible itself, inserting their interpretation directly into the base text that they are interpreting. The present volume respects this tradition by organizing the material canonically rather than topically.

10. See Shepherd, "Targums as Guides to Hebrew Syntax," 49–59.

1

The Messiah in the Pentateuch

GENESIS

Tg. Neof. Gen 1:1

Levey's treatment of messianic renderings in the Targums of the Pentateuch begins with Gen 3:15 because it is the first text for which the term משיחא ("Messiah") is used (see Tg. Ps.-J., Frg. Tg.), but there is one Targum rendering earlier in Genesis that should be taken into consideration, even though the text of this Targum is disputed. Díez Macho's printed text of Tg. Neof. Gen 1:1 reads as follows: מלקדמין בחכמה ברא דייי שכלל ית שמיא וית ארעא ("From the beginning, with wisdom, the Son of the Lord completed the sky and the land"). It has been argued, however, that this extant text is the result of manipulation of a more original text: מלקדמין בחכמה ברא ייי ושכלל ית שמיא וית ארעא ("From the beginning, with wisdom, the Lord created and completed the sky and the land"; cf. Frg. Tg.).[1] According to this view, the word ברא is not the Aramaic word for "Son" (בר) plus a suffixed definite article (א) but the verb ברא ("created"). Furthermore, the following word should be ייי ("the Lord") rather than דייי ("of the Lord"), and what appears in the manuscript to be an erased conjunction ו ("and")

---

1. See Cargill, "Rule of Creative Completion," 90–188. McNamara (*Targum Neofiti 1: Genesis*, 52) suggests restoring the phrase "the Memra of the Lord." See also Tg. Neof. Deut 32:6.

before שכלל ("completed") should be restored. The contention is that the extant text of Neofiti is due to Christian tampering.[2]

There are several problems with the reconstruction proposed here. The first is that the divine name in Neofiti is normally represented by three letters (ייי) rather than four (יייי). The second is that restoration of the erased conjunction ו ("and") before the verb שכלל ("completed") would leave no space in the manuscript between the divine name and what follows it. Thus, it seems that the original text had no conjunction. It was added secondarily. The erasure is a correction intended to restore the original reading.[3] Last but not least, the idea that the extant text of Neofiti is the result of Christian tampering is problematic because there is no other evidence of such tampering anywhere else in the manuscript. Is it plausible that someone would create a distinctively Christian rendering of Gen 1:1 and then leave the remainder of the manuscript untouched? It seems best to accept the text that we have (i.e., the extant text) rather than the text that we do not have (i.e., a hypothetical reconstruction). This forces the reader to think about the possibility of a pre-Christian Jewish interpretation of Gen 1:1 that understands "the Son of Lord" to be the one who from the beginning completed the sky and the land with wisdom.

The idea that God created the world with wisdom is quite prominent in biblical creation theology (see Jer 10:12; 51:15; Ps 104:24; Prov 3:19), but the primary passage through which this interpretation of Gen 1:1 appears to be mediated to Tg. Neof. is Prov 8:22–31. The purpose of the book of Proverbs is to know wisdom (Prov 1:2). Prov 8 is the third and climactic wisdom poem in Prov 1–9 (see also Prov 1:20–33; 3:13–20). These poems personify wisdom as a woman and serve to punctuate the father's addresses to the son in which he commends to him lady wisdom (which leads to life) over against lady folly (which leads to death; see the epilogue in Prov 9).[4]

The opening line of Prov 8:22 features exegesis of the word ראשית ("beginning") in Gen 1:1: יהוה קנני ראשית דרכו. The ESV translates, "The LORD possessed me at the beginning of his work" (cf. Vulg., Luther). The LXX, Syriac Peshitta, and Targum understand the verb קנני to mean

---

2. Targum Neofiti was discovered in the mid-twentieth century by Díez Macho in the Vatican library miscataloged as a manuscript copy of Targum Onqelos. It is a sixteenth-century manuscript copy of a Palestinian Targum whose origins go back to at least the first half of the first millennium CE.

3. This is suggested by Sailhamer, *Introduction to Old Testament Theology*, 222n61.

4. Wisdom is personified as a woman because the grammatical gender of the Hebrew noun חכמה ("wisdom") is feminine.

"created me" rather than "possessed me." The root קנה, however, can also mean "bring forth in childbirth" (e.g., Gen 4:1) or "beget" (e.g., Deut 32:6). This is the way the NAB translates Prov 8:22: "The LORD begot me, the firstborn of his ways." Such a translation is contextually suitable due to the two occurrences of חוללתי ("I was brought forth in childbirth") in Prov 8:24–25. The NAB is also notable for its translation of the phrase ראשית דרכו ("the firstborn of his ways"). Other versions (e.g., Syr., Tg., Luther, ESV) supply a preposition ("at") at the beginning of this phrase, but no such preposition occurs in the Hebrew source text. The NAB thus identifies wisdom as the ראשית (cf. NET), which it interprets to mean "firstborn" rather than "beginning" (see Gen 49:3; Deut 21:17; Pss 78:51; 105:36).

It is easy to see how this understanding of Prov 8:22 has surfaced in Neofiti's version of Gen 1:1. The phrase בראשית from Gen 1:1 has first been interpreted in its temporal sense as מלקדמין ("From the beginning"). Then the same phrase is reinterpreted as בחכמה ("with wisdom") based on the identification of wisdom as the ראשית in Prov 8:22. Finally, Neofiti takes the opportunity afforded by the verb ברא ("created") in Gen 1:1 to introduce its understanding of ראשית as "firstborn son." The verb ברא ("created") becomes the definite Aramaic noun ברא ("the son"), and the combination ברא אלהים ("God created") becomes ברא דייי ("the Son of the Lord"), which requires Neofiti to supply another verb שכלל ("completed").

The text of Prov 8:22–31 goes on to say that wisdom was the agent of creation ("a craftsman" [אמון]) whose delight was in the crowning act of creation, namely, the creation of humanity (Prov 8:30–31; see Gen 1:26–28). The latter end of the book of Proverbs echoes the language of Prov 8:22–31 in the words of Agur: "Who has gone up to heaven and come down? Who has gathered wind in his fists? Who has bound water in his cloak? Who has established all the ends of the earth? What is his name, and what is the name of his son, if you know" (Prov 30:4; cf. John 3:13)? The answer to the question—"What is his name?"—is simple enough. The LORD is the one who has established all the ends of the earth (see Prov 3:19). As for the next question—"What is the name of his son?"—it is sometimes suggested that an appeal should be made to Exod 4:22 to identify Israel as the LORD's firstborn son,[5] but this is an appeal to a text outside the book of Proverbs and does not take into account the clues within the book itself.

The early Jewish interpretation found in Sir 24 identifies wisdom in Prov 8:22–31 with Torah (see Deut 4:6, 8; see also Ps 19:9; cf. Prov 1:7; 9:10;

---

5. E.g., Waltke, "Agur's Apologia," 310.

Job 28:28). According to Gen. Rab. 1:1, God created the world by means of the Torah:

> In human practice, when a mortal king builds a palace, he builds it not with his own skill but with the skill of an architect. The architect moreover does not build it out of his head, but employs plans and diagrams to know how to arrange the chambers and the wicket doors. Thus God consulted the Torah and created the world.[6]

This may very well be connected to the idea that God created by means of his word (Ps 33:6; see Gen 1:3, 6, 9, 11, 14, 20, 24, 26). On the other hand, early Christian interpretation understood Christ to be the embodiment of wisdom (see, e.g., Matt 11:19; 1 Cor 1:24, 30). Indeed, the hymn in Col 1:15–20 makes explicit use of Prov 8:22–31 in its description of Christ: Christ is the "firstborn" of all creation (Col 1:15; cf. Prov 8:22, 24, 25); by means of him all things were created (Col 1:16; cf. Prov 8:30; see also 1 Cor 8:6); and he is the "beginning" (ἀρχή; Col 1:18; cf. LXX Prov 8:22; see also Rev 3:14).

The prologue to John's Gospel appears to combine the idea that God created by means of his word/Torah and the idea that he created by means of Christ. Its opening clause deliberately alludes to Gen 1:1: Ἐν ἀρχῇ ἦν ὁ λόγος ("In the beginning was the Word"; cf. LXX Gen 1:1). The Word was with God, and the Word was God (John 1:1). All things came through the Word (John 1:3). The Word became flesh and dwelt among us, and we beheld his glory (John 1:14). This combination of language comes from the tradition of the Targums.[7] The terms "Word" (ממרא), "Dwelling Presence" (שכינתא), and "Glory" (יקרא) are common substitutes for the divine name in the Targums. Of course, this language of the Targums was not intended to speak of the second person of the Trinity as in Christian theology, but it became a convenient way for John to express his understanding of the relationship of the Word to the Father.

---

6. Freedman, *Midrash Rabbah*, 1.

7. See McNamara, *Targum and Testament Revisited*, 146–66; Evans, *Word and Glory*; Anderson, "Interpretation of Genesis 1:1," 21–29.

Gen 3:15

Several of the messianic renderings of the Targums for the Pentateuch come from the major poetic units of the book (Gen 3:15; 49:1, 10–12, 18; Exod 15:18; Num 23:21; 24:7, 17, 20, 24; Deut 33:5). John Sailhamer has shown that the poems of the Pentateuch (Gen 3:14–19; 49:1–27; Exod 15:1–18; Num 23–24; Deut 32–33) employ major characters on the author's behalf (God, Jacob, Moses, and Balaam) to interpret the narratives that they accompany (Gen 1–11; 12–50; Exod 1–19; Num 11–36; Deut) in an eschatological (Gen 49:1; Num 24:14; Deut 31:29) and messianic (Gen 3:15; 49:8–12; Exod 15:18; Num 24:7–9, 17; Deut 33:5, 7, 20) fashion.[8] The design of these poems is such that they not only are connected with their respective narratives but also are integrally linked to one another. This macrostructural strategy of the Pentateuch's Hebrew text has prompted the messianic interpretations of the Targums. The composer has opted not to litter the book with constant messianic references. Rather, he has chosen to display such references in the most prominent places at the highest level of the book's composition, and the Targums have followed suit.

The text of Gen 3:14–19 consists of divine addresses to the serpent (Gen 3:14–15), the woman (Gen 3:16), and the man (Gen 3:17–19) after the shifting of blame in the previous narrative from the man to the woman and to the serpent (Gen 3:12–13). These addresses concern the curse of the serpent (Gen 3:14) and the curse of the ground (Gen 3:17) that come as a result of the man and woman eating from the forbidden tree of knowledge. The Hebrew text of Gen 3:15 translates as follows: "And enmity/opposition [Syr.: an enemy] is what I will put between you and the woman and between your seed and her seed; as for him, he will bruise [Syr.: trample] you on the head [LXX: he will watch your head; Vulg.: she will crush your head], and as for you, you will bruise [Syr.: strike] him on the heel [LXX: you will watch his heel]." Thus, the conflict will result in a fatal blow to the serpent and a blow to the woman's seed from which he will recover. The identities of the serpent and the woman's seed are made known through innerbiblical exegesis (Isa 27:1; 65:25; Rev 12:9) and via the narratives of the Pentateuch and its poems:

> The conflict in Gen 3:15 unfolds in progressive parallelism from
> the serpent versus the woman to the serpent's seed versus the

---

8. Sailhamer, *Pentateuch as Narrative*, 35–37; Sailhamer, *Meaning of the Pentateuch*, 323–44, 467–81. See also Horbury, *Jewish Messianism*, 27.

woman's seed and finally to the woman's seed versus the serpent. This is not an account of the origin of human fear of snakes (*contra* Josephus). Rather, the reader must continue in order to discover the identity of the woman's seed. Initially, the offspring of the woman perishes in the flood with the exception of Noah, his sons, and their wives. The seventy nations in Genesis 10 come from the three sons of Noah. The biblical narrative then focuses on one particular man (Abraham) and his seed: "I will bless those who bless you and curse those who despise you. . . . To your seed I will give this land" (Gen 12:3a, 7a). These words pass to Isaac (Gen 26:2–5) and then Jacob: "May peoples serve you and nations bow down to you. Be a lord to your brothers, and may the sons of your mother bow down to you. Cursed be those who curse you, and blessed be those who bless you" (Gen 27:29). This finds concrete expression in the life of Joseph (Gen 37:8, 10; 42:6, 9), which in turn becomes a metaphor for the coming king from the tribe of Judah: "The sons of your father will bow down to you. . . . He bows down, he lies down like a lion, and like a lioness who will arouse him" (Gen 49:8b, 9b)? This poetic reflection on the narrative has an echo in the Balaam oracles: "He bows down, he lies down like a lion, and like a lioness who will arouse him? Blessed are those who bless you, and cursed are those who curse you" (Num 24:9). And this is with reference to the king who will lead a new exodus (Num 24:8; cf. Num 23:22) and be exalted over Gog (Num 24:7 [SP, LXX]; cf. Rev 20:8).[9]

Already within the composition of the Pentateuch, the text of Gen 3:15 is understood to project a showdown between a messianic figure and a final enemy to be defeated.

Tg. Onq. does not have an explicitly messianic rendering of Gen 3:15, but Tg. Neof., Tg. Ps.-J., and Frg. Tg. Together share a messianic interpretation of this verse:

> Tg. Neof.: And enmity [lit., an enemy] is what I will put between you and the woman and between your sons and her sons. And so, when her sons keep the Torah and do the commandments, they will turn themselves to you and strike you on your head and kill you; and when they forsake the commandments of the Torah, you will turn yourself and bite him on his heel (בעקבה) and make him sick. But his son will have healing, and you, O serpent, will not have healing, for they are about to make his appeasement in the end (בעוקבה), in the day of King Messiah.

9. Shepherd, *Text in the Middle*, 15–16.

Tg. Ps.-Jon.: And enmity is what I will put between you and the woman, between the offspring of your sons and the offspring of her sons. And so, when the sons of the woman keep the commands of the Torah, they will turn themselves and strike you on your head; and when they forsake the commands of the Torah, you will turn yourself and bite them on their heels (בעיקביהון). But they will have healing, and you will not have healing, and they are about to make appeasement in the end (בעיקבא), in the days of King Messiah.

Frg. Tg. (Paris): And enmity [lit., an enemy] is what I will put between the serpent and the woman and between the offspring of your sons and the offspring of her sons. And so, when the sons of the woman work in the Torah and keep the commandments, they will turn themselves and strike you on your head and kill you; and when the sons of the woman withhold themselves so that they do not work in the Torah and do not keep the commandments, you will turn yourself and bite them on their heels (בעוקביהון) and make them sick. But the sons of the woman will have healing, and you will not have healing. But these are about to make appeasement in the end (בסוף עקב), in the days of King Messiah.

Frg. Tg. (Vatican): And so, when the sons of the woman work in the Torah and keep the commandments, they will turn themselves and strike you on your head and kill you; and when the sons of the woman forsake the commands of the Torah and do not do the commandments, you will turn yourself and bite them on their heels (בעקביהון) and make them sick. But the sons of the woman will have healing, and you, O serpent, will not have healing. But these are about to make appeasement with one another in the end (בעיקבא), in the end of days (בסוף עקב יומייא), in the days of King Messiah.

The general outline of the interpretation is the same in each of these Targums, although they do vary in detail. They each interpret Hebrew זרע ("seed") in a collective sense ("sons/children"), but Neofiti combines this with an interpretation of the woman's seed as an individual ("you will turn yourself and bite him on his heel and make him sick. But his son will have healing"). When the woman's sons/children devote themselves to the Torah and keep its commands, then they will strike the serpent on its head and kill it; but when they forsake the Torah's commands, the serpent will bite them on their heels (Tg. Neof.: "bite him on his heel").[10] The sons/children

10. The Palestinian Targum tradition (Tgg. Neof., Ps.-J., Frg. Tg.) refers to the Torah

of the woman (Tg. Neof.: "his son") will be healed, but the serpent will not be healed. The woman's sons/children will make appeasement (Frg. Tg. [Vatican] adds: "with one another") in the end, in the day(s) of King Messiah (cf. Isa 11:6–8; 65:25; see also Gen. Rab. 20:5).[11] This links Gen 3:15 to the references to the last days and the coming of the Messiah in the other poems of the Pentateuch (Gen 49:1, 8–12; Num 24:7–9, 14, 17). As noted in the previous translations, each of the Targums plays on the Hebrew word עקב ("heel") to create the phrases "on their heels" (Tg. Neof.: "on his heel") and "in the end" (see also Tg. Onq.).

The consistent choice of the verbs מחי ("strike") and נכת ("bite") helps to disambiguate the sense of the double usage of the rare Hebrew verb שוף ("bruise"; cf. Ps 139:11; Job 9:17). It also connects Gen 3:14–19 to other ancient Hebrew poems in which a messianic figure or God "strikes" (מחץ) the head of the enemy (see Num 24:17; Hab 3:13; Pss 68:21; 110:6; see also Judg 5:26). This connection is heightened by Neofiti's rendering "his son" for Gen 3:15 where the other Targums have "her sons." Pauline Paris Buisch points to Targum Jonathan's singular ברך ("your son") for the Hebrew זרעך ("your seed") in 2 Sam 7:12 and suggests that "his son" in Neofiti's version of Gen 3:15 refers to David's son (see also Gen 49:8–12).[12] Another possibility is that "his son" refers back to "the Son of the Lord" in Neofiti's rendering of Gen 1:1 (see LAE 44[26]:3). Of course, David's son in 2 Sam 7:12 is also God's son in 2 Sam 7:14 (see also Ps 2:6–7; cf. Ps 110:3 [LXX 109:3]; Prov 8:23).[13]

According to Levey, "the Targum's influence on Christian Messianic thought on this passage is unmistakable."[14] Of course, this does not mean that the NT authors and the earliest church fathers were necessarily working from written copies of the Targums comparable to the extant manuscripts available today.[15] Rather, it means that Christians were heirs to a similar

---

already in its rendering of Gen 2:15 and speaks elsewhere of the consequences of keeping or forsaking the commands of the Torah (see Gen 3:22, 24; 27:40; Deut 32:14, 29, 30). See Shepherd, *Textual World of the Bible*, 97–107.

11. Levey (*Messiah*, 2) considers the Aramaic noun שפיותא ("appeasement") to be a play on the Hebrew תשופנו ("you will bruise him").

12. Buisch, "Rest of Her Offspring," 395.

13. The notion that "his son" will have healing raises the issue of the suffering of the son. This issue will be revisited later in the treatments of Isa 52:13—53:12 and Zech 12:10.

14. Levey, *Messiah*, 3.

15. See Buisch, "Rest of Her Offspring," 400–401. See also Chilton, *Judaic Approaches*

exegetical tradition that later surfaced in the written Targums known to us. One example of this from the NT documents is Rom 16:20a: "The God of peace will crush Satan under your [pl.] feet quickly" (cf. Isa 26:6; Mal 4:3; Ps 91:13; Mark 16:18; Luke 10:19; Acts 28:3–6). This follows the collective interpretation of the woman's seed found in the Targums. A more outstanding example is Rev 12 for which the exegesis of Gen 3:15 found in the Targums provides the basic characters (the woman, the serpent, and the male child), plot (conflict and resolution), and setting (eschatological).[16] Furthermore, Rev 12:17 features some of the same wording found in the Targums: "And the dragon was angry at the woman and he departed to make war with the rest of her seed/offspring who keep the commands of God and have the testimony about Jesus" (cf. Rev 14:12; see also Dan 7:21).[17] Buisch suggests that the lack of reference here to the possibility of forsaking the commands may indicate the presence of an earlier tradition:

> The fact that Revelation 12 omits the oscillation of the struggle depending on the children's obedience could simply indicate that that element of the tradition had not yet been developed. Levy argues that the expansions within *Targum Neofiti* (and the other Palestinian Targums by extension) originally existed separately from the translation as independent midrash and were only later incorporated into the translation of the text. If this were the case with our particular expansion, it is possible to imagine that the original interpretation simply identified the victorious seed of the woman as those who keep the law. Only later, once the expansion was interwoven with the translation itself, was the condition of the children's obedience added in order to fit the reciprocal language of the blow to the head and the blow to the heel.[18]

---

to the Gospels, 305–15.

16. See Buisch, "Rest of Her Offspring," 395–99. Rev 12 is part of a vision (Rev 4–16) that John received, but he had to have some kind of recognizable means of communicating in written form what he saw. Gen 3:15 among other texts (e.g., Dan 7) provided a way to depict this portion of his vision.

17. See McNamara, *New Testament and the Palestinian Targum*, 221–22.

18. Buisch, "Rest of Her Offspring," 400. The origin of the tradition thus likely predated any major Jewish-Christian polemics and should not be viewed as distinctively Jewish over against Christian or distinctively Christian over against Jewish.

Tg. Ps.-J. Gen 35:21

There is nothing particularly messianic about the Hebrew text of Gen 35:21 ("And Israel journeyed and pitched his tent beyond Migdal-eder"; > LXX) or its immediate context, although Jacob in Gen 49:4 does refer back to the incident in Gen 35:22 to explain why the kingship will come from the line of Judah (Gen 49:8–12) and not from the line of his firstborn, Reuben (Gen 49:3–4). It is also possible that Gen 35:16b–17 alludes back to Gen 3:15–16. The account of Gen 35 is primarily concerned with Jacob's second encounter with God at Bethel (Gen 35:1–15; cf. Gen 28), the birth of Benjamin and the death of Rachel (Gen 35:16–22a), and the listing of Jacob's sons, which concludes with a brief narrative about the death and burial of Jacob's father Isaac (Gen 35:22b–29).

Tg. Ps.-J., however, renders Gen 35:21 in an explicitly messianic fashion, and it is the only Targum to do so: "And Jacob journeyed and pitched his tent beyond the tower of Eder, the place where King Messiah will be revealed [or: will reveal himself] in the end of days." This interpretation of Migdal-eder is under the influence of an exegesis of Mic 4:8 found in Tg. Jon., which addresses Migdal-eder as the Messiah of Israel who is currently hidden because of the sins of the assembly of Zion. That exegesis will be discussed more fully in a later section on Tg. Jon.'s rendering of Mic 4:8. Suffice it to say here that the proximity of Migdal-eder to Bethlehem Ephrathah (Gen 35:19; Mic 5:2), David's hometown (1 Sam 16:1, 4, 18; 17:12, 58 [MT]), and to Zion/Jerusalem (Mic 4:8; m. Sheqal. 7:4), the royal city, in addition to other factors in the Micah context, has prompted a messianic interpretation. Tg. Ps.-J.'s rendering of Gen 35:21 shares with the Palestinian Targum tradition of Gen 3:15 an interest in an eschatological King Messiah. This is also something that it has in common with the major poetic units of the Pentateuch (see again Gen 49:1, 8–12; Exod 15:18; Num 24:7–9, 14, 17; Deut 31:29; 33:7).

According to Levey, "PsJ sees in this verse a reflection of the history of the Jew, and from his standpoint it could be translated: 'And Israel wandered on, pitching his tent, thenceforth until the coming of the Messiah.' The coming of the Messiah will end Israel's wandering." The messianic interpretation of Mic 4–5 in conjunction with Gen 35:16–22a exerted a great influence on the accounts of Jesus' birth in Matt 2:1–12 and Luke 2:1–21. More will be said about this later. For now, it is enough to note that the connection between Migdal Eder and Bethlehem Ephrathah in Gen 35:19, 21 was and is significant for the Micah context (Mic 4:8; 5:2).

Gen 38:26 (Cairo Genizah Ms FF)

The witnesses to the Palestinian Targum tradition each have a slightly different version of the same lengthy expansion of Gen 38:25–26, which is where Judah has Tamar brought forth to be burned for her alleged harlotry. According to this expansion, Tamar is initially unable to locate her three "witnesses" (the seal, the cord, and the staff). She thus prays for these witnesses to be granted to her and promises in return to provide from the descendants of her offspring three faithful witnesses for the Lord in the fiery furnace: Hananiah, Mishael, and Azariah (Dan 1:6–7; 3:13–30). The Lord responds by sending Michael to give her the three witnesses, but Tamar does not name Judah as the man by whom she is pregnant. Rather, she is confident that the three witnesses will move him to confess his wrongdoing. Judah does confess, concluding that it would be better for him to burn with extinguishable fire in this world than to burn with inextinguishable fire in the world to come, and that it would be better for him to be ashamed in this passing world than to be ashamed before his fathers in the world to come.[19] Judah says that Tamar is more righteous than he is because he did not give his son Shelah to her (see Gen 38:11; cf. 44:16). A heavenly voice, however, declares both Judah and Tamar to be innocent.

The Cairo Genizah Ms FF is the only Targum witness that provides a rationale for the declaration of Judah's innocence: "for from him the Messiah of the Lord will come and rule over all the peoples and bring my people out from among the peoples to the sanctuary." This rationale is obviously influenced by Jacob's blessing of Judah in Gen 49:8–12, which looks forward to a messianic king from the tribe of Judah to whom the obedience of the peoples will belong. The Targum respects the interpretive function of the poetry in Gen 49 in relation to its preceding narratives. Unlike Reuben, Simeon, and Levi, who are unable to overcome the ways in which they have displeased their father (Gen 34:25, 30; 35:22; 49:3–7), Judah redeems himself with his confession (Gen 38:26) and his willingness to sacrifice himself for his brother (Gen 44:33; cf. 37:26–27). Thus, the kingship will belong to Judah and not to his three older brothers who would otherwise have the priority according to their birth order.

---

19. The Targums also make the connection between the wording of Gen 37:32–33 and that of Gen 38:25–26.

Gen 49:1, 10–12, 18

In Gen 49:1, Jacob summons his sons so that he can tell them what will happen to them "in the end of days" (באחרית הימים). This naturally lends itself to an eschatological interpretation. The strategic use of this phrase with the poems of the Pentateuch (Gen 49:1; Num 24:14; Deut 31:29; see also Deut 4:30) and with the programmatic texts of the Prophets (Isa 2:2; Hos 3:5) and their restoration sections (Jer 30:24; Ezek 38:16; Mic 4:1; see also Jer 23:20; 48:47; 49:39; Dan 2:28; 10:14) always points to the messianic future for the people of God (see Gen 49:1, 8–12; Num 24:7–9, 14, 17; Deut 31:29; 33:7; Isa 2:1–5; Jer 30:9, 21, 24; Ezek 34:23; 37:24; 38:16; Hos 3:5; Mic 4:1–5; see also Dan 2:28, 34–35, 44–45). It is no surprise then that a messianic interpretation of Gen 49:1 surfaces in the Targums.

An explicitly messianic interpretation of Gen 49:1 only appears in Ps.-J. and the Paris Frg. Tg., although Tg. Neof. and the Vatican Frg. Tg. do share other features of the expansion. The translation of Gen 49:1 in Tg. Onq. is straightforward, but Onqelos does introduce a messianic interpretation later in Gen 49:10.

> Tg. Ps.-J.: And Jacob summoned his sons and said to them, "Purify yourselves from uncleanness, and I will tell you the concealed mysteries, the hidden times of the end, and the giving of the reward of the righteous and the payback of the wicked, and what the tranquility of Eden will be." The twelve tribes of Israel gathered together around the bed of gold on which he was lying. And as soon as the glory of the dwelling presence of the Lord was revealed, the time when King Messiah would come, it was concealed from him. And then he said, "Come and I will tell you what will happen to you in the end of days."

> Frg. Tg. (Paris): And Jacob summoned his sons and said to them, "Gather together and I will tell you what will happen to you, the giving of the reward for the righteous and the payback that is about to come for the wicked at the time when they are gathered together in the end of days." They thought that he would reveal to them all that was about to come in the end times of the Messiah. As soon as it was revealed to him, it was concealed from him. And Jacob arose and blessed them. Each man according to his blessing he blessed them.

According to Pseudo-Jonathan, Jacob says to his sons that he will tell them "the concealed mysteries" (רזייא סתימיא) about the hidden times of the end, the vindication of the righteous and the judgment of the wicked, and what the new garden of Eden will be (cf. Isa 51:3; Ezek 36:35).[20] The Aramaic word רז ("mystery" or "secret") refers to something previously undisclosed that must be revealed by God in order to be known. In biblical literature, this word occurs in Dan 2:18, 19, 27, 30, 47 with reference to the dream and its interpretation that were revealed to Daniel by God (see also Dan 4:9). Daniel himself confesses that his God is the one who reveals mysteries (Dan 2:28, 29; see also 2:47). For the story of Daniel, the mystery that is revealed concerns what will happen "in the end of days" (Dan 2:28; cf. 10:14) with regard to the kingdoms of the world and the everlasting kingdom of the Messiah (Dan 2:31–45; cf. Dan 7; see also 2:21; 4:17).[21] The term רז appears frequently in the nonbiblical manuscripts from Qumran.[22] In the Greek NT, the equivalent term is μυστήριον (cf. Greek Dan), which, according to Rom 16:25–27, is something that was kept silent in ages past but is now made manifest through the prophetic writings (see Rom 1:2; 3:21–22; Eph 3:9; Col 1:26; Rev 10:7).

When Jacob's sons gather around his golden bed (Tg. Ps.-J.), they assume that he will tell them about the end times of the Messiah (Frg. Tg.), and indeed the time of the coming of the Messiah is revealed to him (Tg. Ps.-J.), but as soon as it is revealed it is concealed.[23] Thus, Jacob is unable

20. According to Gen. Rab. 98:2, he showed them the downfall of Gog and Magog (see Num 24:7 [SP, LXX]; Ezek 38–39; Rev 20:8) and the rebuilding of the temple (see Ezek 40–48).

21. Gen. Rab. 98:2 says that the end was revealed to two men, Jacob and Daniel, only to be hidden from them again (see Dan 12:4).

22. CD 3:18; 1QS 3:23; 4:6, 18; 9:18; 11:3, 5, 19; 1QpHab 7:5, 8, 14; 1QM 3:9; 14:9, 14; 16:11, 16; 17:9; 1QHa 5:17, 19, 30; 6:13; 8:10; 9:13, 15, 23, 31; 10:15; 12:28; 13:27, 38; 15:30; 16:7, 12; 17:23; 18:5; 19:13, 19; 20:16, 23; 21:27; 24:9, 28; 26:15-16; 1Q26 f1:1, 4; 1Q27 f1ii:2-4, 7; f13:3; 1Q30 f4:1; 1Q36 f9:2; f16:2; 1Q40 f1:2; 4Q176 f16:2; 4Q256 18:2; 4Q257 5:3; 4Q258 8:3; 4Q259 3:17; 4Q264 f1:7; 4Q270 f2ii:13; 4Q286 f1iii:8; 4Q299 f3aii_b:11, 15; f3c:5; f5:2; f43:2; 4Q300 f1aii_b:2; f3:2-4, 6; f8:5, 7; 4Q301 f1:2; 4Q369 f1ii:2; 4Q385a f3a_c:8; 4Q401 f14ii:2; f17:6; 4Q403 f1ii:19; f1iii:27; 4Q405 f3ii:9; f13:3; 4Q415 f6:4; f24:1; 4Q416 f2i:5; f2ii:8; f2iii:9, 14, 18, 21; f17:3; 4Q417 f1ii:2-3, 6, 8, 13, 18, 21, 25; f1iii:3; f2i:10; 4Q418 f5:1; f8:8; f9+9a_c:8, 15; f10a_b:1, 3; f17:4; f43_45i:1-2, 4, 6, 10, 14, 16; f77:2, 4; f123ii:4; f172:1; f177:7; f179:3; f184:2; f190:2; f219:2; 4Q418a f11:1; 4Q418c f1:8; 4Q423 f3:2; f5:2; f7:7; 4Q427 f7i:19, 21; f8ii:18; f11:4; 4Q428 f9:1; f11:2; 4Q429 f3:10; 4Q432 f1:1; 4Q437 f6:1; 4Q440 f3i:23; 4Q464a f1:3; 4Q491 f8_10i:7, 12; f10ii:11; f11i:10; f11ii:9, 13; 4Q511 f2ii:6; f44_47:6; f48_49+51:7; f63i:6; 11Q11 3:8. See VanderKam and Flint, *Meaning of the Dead Sea Scrolls*, 236-37.

23. Gen. Rab. 98:2 compares this to a king's friend who says to his children on his deathbed that he will reveal the king's secrets to them, but when he looks up and sees the king, he refrains from doing so out of respect for the king.

to disclose the time of the Messiah's coming,[24] but he is able to tell his sons what will happen to them in the end of days (Tg. Ps.-J.) and to bless each one according to his blessing (Frg. Tg.; see Gen 49:28). This sets up Jacob's words in Gen 49:3–27 wherein he does not give a chronology of events to come but he does utter a prophecy about the Messiah (Gen 49:8–12). The timing of the Messiah's coming is discussed in b. Sanh. 97–99 (see also Tg. Eccl 7:24).

This notion about what is revealed or concealed about the Messiah has an important point of contact with several NT documents and their understanding of the nature of biblical prophecy. The text of 1 Pet 1:10–11 is explicit that messianic prophecy is not about chronological details but about the sufferings of Christ and the glories to follow (cf. Luke 24:26): "Concerning which salvation prophets who prophesied concerning the grace to you searched and sought, seeking as to what person or time the Spirit of Christ within them was indicating when he testified beforehand about the sufferings of Christ and the glories to follow" (cf. Luke 10:24).[25] Likewise, Acts 1:7 speaks of the timing of the "second" coming of Christ (see Heb 9:28) as that which is set by the Father's authority and is not for the followers of Christ to know (cf. Matt 24:36; Mark 13:32). Thus, the return of Christ in the imminent Day of the Lord will come like a thief in the night for which believers must always be prepared (Matt 24:43–44; Luke 12:39–40; 1 Thess 5:2, 4; 2 Pet 3:10; Rev 3:3; 16:15).

Jacob's words of blessing for his sons concerning what will happen to them in the end of days begin with an indication of why the kingship will not come from the first three sons born to him (Gen 49:3–7; see 34:25, 30; 35:22). The remainder of his words is disproportionately devoted to Judah (Gen 49:8–12) and Joseph (Gen 49:22–26). This is to be expected from the roles that these two characters play in the narrative leading up to Gen 49.[26] The text of Gen 49:8 picks up the image of Joseph's brothers bowing down to him (see Gen 27:29; 37:6–11; 42:6, 9) and interprets it to be a prefiguration of the brothers bowing to Judah in the last days. Genesis 49:9 compares Judah to a lion that has gone up from its prey and settled (cf. Num 24:9). No one dares to disturb it. This is a royal metaphor for a king who has defeated

---

24. According to Zech 14:7, the day is known only to God.

25. This should give interpreters pause concerning the intended chronological precision of Dan 9:24–27.

26. The role of Joseph in the previous stories is obvious enough. For Judah, see Gen 37:26–27; 38; 43:1–14; 44:16–34; 46:28.

his enemies (see Tg. Neof.; Gen. Rab. 98:7; cf. Ezek 19:1–9; Nah 2:11–12; see also Rev 5:5).

According to Gen 49:10, a scepter will not depart from Judah, nor a ruler's staff from between his feet (i.e., from his progeny; SP: from between his banners), until the one to whom it belongs comes (LXX: until the things stored away for him come; Vulg.: until the one who is sent comes; Luther: until the hero comes), and to whom will belong the obedience of peoples (LXX: and he is the expectation of the nations). This envisions a king whose rule extends beyond Israel to include all the nations (see Jub. 31:18). Richard Steiner has demonstrated four different innerbiblical interpretations of Gen 49:10 based on their understanding of the word עד ("until" or "[for] ever").[27] These occur in prophecies that correspond to the rise, decline, fall, and renewal of the Davidic dynasty: (1) a scepter will not depart from Judah . . . ever (עד) (i.e., it will not ever depart; see the covenant with David in 2 Sam 7:15–16; 1 Chr 17:13–14); (2) a scepter will not depart from Judah . . . forever (עד) (i.e., it will not always depart; see the division of the kingdom in 1 Kgs 11:39); (3) a scepter will not depart from Judah . . . until (עד) (indicating a point of cessation; see Ezek 21:37, which anticipates the coming of Nebuchadnezzar);[28] and (4) a scepter will not depart from Judah . . . until (עד) (indicating a point of culmination; see the coming of the Messiah in Zech 9:9–10).[29]

All extant Targums interpret Gen 49:10 in a messianic sense.[30] The key word in the Hebrew text for this interpretation is the mysterious שילה (mlt Mss, SP[Mss]: שלה), which has been understood primarily in three different ways in the history of exegesis: (1) as either a place name or a personal name—Shiloh (e.g., KJV),[31] (2) as a combination of the noun שי ("tribute") and the

27. Steiner, "Four Inner-Biblical Interpretations," 33–60.

28. See also Shepherd, *Text in the Middle*, 48.

29. Tg. Onq. has a double rendering of עד that combines options 2 and 4: "a ruler will not depart from the house of Judah . . . forever, until the Messiah to whom the kingdom belongs comes."

30. A messianic interpretation has also been found among the Dead Sea Scrolls in 4Q252: "Until the Messiah of righteousness, the Branch of David, comes. For to him and to his seed has been given the covenant of the kingship of his people for everlasting generations" (cf. 2 Sam 7:12–16; Isa 4:2; 11:1; Jer 23:5–6; Zech 6:12–13).

31. According to b. Sanh. 98b, Shiloh is the personal name of the Messiah. See also Gen. Rab. 98:8. The numerical value (gematria) of משיח ("Messiah") is 358, which is the same as that of יבא שילה ("Shiloh comes").

prepositional phrase לה ("to him")—"until tribute comes to him" (NRSV), or (3) as a combination of the relative ש ("which") plus the prepositional phrase לה ("to him")—"until the one to whom it belongs comes" (see Syr., RSV, NIV, NET; see also BDB, 1010).[32] Tg. Onq., which is the most conservative of the renderings found among the Targums, simply says: "until the Messiah to whom the kingdom belongs comes, and whom the peoples will obey." Tg. Neof. speaks of kings and Torah scholars not ceasing from Judah "until King Messiah to whom the kingdom belongs comes, and to whom all the kingdoms will be subdued" (cf. Frg. Tg.; see also Isa 2:1–5; Mic 4:1–5). Tg. Ps.-J. likewise speaks of kings and Torah scholars, but its view of the nations is more negative: "until the time when King Messiah comes, the youngest of his sons,[33] and because of him the peoples will melt away." This anticipates the warrior image of Gen 49:10–11 according to which the Messiah will defeat his enemies from among the nations and incorporate those who submit to him into his kingdom.

The Hebrew text of Gen 49:11, which depicts the Messiah binding his young donkey to a grapevine and washing his clothing in wine (cf. Zech 9:9–10; see also 2 Sam 18:9; 1 Kgs 1:33; b. Ber. 57a),[34] has been understood in two very different ways. One way says that this is an image of abundance in the messianic kingdom, which allows items of luxury to be used for menial tasks.[35] Another says that it is an image of a warrior king whose garments are stained with the blood of his defeated enemies. It is this latter understanding that finds its way into innerbiblical interpretation.[36] Isaiah 63:1–6 presents the Messiah as one whose garments are red like those of one who treads in a winepress. The text goes on to say that his garments are red because of the spattered blood of his enemies whom he has trampled in his fury. This then influences the depiction of Christ in Rev 19:13, 15 where his bloodstained garment is due to trampling the "winepress" of God's wrath (see Rev 14:19–20). Genesis 49:12 completes the image of the warrior king with a picture of one who has enjoyed the spoils of battle after victory: "Dull

32. See LXX ("until the things stored up for him come, and he is the expectation of the nations") and Latin Vulgate ("until the one who is sent comes, and he will be the expectation of the nations"; cf. Vulg. Hag 2:7).

33. Levey (*Messiah*, 9) says that Tg. Ps.-J. has interpreted שילה in the sense of שיל, "embryo."

34. See also Matt 21:1–11; John 12:12–19.

35. See Calvin, *Commentaries on Genesis*, 460–61; Keil, *Pentateuch*, 258–59.

36. See Shepherd, *Text in the Middle*, 49.

of eyes from wine, and white of teeth from milk" (cf. NET; see Isa 53:12; see also Gen 43:34; Amos 9:11–15; Ps 23:5 [LXX 22:5]; John 2:1–12).[37]

Tg. Onq. takes the view that Gen 49:11–12 is a picture of royal splendor and agricultural abundance. The clothing washed in wine (Gen 49:11) is the purple and brightly dyed clothing of the king. The wine and milk of Gen 49:12 stand for mountains red with vineyards (and overflowing vats) and for valleys white with grain and flocks of sheep (cf. Deut 32:14). On the other hand, the Palestinian Targum tradition (Tgg. Neof., Ps.-J., Frg. Tg.) adopts the view of Isa 63:1–6 and interprets Gen 49:11 to be an image of a warrior King Messiah who makes the mountains red with the blood of his slain enemies and whose garments are thus like those of one squeezing grapes.[38] This is balanced, however, by a picture of agricultural abundance in Gen 49:12 similar to that found in Targum Onqelos. The witnesses to the Palestinian Targum tradition also speak of the great beauty of the Messiah (Gen 49:11) and the beauty of his eyes (cf. 1 Sam 16:12) that have not seen the uncovering of nakedness or the shedding of innocent blood (Gen 49:12; see also Vulg.). His teeth are whiter than milk because he has not eaten anything that has been stolen or taken by force.

The Palestinian Targum tradition (Tgg. Neof., Ps.-J., Frg. Tg.) expands the short text of Gen 49:18 ("For your salvation I wait, O LORD") at the conclusion of Jacob's words for Dan (Gen 49:16–18) so that Jacob says that he does not hope for the deliverance of Gideon or for the deliverance of Samson (from Dan) but for the deliverance of the Lord. The Cairo Genizah Ms FF is unique in that it indicates how Jacob's hope is specifically for the deliverance of King Messiah. This may have been motivated by the image of a serpent biting the heels of a horse in Gen 49:17, which is reminiscent of Gen 3:15. Another contributing factor may have been the refrain of the book of Judges where the stories of Gideon (Judg 6–8) and Samson (Judg 13–16) are found: "In those days there was no king in Israel, everyone did what was right in his own eyes" (Judg 17:6; 18:1; 19:1; 21:25; cf. Deut 12:8). This hope then becomes the great theme of the Former and Latter Prophets

37. Some translations understand the Hebrew text to mean something like, "Eyes darker than wine, and teeth whiter than milk" (e.g., NIV, NRSV), but this is not the most likely understanding of the syntax. In any case, if the writer had wanted to say this, he could have been much clearer about it.

38. "There are no known texts in rabbinic literature reflecting the Pal. Tg. paraphrase of v. 11. This particular paraphrase is believed to be very old and probably pre-Christian" (McNamara, *Targum Neofiti 1: Genesis*, 220n27).

(1 Sam 2:10; 2 Sam 7:12–16; Isa 9:6–7; 11:1–10; Jer 23:5–6; et al.; see also Ps, Dan, Chr).

EXODUS

Exod 12:42; 15:18

The Hebrew text of Exod 12:42 calls the night of the Passover a night of watching for the LORD to bring the people out of the land of Egypt. This same night for or to the LORD is one of watching or observance for all the children of Israel throughout their generations. The Palestinian Targum tradition expands this text considerably and speaks of four nights recorded "in the Book of Remembrances" (בספר דוכרנייא) (cf. Exod 17:14; Mal 3:16). The first is the night when the bright Word of the Lord revealed himself to the world to create the world, which was dark (Gen 1:2–3; cf. John 1:1–5). The second is the night when the Word of the Lord revealed himself to Abraham, although the Targums speak here of everything from the making of the covenant "between the pieces" (Gen 15:17–18; Frg. Tg. V, N; Cairo Genizah Ms FF) to Abraham having a child at the age of one hundred (Gen 17:17; 21:5) and to Isaac being offered on the altar at the age of thirty-seven (Gen 22). The third is the night when the Word of the Lord revealed himself to the Egyptians in the middle of the night to slay their firstborn (Exod 12:29), sparing his own firstborn, Israel (Exod 4:22). The fourth is the night when the world will be completed:

> Frg. Tg. (Vatican): The fourth night, when he will complete the world, the end time for it to be redeemed, evildoers will be destroyed, and the yokes of iron will be broken.[39] Moses will go forth from the midst of the wilderness to heaven, and King Messiah from the midst of Rome. The one will lead at the head of the flock [Cairo Genizah Ms FF: at the head of the people; Levey: on top of a cloud], and the other will lead at the head of the flock [Cairo Genizah Ms FF: at the head of the people; Levey: on top of a cloud], and the Word of the Lord will be between the two of them, and I and they will walk together. That is the night of the Passover before the Lord, [Cairo Genizah Ms FF adds: which the Master of all the worlds called the fourth night, at the end of the world],

---

39. The reference to the breaking of iron yokes may be an allusion to the messianic prophecy in Jer 30:8–9 (cf. Ezek 34:23; 37:24; Hos 3:5).

watched and prepared for the children of Israel throughout their generations.

The Frg. Tg. is the only Targum that preserves an explicitly messianic ("King Messiah") version of the expansion for Exod 12:42,[40] although all the Targums of the Palestinian tradition are eschatological. Both Tg. Neof. and the Cairo Genizah Ms FF have a gap where the messianic reference should be, and they appear to presuppose it. Tg. Onq. does not have the expansion at all, and Tg. Ps.-J. has a very short version of it. Neofiti and the Cairo Genizah Ms FF are the closest to the Frg. Tg.

Certainly one of the most striking features of the expansion in the Targum cited above is the pairing of Moses and the Messiah.[41] Already within the Pentateuch, the expectation of a prophet like Moses (Deut 18:15, 18) is interpreted to be a prophecy of a single messianic figure who is yet to come (Deut 34:10), and this understanding had a great influence on early Christian thinking about Jesus (see, e.g., John 6:14; Acts 3:22; 7:37). The four nights of the Targum's expansion are said to be recorded "in the Book of Remembrances," and this may allude to the "Book of Remembrance" (ספר זכרון) mentioned in Mal 3:16 where the reference is likely to the Book of the Twelve (Hos–Mal).[42] It is worth noting then that the end of the Book of the Twelve concludes with a call to remember the Torah of Moses and to expect the coming of a prophet like Elijah (in NT = John the Baptist [e.g., Mark 1:2–8]) before the coming of the Day of the LORD (Mal 4:4–5; see also Mal 3:1).

According to the Frg. Tg., both Moses and the Messiah will lead "at the head of the flock" (בריש ענה), and the Word of the Lord will be between the two of them. The Cairo Genizah Ms FF says that they will lead "at the head of the people" (בראש עמא). This image of the shepherd-king

---

40. The Frg. Tg. (Paris) for Exod 15:18 ("The LORD, he will be king forever and ever") also has this expansion about the four nights, including the coming of King Messiah on the fourth night (cf. 4QFlor).

41. "Compare the parallels in the lives of Moses and Jesus implied in the Synoptics, such as being hidden in the basket and in the manger (Luke 2:7); the threat of Pharaoh and the threat of Herod (Matt. 2:13); flight to Egypt and return of Jesus (Matt. 2:13ff.); the forty days of seclusion (Mark 1:13); the Torah handed down from the mountain and the Sermon on the Mount (Matt. 5:1ff.), etc." (Levey, *Messiah*, 13). Levey also points to the Gospel accounts of the transfiguration "in which Moses, Elijah, and Jesus constitute a trio, and the voice of God speaks from a cloud" (Levey, *Messiah*, 3; see also Gen. Rab. 18:12).

42. See Shepherd, *Commentary on Book of the Twelve*, 504–5.

leading the people like a flock likely comes from Mic 2:12–13 (see also Mic 4:6–7; 5:4), which compares the people to a flock and says, "And their king passes through before them, and the LORD is at their head (בראשם)." This juxtaposition of a messianic ruler and the LORD as king is not unusual in the Tanakh.[43] Levey, however, translates the phrase בריש ענה in the Fragmentary Targum as "on top of a cloud" and takes it to be a reference to the coming of the Son of Man with/on a cloud in Dan 7:13 (cf. 2 Sam 22:10; Isa 19:1; Nah 1:3; Ps 104:3; see also b. Sanh. 98a).[44]

The latter part of the expansion of Exod 12:42 in the Palestinian Targum tradition calls the fourth night the night of the Passover, which will occur "at the end of the world" according to the Cairo Genizah Ms FF. This is intriguing given the many connections in biblical literature between the hope of a new exodus in the last days and the expectation of a messianic deliverance (see, e.g., Num 23:22; 24:7–8; Hos 1:1, 5, 11; Matt 2:15). John presents Jesus as the Passover lamb of God who takes away the sin of the world (John 1:29, 36), and all the passion narratives of the Gospels make the connection between the substitutionary death of Jesus and the Passover festival (see also 1 Cor 5:7; 1 Pet 1:19; Rev 5:6). Already in the account of the binding of Isaac, a שה ("small, individual animal of livestock"), which is the same word used for the substitutionary Passover lamb (Exod 12:3), is offered "in place of" (תחת) of Isaac (Gen 22:8, 13).[45] The subsequent narrative of Genesis then depicts Judah as one who offers himself as a substitute "in place of" (תחת) his brother Benjamin (Gen 44:33), which serves to prefigure the Messiah from the tribe of Judah (Gen 49:8–12). Thus, Isa 52:13—53:12 presents the messianic servant of the LORD as one who is a substitutionary שה ("lamb") led to the slaughter to die for the sins of the people as an אשם ("guilt offering") on their behalf (Isa 53:4–7, 10–12; see also Lev 1–7). Likewise, the suffering servant song of Ps 22 draws upon the description of the Passover lamb in Exod 12:46 to describe the servant's

---

43. "In the Pentateuch these prophecies are uttered by Jacob and Balaam, especially in the form of the Shiloh oracle and the star oracle (Gen. 49.10; Num. 24.17), both of which foretell a specifically Israelite ruler and are introduced as relating to 'the latter days' (aharit hayamim). These oracles of an Israelite king alternate in the Pentateuch with the prophecies of the kingdom of God and the blessings of Israel in the two songs of Moses and the blessing of Moses (Exod. 15; Deut. 32–33)" (Horbury, *Jewish Messianism*, 27). See also 4QFlor.

44. Levey, *Messiah*, 12–13.

45. The small animal is identified in Gen 22:13 as an איל ("ram").

suffering (Ps 22:17; see also 34:20), and John puts both texts together in his account of Jesus' crucifixion (John 19:24, 37).

Exod 17:16

The text of Exod 17:14–16 concludes the account of the battle with Amalek in which Joshua leads the Israelite army while Moses keeps his hands raised with the staff of God (Exod 17:8–13). The army prevails as long as Moses does not relax his hands. Thus, Aaron and Hur come alongside Moses to provide support for him. The LORD then instructs Moses to record the victory over Amalek as "a memorial in a book" (זכרון בספר) because he will wipe out any memory of Amalek from under the sky (Exod 17:14). This has a connection to the Palestinian Targum tradition of Exod 12:42 discussed previously, which speaks of what is recorded "in the Book of Remembrances" (cf. Mal 3:16), including the coming of the Messiah. Moses subsequently builds an altar and calls it, "The LORD (is) My Banner" (יהוה נסי),[46] but the following explanation of this name in the MT seems to bear no relationship to it: "For a hand upon the כס of Yah [abbreviated divine name], the battle belongs to the LORD against Amalek from generation to generation" (Exod 17:16; cf. 14:14; 1 Sam 17:47).[47] The word כס is unknown, but the Samaritan Pentateuch has כסא ("throne"): "For a hand upon the throne of Yah" (cf. Syr., Vulg., Luther). The Targums interpret this to be the lifting up of a hand in the taking of an oath (see, e.g., Ezek 20:5–6), but again this would have little to do with the naming of the altar in the previous verse.[48] The LXX interprets כס יה as if it were a single word modifying "hand": "for with a hidden (כְּסָיָה) hand the Lord wages war against Amalek from generation to generation."

It is likely that כס (?) is the result of a very early error in transmission for נס ("banner") due to the similarity between כ and נ in the Old Hebrew script (see BDB, 490).[49] The Samaritan Pentateuch's כסא ("throne") and the

46. The building of the altar is another kind of memorial (cf. Gen 12:8; 13:18; 35:7; Josh 22:27, 34), a visual reminder that the LORD is the one who leads his people's army.

47. The latter part of this verse is usually understood to mean that the LORD will have war with Amalek continually, but this hardly corresponds to Exod 17:14, which says that he will wipe out the memory of Amalek. The idea seems rather to be that the LORD will always have victory against Amalek.

48. Another possibility, still unrelated to the previous verse, is that יד means "monument" here rather than "hand" (see 1 Sam 15:12; 2 Sam 18:18; Isa 56:5).

49. This suggestion was first made by J. Clericus in the seventeenth century (see Childs, *Book of Exodus*, 311–12).

LXX's "hidden" (= כסיה) are attempts to make sense of the erroneous כס. Once the original reading נס ("banner") is restored, verses 15 and 16 of Exod 17 read together quite nicely: "And Moses built an altar and called its name, 'The LORD (is) My Banner (נסי),' and said, 'For a hand upon the banner (נס) of Yah, the battle belongs to the LORD against Amalek from generation to generation.'" The image of the hand upon the banner bearing the standard or emblem of the LORD's army recalls from the story the raised staff in the hand of Moses (Exod 17:9b). It indicates trust in the LORD. Thus, as long as Israel trusts in the LORD, the LORD will make Amalek their defeated enemy throughout their generations.

Tg. Neof., the Frg. Tg., and witnesses from the Cairo Genizah (Mss AA, J) all have the same considerable expansion of Exod 17:16 that speaks of Saul's war with the house of Amalek (1 Sam 15) and the destruction of Amalek's remnant in the time of Mordecai and Esther (see Haman the Agagite, a descendant of the Amalekite king [Esth 3:1]). Tg. Ps.-J. is the only Targum that features a messianic rendering in its expansion of Exod 17:16:

> Tg. Ps.-J.: And he said, "For the Word of the Lord has sworn by his glorious throne that by means of his Word he will wage war against those of the house of Amalek and destroy them for three generations—from the generation of this world and from the generation of the Messiah and from the generation of the world to come.[50]

Levey suggests that the phrase "from generation to generation" (מדר דר) in Exod 17:16 has prompted this messianic interpretation (cf. Exod 12:42, "throughout their generations" [לדררתם]),[51] but there may be more to it than this. Tg. Ps.-J. has interpreted the MT's כס to mean "throne" (cf. SP), and this may have been enough to suggest a messianic sense, but the name of the altar ("The LORD [is] My Banner [נסי]") in the previous verse may also have influenced the interpretation.[52] According to Tg. Jon.'s render-

---

50. "R. Joshua says: 'From generation,' that is, from the life of this world; 'to generation,' that is, from the life of the world to come. R. Eleazar of Modi'im says: From the generation of Moses and from the generation of Samuel. R. Eliezer says: From the generation of the Messiah which really consists of three generations. And whence do we know that the generation of the Messiah consists of three generations? It is said: 'They shall fear Thee while the sun endureth and so long as the moon, a generation and two generations' (Ps. 72.5)" (Lauterbach, *Mekhilta de-Rabbi Ishmael*, 270).

51. Levey, *Messiah*, 14.

52. It is also possible that Tg. Ps.-J. shows an awareness of two different understandings

ing of Isa 11:1, 10, the Messiah is the one who will be a "banner" (נס) to the nations.[53] The text of Num 24:17–24, which the Targums interpret messianically and eschatologically, refers to the beginning and the end of Amalek (Num 24:20). Amalek was the first of the nations to come against Israel after their departure from Egypt (Exod 17:8–13); and Amalek's end, according to Tg. Ps.-J.'s rendering of Num 24:20 (see also Tg. Ps.-J. Deut 25:19), will come in the days of King Messiah (Tg. Neof.: "in the end of days of Gog and Magog"). The image of the Messiah striking his enemies in Num 24:17 strongly suggests that Amalek's ultimate demise will come at the hands of the messianic king (cf. Gen 49:11). Thus, the idea that the war against Amalek will be waged by means of the Word of the Lord (Tg. Ps.-J. Exod 17:16) and the picture of the Messiah destroying Amalek are not mutually exclusive.

Tg. Ps.-J. Exod 40:9–11

Tg. Ps.-J. is the only Targum that preserves a messianic interpretation of Exod 40:9–11:

> Tg. Ps.-J.: And you will take the anointing oil and anoint the tabernacle and all that is in it and sanctify it because of the crown of the kingdom of the house of Judah and King Messiah who is about to redeem Israel in the end of days. And you will anoint the altar of burnt offering and all its vessels, and you will sanctify the altar, and the altar will be most holy, because of the crown of the priesthood of Aaron and his sons and Elijah the high priest who is about to be sent at the end of the exiles. And you will anoint the basin and its base and sanctify it because of Joshua your servant, the leader of the Sanhedrin of your people, by whose hands the land of Israel is about to be divided, and the Messiah the son of Ephraim who will go forth from him, by whose hands the house of Israel is about to be victorious against Gog and his troops in the end of days.

Levey points to the phrase שמן המשחה ("the anointing oil") and the threefold occurrence of ומשחת ("and you will anoint") in the Hebrew text of Exod 40:9–11 as motivating factors for Tg. Ps.-J.'s messianic rendering

---

of כס ("throne" and "banner"). As noted in the earlier discussion of שלה in Gen 49:10, the Targums sometimes give more than one interpretation of the same word at the same time.

53. The Targum renders נס ("banner") in Isa 11:10 as את ("sign") (cf. Isa 66:19). See also John 3:14; 12:32.

(Aram.: משיחא).[54] The anointing of the tabernacle prompts the Targumist to think of the crown of the kingdom of the house of Judah and King Messiah who is about to redeem Israel in the end of days (see again Gen 49:1, 8–12). This is likely due to Nathan's prophecy about the son of David who will build a temple and reign over an everlasting kingdom (see 2 Sam 7:13; Zech 6:12–13; see also Ezek 40–48). The anointing of the altar moves the Targumist to think of the crown of the priesthood of Aaron and his sons and Elijah the high priest who is about to be sent at the end of the exiles (cf. Tg. Ps.-J. Exod 6:18; Tg. Ps.-J. Deut 30:4; Tg. Lam 4:22; see also b. Sukkah 52b). The prophet like Elijah will prepare the way for the messianic prophet like Moses before the Day of the LORD (see Deut 18:15, 18; 34:10; Mal 3:1; 4:4–6; see also Isa 40:3; Mark 1:2–11; Luke 1:17). The anointing of the basin brings to mind for the Targumist Moses' servant Joshua from the tribe of Ephraim (Num 13:8) who will divide the land of Israel and from whom will descend the Messiah the son of Ephraim by whose hands the house of Israel will be victorious against Gog and his troops in the end of days (see Ezek 38–39; Rev 20:8). According to the Samaritan Pentateuch's version of Num 24:7b (see also LXX Num 24:7), the messianic king will be exalted over Gog (cf. Tg. Neof, Frg. Tg. Num 11:26; Tg. Neof. Num 24:20).[55]

Levey's comments about the Messiah the son of Ephraim are worth reproducing here:

> The Ephraimite Messiah does not figure too prominently or clearly in rabbinic thought. Such a personality was probably built up as a psychological reaction to the death of Bar Kokhba; he will be a conquering hero who will actually lead in the final battle, and will be slain and mourned. The implication of PsJ is that the Ephraimite Messiah will do the fighting and vanquish Gog, while the Davidic King Messiah will be the symbol of deliverance. Rabbinic sources do not indicate the reason why this personality is depicted as of Ephraimite descent, but it may be conjectured that this represents that phase of the Messianic hope in which a reunion of the Northern and Southern Kingdoms was expected.[56]

The Messiah the son of Ephraim is also mentioned alongside the Messiah the son of David in Tg. Song 4:5 and 7:4 where the two are compared to

---

54. Levey, *Messiah*, 15.

55. The MT historicizes this so that it is a prophecy about Saul's defeat of Agag (1 Sam 15).

56. Levey, *Messiah*, 16.

Moses and Aaron. According to b. Sukkah 52a, the mourning mentioned in Zech 12:10, 12 is on account of the Messiah the son of Joseph who was killed (cf. 4 Ezra 7:28–29). A marginal reading to the Targum of Zech 12:10 in Codex Reuchlinianus (1105 CE) from a no longer extant Palestinian Targum of the Prophets also refers to the Messiah the son of Ephraim:

> And I will let rest upon the house of David and upon the inhabitants of Jerusalem the Spirit of prophecy and true prayer. Afterwards the Messiah the son of Ephraim will go out to wage war with Gog, and Gog will kill him before the gate of Jerusalem. And they will look at me and ask why the peoples pierced the Messiah the son of Ephraim, and they will mourn over him.[57]

The creation of an Ephraimite Messiah appears to be designed to avoid the conclusion that the Davidic Messiah might suffer and die (but see again Tg. Neof. Gen 3:15).[58] On the other hand, the NT authors accept that the Davidic Messiah will not only suffer and die but also rise up and reign over an everlasting kingdom (see, e.g., Matt 24:30; John 19:37; Rev 1:7).

NUMBERS

Num 11:26

Num 11 is an account of God's provision for the people in the wilderness that runs parallel to the account in Exod 16.[59] The account in Exod 16 focuses on the instruction for the Sabbath, which becomes known as the sign of the covenant (Exod 31:12–17). Num 11, on the other hand, focuses on the gift of the Spirit,[60] and it is this feature of the account that ultimately leads to the messianic interpretation found in the Targums. Moses receives instruction to gather seventy elders to the tent of meeting where the LORD will take some of the Spirit that is on Moses and put it on the elders so that they can bear some of the burden of the people with Moses (Num 11:16–17; cf. Exod 18). Moses follows this instruction; and when the LORD does what he said he would do, the Spirit rests upon the elders, and they prophesy (Num 11:24–25; cf. Mic 3:8; 2 Chr 15:1; 20:14; 24:20).[61] Two men,

---

57. Cf. b. Pesah. 118a.

58. See also the later discussion of the Targum of Isa 52:13—53:12 (cf. Dan 9:24–27).

59. See Sailhamer, *Pentateuch as Narrative*, 278.

60. See Shepherd, *Text in the Middle*, 64–71.

61. Normally the niphal נבא would be used for prophetic discourse, whereas the

Eldad and Medad, remain in the camp;[62] nevertheless, the Spirit rests upon them too, and they prophesy (Num 11:26). This is subsequently reported to Moses who then expresses the desire that the LORD would make all the people prophets, that is, that he would put his Spirit upon them all (Num 11:27–29; cf. Joel 2:28–29; Acts 2; see also Ezek 11:19–20; 36:26–27; 39:29; Zech 12:10).

The reference to the Spirit of prophecy in the Hebrew text of Num 11:26 serves as an impetus for an eschatological and messianic interpretation in the Targums. The same Spirit rests upon Balaam prior to the delivery of his third and fourth oracles in which he speaks of a messianic figure who will defeat his enemies in the last days (Num 24:2, 7–9, 14, 17; see again the earlier discussion of Tg. Ps.-J. Exod 40:9–11).[63] The Targums interpret these oracles in an eschatological and messianic fashion as well. The Palestinian Targum tradition seeks to supply from these oracles (and from Ezek 38–39) the prophecy of Eldad and Medad, which is missing from the Hebrew text of Num 11:26. Tg. Ps.-J.'s version of their joint prophecy in Num 11:26 is eschatological but not messianic. It draws upon the image of the birds and wild animals feasting on the dead bodies of the slain in Ezek 39:17–24 (cf. Rev 19:17–18; 20:8) to depict the Lord's defeat of Gog in the last days (see Num. Rab. 15:19) and looks forward to the resurrection of Israel's dead (Ezek 37).[64] Tg. Neof. and the Frg. Tg., however, are both eschatological and messianic in their renderings of Num 11:26:[65]

---

hithpael, which is used in Num 11:25–27, would be used for ecstatic behavior, but see Levison, "Prophecy in Ancient Israel," 503–21.

62. There is some debate about whether Eldad and Medad were counted among the seventy elders (see b. Sanh. 17a).

63. See also Horbury, *Jewish Messianism*, 29, 61–62.

64. According to b. Sanh. 17a, the text of Ezek 38:17 refers specifically to this prophecy of Eldad and Medad: "Are you [i.e., Gog] not the one of whom I spoke in former days by the agency of my servants the prophets of Israel who prophesied [> LXX] in those days, years (שנים), to bring you against them?" This likely refers to Jeremiah's prophecy about the enemy from the north, but the Talmud interprets שנים ("years") to be the number "two" with reference to the two prophets Eldad and Medad.

65. B. Barry Levy suggests that Tg. Neof. preserves an earlier form of the prophecies than Tg. Ps.-J. or the Frg. Tg.: "Minor additions that break the rhythm and parallelism and rearrangements that destroy the rhyme all point to a period of transmission during which the poetic qualities were either unnoticed or disregarded. Unless we are prepared to assume that some transmittor [*sic*] of N converted the prose accounts found in these other texts into poetic form, we must conclude that N, as the most poetic text, preserves the earliest version of these lines" (Levy, *Targum Neophyti 1*, 83).

> Tg. Neof.: And two men were left in the camp. The name of one was Eldad, and the name of the other was Medad.[66] And the Holy Spirit rested upon them. Eldad was prophesying and said, "Look, quail is about to come up from the sea and become to Israel [Frg. Tg. (Paris): the children of Israel] a stumbling block."[67] And Medad was prophesying and said, "Look, Moses the prophet [Frg. Tg. (Paris): the scribe of Israel] is about to be taken up from the camp,[68] and Joshua the son of Nun is about to serve in his position of leadership after him [Frg. Tg. (Paris): and Joshua the son of Nun, that servant, is about to receive prophecy after him]."[69] And the two of them were prophesying together and saying, "In the end of days, Gog and Magog [Frg. Tg. (Paris, Vatican) adds: and their armies] will come up to Jerusalem, and into the hands of King Messiah they will fall. And for seven years the children of Israel will kindle fires from their weapons, and to the forest they will not go out [Frg. Tg. (Paris, Vatican) adds: and a tree they will not cut down]." And they were from the seventy wise men who were set apart [Frg. Tg. (Paris) adds: by their name but did not go out], and the seventy wise men did not go out from the camp while Eldad and Medad were prophesying in the camp.[70]

According to the Targums, the Spirit that rests upon Eldad and Medad is "the Holy Spirit" (see Isa 63:10). The two men prophesy individually before they prophesy together. Eldad prophesies about the coming quail. The fulfillment of this prophecy is subsequently narrated in Num 11:31–34. Medad prophesies about the transfer of leadership from Moses to Joshua (see Num 27:15–23; Deut 34:9–10). As noted in the above translation, the Frg. Tg. (Vatican) and Tg. Ps.-J. attribute these prophecies to the opposite men. The reader's ability to identify the historical fulfillments of these individual

---

66. Tg. Ps.-J. adds: "the sons of Elizaphan son of Parnach, to whom Jochebed the daughter of Levi bore to him at the time when Amram her husband had sent her away, but she had been taken back to him for a wife before she bore Moses" (see b. Sotah 12a).

67. Frg. Tg. (Vatican) and Tg. Ps.-J. attribute this prophecy to Medad.

68. It is not uncommon for the Targums to designate prophets as scribes. This shows an early recognition of what modern scholarship now calls "scribal prophecy" (see Toorn, *Scribal Culture*, 107, 169, 185).

69. Frg. Tg. (Vatican) and Tg. Ps.-J. attribute this prophecy to Eldad. Tg. Ps.-J. adds that Joshua will bring the people into the land of the Canaanites and cause them to inherit it.

70. Tg. Ps.-J.: "Now they were among the elders who had gone up in the written registry but had not gone out to the tabernacle, for they had hidden so as to flee from official leadership, and they prophesied in the camp."

prophecies instills confidence in the following joint prophecy about the last days.

When Eldad and Medad prophesy together, they turn their attention to "the end of days" (cf. Gen 49:1; Num 24:14; Deut 4:30; 31:29) when Gog and Magog will come up to Jerusalem (see Ezek 38–39; Rev 20:8–9) and fall into the hands of King Messiah (see SP, LXX Num 24:7). For seven years the people of Israel will use Gog's weapons for kindling and will thus have no need to go into the forest to cut down trees. This latter part of the prophecy comes directly from the description of the aftermath of Gog's defeat in Ezek 39:9–10. The conclusion to the expansion in the Targums then identifies Eldad and Medad as members of the seventy wise men (i.e., elders). The relatively early nature of the exegetical tradition represented in this expansion can be seen in a comparison with Rev 20:8–9. The prophecy about Gog in Ezek 38–39 does not mention anything about Gog coming against the city of Jerusalem in particular, yet the Targums (Tg. Neof., Frg. Tg.) and Rev 20:8–9 ("the beloved city") include this feature. This is a unique combination of material from Ezek 38–39 (the battle of Gog) with Zech 12 and 14 (the battle of Armageddon) where the enemies of the people of God come against the holy city (cf. Rev 16:16; see also Luke 21:20).

Num 23–24

The Balaam oracles in Num 23–24 form yet another substantial poetic section of the Pentateuch in which the Targums take great interest for its eschatological and messianic message (see again Gen 3:14–19; 49:1–28; Exod 15:1–18; see also Deut 32–33). In Num 22, the Moabite king Balak summons Balaam to come and curse the people of Israel as they move into the territory east of the Jordan. Balaam's first oracle in Num 23:7–10 expresses his inability to curse a people whom God has blessed (see Gen 12:3; 27:29; Num 22:6; 24:9). The second oracle in Num 23:18–24 continues this thought and speaks of Israel as a people whose God is with them and among whom is a shout of a king's acclamation (Num 23:21; cf. 24:7, 17). The text goes on to refer to the exodus from Egypt (Num 23:22; cf. 24:8) and then compares Israel to a lion (Num 23:24; cf. Gen 49:9; Num 24:9).

Tg. Onq. and the Frg. Tg. (Paris) interpret the "shout of a king" (תרועת מלך) in Num 23:21 to be "the Dwelling Presence of their King" (שכינת מלכהון) and "the shout [or, trumpet blast] of the splendor of the Glory of their King" (יבבות זיו איקר מלכהון) respectively (cf. Syr.). Thus, according to this view, the king in Num 23:21 is the divine king (cf. Exod 15:18). Tg. Neof. and the Frg. Tg. (Vatican), however, have "the shout [or, trumpet blast] of the splendor [of the splendor > Frg. Tg. (Vatican)] of the glory of their kings" (יבבות זיו איקר מלכיהון), although some still interpret מלכיהון in these Targums to be singular ("their king"). The plural "kings" in the phrase "the glory of their kings" fits with the LXX rendering of Num 23:21: "the glories of rulers." This anticipates a succession of kings in Israel (cf. Gen 17:16; 35:11).

The phrase "shout of a king" (תרועת מלך) in Num 23:21 could be understood as a reference to Moses as king (see Deut 33:5), but Tg. Ps.-J. understands it to mean "the shout [or, trumpet blast] of King Messiah" (יבבות מלכא משיחא) (cf. Vulg.; see also Isa 27:13; Zech 9:14; Gen. Rab. 56:9). This interpretation takes its cue from Balaam's third and fourth oracles, which speak of a messianic king who will be delivered in a new exodus and who will be comparable to a lion (Num 24:7–9, 17). Thus, what happens with Israel historically (Num 23:22, 24) prefigures what happens with the Messiah eschatologically (Num 24:7–9, 14, 17).

The MT and the LXX *Vorlage* differ considerably for Balaam's third oracle (Num 24:3–9), especially for Num 24:7. According to the MT, "Water will flow from his buckets, and his seed will be in many waters (יזל מים מדליו וזרעו במים רבים); and his king will be higher than Agag (אגג), and his kingdom will be lifted up." This text is a prophecy about King Saul and his defeat of the Amalekite king Agag (see 1 Sam 15),[71] which is the way Tg. Onq. and Tg. Ps.-J. understand it. According to the LXX *Vorlage*, however, "A man will go forth from his seed, and he will rule over many nations (יאזל אדם מזרעו וימשל בגוים רבים); and his kingdom will be higher than Gog (גוג), and his kingdom will be made to grow" (cf. Syr.). This reconstruction is partially confirmed by the Samaritan Pentateuch, which has גוג ("Gog") instead of אגג ("Agag"). It is a prophecy about the Messiah and his defeat of a future and final enemy named Gog (see Ezek 38–39; Rev 20:8; see also the earlier discussion of Exod 40:9–11; Num 11:26). The word "man" in certain contexts is something of a technical term for the Messiah in both the MT (Zech 6:12–13; cf. John 19:5) and the LXX (Num 24:17; Isa 19:20).[72]

---

71. It is not a prophecy about David and his men rescuing their families from the Amalekites in 1 Sam 30—a story that does not feature the Amalekite king Agag.

72. See 2 Sam 23:1 (4QSam^a); 2 Sam 23:3 (LXX); Dan 7:13; 1 Tim 2:5. See also Horbury, *Jewish Messianism*, 28–30, 34–35, 43–45; Shepherd, *Text in the Middle*, 85–88.

Tg. Neof. and the Frg. Tg. both have messianic interpretations of Num 24:7:

> Tg. Neof.: Their king will rise up from among them [Frg. Tg. (Vatican): Their king will rise up for their children], and their redeemer will be from them [Frg. Tg. (Paris, Vatican) adds: and with them]. He will gather to them their exiles from the provinces of their enemies, and his sons will rule over many peoples [Frg. Tg. (Paris, Vatican): and their sons will rule over peoples]. He will be stronger than Saul who had compassion on Agag the king of the Amalekites, and the kingdom of King Messiah will be exalted.

The image of the king rising up from among the people may allude to the prophecy of the coming prophet like Moses, which says that he will be from among his fellow Israelites (Deut 18:15, 18; 34:10; Acts 3:22; 7:37). The description of this king as the people's "redeemer" (פרוק) depicts him as a leader of a new exodus (cf. Tg. Neof. Lev 11:45; 22:33; 25:38, 45; Num 15:41; 24:17). Just as God brought the people out of Egypt according to Num 23:22 (אל מוציאם ממצרים ["God brings them out of Egypt"]), so will he bring his messianic king out of Egypt according to Num 24:8 (אל מוציאו ממצרים ["God brings him out of Egypt"]).[73] Just as the people rose up like a lion according to Num 23:24 and would not lie down until they defeated their enemies, so will the messianic king lie down undisturbed like a lion after he defeats his enemies (Num 24:9a; cf. Gen 49:9); and the lost blessing of life and dominion in the land (Gen 1:26–28) will be restored through him (Num 24:9b; cf. Gen 12:3; 22:18; 27:29; Jer 4:2; Ps 72:17; Gal 3:16, 28–29).

The latter part of the above messianic rendering of Num 24:7 in Tg. Neof. and the Frg. Tg. presupposes the Assyrian and Babylonian captivities and assumes that full restoration from these will only take place in the messianic age. This is in agreement with the outlook of the Prophets (e.g., Isa 40–66; Jer 3:14–18; Ezek 34–37; Zech 9–10). According to Tg. Neof., the Messiah's sons ("his sons") will rule over many peoples, which seems to envision a messianic dynasty. On the other hand, the Frg. Tg. says that the people's sons ("their sons") will rule over peoples. This seems to anticipate a scenario in which the Messiah will rule, but the people will reign with him (see Isa 32:1; Jer 23:4–5; Mic 5:5–6; Dan 7:13–14, 27; Rev 5:10; 20:6). The Messiah will be stronger than Saul who spared the Amalekite king Agag

---

73. See Hos 11:1, 5, 11; Matt 2:15 (Sailhamer, "Hosea 11:1 and Matthew 2:15," 87–96; Shepherd, *Commentary on Book of the Twelve*, 92–98).

contrary to orders (1 Sam 15:3, 9). Like David, the Messiah will be "better" than Saul (see 1 Sam 15:28). He will eradicate his foes, and his kingdom will be elevated (cf. Num 23:24). Thus, despite the fact that Tg. Neof. and the Frg. Tg. are following a Hebrew text with "Agag" instead of "Gog," they nevertheless interpret the text in an eschatological and messianic fashion.[74]

Balaam explicitly introduces his fourth and final oracle (Num 24:15–24) as eschatological: "what this people [i.e., Israel] will do to your people [i.e., Balak's people, Moab] in the end of days" (Num 24:14; cf. Gen 49:1; Deut 4:30; 31:29). It is evident from the content of this oracle that it applies not only to Moab but to all the enemies of the people of God. As is the case with Gen 49:10, all Pentateuchal Targums interpret Num 24:17 in an eschatological and messianic sense, although Tg. Onq. and Tg. Ps.-J. are more explicit about this than Tg. Neof. and the Frg. Tg. Gen 49:10 and Num 24:17 are the only two texts for which Tg. Onq. has a messianic rendering.

According to the Hebrew text of Num 24:17, Balaam says that he sees someone but not now, he sees him but not near. A "star" (כוכב) treads from Jacob, and a "scepter" (שבט) rises from Israel. The Targums uniformly interpret the star to be a metaphor for a king (see Mal 4:2; Matt 2:2; 2 Pet 1:19; Rev 22:16; T. Jud. 24:1; see also 1QM 11:6; 4Q175 [4QTest]; CD-A 7:18–21). The LXX translates that a star "will rise" (ἀνατελεῖ = זרח) from Jacob. This connects the prophecy to other texts for which the LXX translates the messianic title צמח ("Branch") as ἀνατολή ("sunrise") (Jer 23:5; Zech 3:8; 6:12; see also Ps 110:3 [LXX 109:3]).[75] Tg. Onq. and Tg. Ps.-J. render "scepter" as "Messiah" (cf. Syr.: "leader"; LXX: "a man" [see again LXX Num 24:7]). Tg. Neof. and the Frg. Tg. render "scepter" as "redeemer and ruler," which is similar to their designation of the messianic king in Num 24:7 as "redeemer."[76] The latter part of Num 24:17 in Tg. Onq. says that the Messiah will kill the leaders of Moab (MT: "and he will strike the temples [LXX, Syr., Vulg.: rulers] of Moab") and rule over all humanity (MT: "and tear

---

74. The MT's historicization of the prophecy in Num 24:7 is at odds with the connection between Num 24:9 and Gen 49:9. In Gen 49:9, the lion-like king comes out of the tribe of Judah. MT Num 24:7, however, anticipates the coming of Saul from the tribe of Benjamin (1 Sam 9:21). This incongruity betrays the secondary nature of the MT's version of the prophecy. Such a tendency in the MT to historicize otherwise eschatological and/or messianic prophecies may be observed elsewhere (see, e.g., MT Gen 49:10b ["Shiloh"]; MT 2 Sam 23:1 [cf. 4QSamᵃ, LXX]; MT Jer 25:9, 11 [cf. LXX]).

75. See Horbury, *Jewish Messianism*, 92–96.

76. "[W]ere it not for their messianic content they would be worthy of almost no special mention" (Levy, *Targum Neophyti 1*, 148).

down [וקרקר; SP: and the top of the head of (וקדקד)] all the sons of Seth [שת; Jer 48:45: the sons of destruction (שאון)]) (cf. Gen 4:25).[77] Tg. Ps.-J. designates the sons of Seth as the army or armies of Gog (see Num 24:8 [SP, LXX]; Ezek 38–39; Rev 20:8; see again the earlier treatments of Exod 40:9–11; Num 11:26; see also Tg. Neof. Num 24:20).

Tg. Ps.-J. explicitly identifies the subject of Num 24:19 as a "ruler," which is not a feature of Tg. Onq. (see also MT, SP, LXX, Vulg.). Tg. Neof. and the Frg. Tg. identify this same subject as a "king." According to Tg. Ps.-J.'s rendering of Num 24:20, Amalek was the "beginning of nations" (MT) in the sense that the house of Amalek was the first nation to wage war against Israel (see again Exod 17:8–16 and earlier discussion), and Amalek's end will be destruction (MT) in the sense that the end of the Amalekites will come in the days of King Messiah when they wage war (along with all the sons of the east) against the house of Israel. According to the Frg. Tg., this latter war will take place "in the end of days," and Tg. Neof. says that it will occur "in the end of days of Gog and Magog."

Gog also comes into view in some witnesses to the Greek text of Num 24:23. The MT introduces the last subsection of Balaam's oracle very simply ("And he took up his discourse and said"), but the LXX has an addition prior to this: "And when he saw Og he took up his discourse and said" (see Num 21:33–35; cf. 24:20, 21). The Göttingen Septuagint (Wevers) indicates that manuscript group b (19-108-118-314-537) attests to the reading "Gog" instead of "Og." This is remarkable when it is considered that the phrase "ships from Kittim" (Tgg.: Rome; Vulg.: Italy) in Num 24:24 recurs later in the prophetic vision of Dan 10–12 (see Dan 11:30), which culminates with the defeat of the final enemy (Dan 11:36–45) and the resurrection (Dan 12:1–3).[78] According to Tg. Ps.-J.'s version of Num 24:24, the end of Assyria, the sons of Eber (Tg. Onq.: "those beyond the Euphrates"), and those from the west (Kittim = Cyprus to the west) will be to fall by the hand of King Messiah and be destroyed forever.

---

77. See again Gen 3:15; Judg 5:26; Hab 3:13; Pss 68:21; 110:6. See also Deut 33:20.

78. See Shepherd, *Daniel in the Context*, 101–4.

DEUTERONOMY

Tg. Ps.-J. Deut 25:19

Deut 25:17–18 calls for remembrance of what Amalek did to the people when they came out of Egypt (see again Exod 17:8–16; Num 24:20). When the LORD gives the people rest in the land of the covenant, they are to wipe out the memory of Amalek and must not forget to do so (Deut 25:19). A partial fulfillment of this occurs in the story of 1 Sam 15, but a remnant of Amalek remains (Esth 3:1). Thus, the complete destruction of Amalek is left for the future (Num 24:20). According to Tg. Ps.-J., this will take place in the days of King Messiah. Tg. Ps.-J. is the only Targum that connects the ultimate fate of Amalek, descendant of Esau (Gen 36:12), with the coming of the Messiah in the last days, and it does so in all three passages that speak of Amalek's future (Exod 17:16; Num 24:20; Deut 25:19).

Tg. Ps.-J. Deut. 30:4

Deut 29:1 begins a new section (cf. Deut 1:1; 4:44; 12:1) that looks beyond the failure of the people under the old covenant made at Sinai to the words of a new covenant that the LORD commanded Moses to make with the children of Israel in the land of Moab apart from the covenant that he made with them at Horeb. This does not anticipate a renewal of the Sinai covenant, nor does it speak of the making of a new covenant already in the land of Moab.[79] Rather, it sets up the words that the LORD commanded Moses in the land of Moab. In other words, the new covenant is revealed to Moses but not yet made. For the time being, the people do not yet have the kind of heart/mind that they need to know the LORD (Deut 29:4). Thus, the old covenant relationship will end in failure in accordance with the covenant curses outlined in Deut 28 (Deut 29:22–29). The new covenant will address the need for new, circumcised hearts (Deut 30:6)—spiritual circumcision. This inspires the hope of a new covenant relationship found in the Prophets (e.g., Jer 4:4; 31:31–34; 32:39–40; Ezek 11:19–20; 18:31; 36:26–27; see also Rom 2:28–29; Col 2:11; 4Q434).

The text of Deut 30:1b–7 outlines the restoration of the people of God beyond their experience of the blessing and the curse of the old covenant

---

79. See Sailhamer, *Pentateuch as Narrative*, 471–74. See also McConville, *Deuteronomy*, 37.

(Deut 30:1a; see Deut 28).[80] Even if they are banished at the end of the sky, from there the LORD will gather them and take them (Deut 30:4). Tg. Ps.-J. says that the Word of the Lord will gather them by the hands of Elijah the high priest and bring them near by the hands of King Messiah. This is reminiscent of Tg. Ps.-J.'s rendering of Exod 40:9–11 (see also Tg. Lam 4:22). According to Mal 4:5–6, Elijah will cause the heart of the fathers to return in addition to the heart of the children before the coming of the Day of the LORD (cf. Luke 1:17). The association of the Messiah with the making of a new covenant is likely motivated by the connection that is made in the Prophets (see, e.g., Isa 9:2, 6–7; 11:1–2; 42:1, 6; 49:6, 8; 61:1, 8; Jer 4:1–4; 23:5–6; 30:8–9; 31:31–34; 32:39–40; Ezek 34:23, 25; 37:24, 26; see also Luke 22:14–23; 1 Cor 11:23–25).

The LORD will circumcise the hearts of the people to love him with all their heart (Deut 30:6; cf. 6:5). According to Targum Pseudo-Jonathan, he will remove the stupidity of their hearts (cf. Tg. Onq.), for he will bring to an end the evil inclination of the world and create a good one. Tg. Neof. says that the Lord will circumcise the hearts of the people to love the instruction of the Torah with all their heart. This aligns with the new covenant passage in Jer 31:31–34, which says that the LORD will write his Torah not on tablets of stone (Exod 31:18) but on the hearts of the people (cf. Ezek 11:19–20; 36:26–27; 2 Cor 3:3, 6).

Deut 33:5

The last two poems of the Pentateuch are the Song of Moses (Deut 32:1–43) and the Blessing of Moses (Deut 33). The Song of Moses serves as an ongoing "witness" against the people (Deut 31:19) in anticipation that they will act corruptly after the death of Moses and thus find that calamity befalls them "in the end of days" (Deut 31:29; cf. Gen 49:1; Num 24:14; Deut 4:30). The Blessing of Moses for the twelve tribes of Israel has several points of contact with Jacob's blessing for his twelve sons (Gen 49:1–27), including the hope of a coming messianic figure from the tribe of Judah (Deut 33:7; cf. Gen 49:10; Mic 1:15; 4:8) who will be like a lion (Deut 33:20; cf. Gen 49:9).[81]

---

80. See Shepherd, *Text in the Middle*, 96–99.

81. Deut 33:20 is not about Gad. It is about one who enlarges Gad. He dwells like a lioness and tears an arm, also the top of the head (cf. SP Num 24:17).

Moses' blessing for the twelve tribes is framed by an introduction (Deut 33:1–5) and a conclusion (Deut 33:26–29). The introduction is remarkable for several reasons, but the clause of interest for the present discussion is Deut 33:5a: "And he was king in Jeshurun." Many English translations supply "the LORD" as the subject of this clause (e.g., ESV, NET, NLT, TEV), although this is not a feature of the Hebrew text. Others leave the subject unidentified (e.g., NAB, NIV). It is arguable that the most natural understanding of the text is that Moses is the subject (see Ibn Ezra), given the fact that he is the grammatical subject of the previous verse (Deut 33:4). This makes Moses a kind of messianic prototype (see again Deut 18:15, 18; 34:10; John 6:14; Acts 3:22; 7:37).[82]

The Targums do not employ the term "Messiah" or "King Messiah" in their renderings of Deut 33:5. Nevertheless, some of the Targums do have what may be considered messianic interpretations of the text. Tg. Onq. and Tg. Ps.-J. are not messianic. They render Deut 33:5 in a fairly straightforward fashion and do not identify the subject of the clause in question. Tg. Neof. and the Frg. Tg. (Vatican), however, render, "And a king will arise (יקום) from those of the house of Jacob. When he gathers together the heads of the people, all the tribes of the children of Israel will listen to him" (cf. Num 24:17; Deut 18:15, 18–19). The Cairo Genizah Ms DD has for the first part, "And a king [and a ruler] will arise from those of the house of Jacob."[83] This interpretation understands Moses to be a prefiguration of one who is yet to come.

FINAL THOUGHTS ON THE MESSIAH OF THE PENTATEUCHAL TARGUMS

Tg. Onq. is the least messianic of the Targums of the Pentateuch (Gen 49:10; Num 24:17). Tg. Ps.-J. is the most messianic, although its renderings in the passages cited previously do not always have a messianic interpretation. The Palestinian Targum tradition has at least one representative with a messianic rendering for each of the texts discussed in this chapter. The messianism of these Targums is largely driven in one way or another by their Hebrew source texts, particularly the great poems of the Pentateuch and

---

82. See Sailhamer, *Pentateuch as Narrative*, 477; Horbury, *Jewish Messianism*, 31, 49–51.

83. Cf. LXX: "And there will be in the beloved a ruler [or, And he will be in the beloved a ruler]."

their interpretive relationship to the narrative blocks that precede them—a relationship that is eschatological and messianic in nature. There is hardly a messianic text in the Pentateuch that the Targums miss,[84] and the Targums show great restraint in not multiplying their messianic renderings beyond reason. Because the Pentateuch itself motivates the Targums in this regard, it is not surprising to find that the Targums are in many instances heirs to a very early exegetical tradition that has also influenced the LXX, the Dead Sea Scrolls, the NT, the Syriac Peshitta, the Latin Vulgate, and the rabbinic literature. That is, because the tradition began with a certain kind of fidelity to the Hebrew text of the Pentateuch, it found many adherents among early interpreters and translators who likewise sought to be faithful to the Scripture that they received.

---

84. The passage in Deut 17:14–20 anticipates the establishment of a monarchy in general and should not necessarily be expected to generate messianic interpretation among the Targums.

2

The Messiah in the Prophets

SAMUEL

1 Sam 2:10

THE PRAYER OF HANNAH (1 Sam 2:1–10) is somewhat unsettled among textual witnesses to the book of Samuel (4QSam[a], LXX, and MT), in each case occupying a slightly different position between 1 Sam 1:28 and 2:11 and featuring different content (especially 1 Sam 2:8b–9a; cf. Ps 113:7–8).[1] What this tells the reader is that Hannah's prayer has been deliberately placed between 1 Sam 1:28 and 2:11 to interrupt the flow of the narrative. The content of the prayer rises above the level of Hannah's personal situation (1 Sam 1) and speaks in general terms about how God exalts the

---

1. "According to MT, an unidentified person bows before the Lord prior to Hannah's Song. In a similar way, according to 4QSam[a], Hannah prostrates herself before the Lord before the Song, and at that point she leaves Samuel at the temple. On the other hand, according to the LXX, Hannah leaves Samuel at the temple after the Song. Since the actions themselves are more or less identical, the data could also be presented as the insertion of the Song at two different positions, according to 4QSam[a] after Hannah's actions, and according to the LXX before these actions. MT resembles the scroll inasmuch as it describes an action before Hannah's Song, but it differs from the LXX and 4QSam[a] since it ascribes the actions to Elkanah. The insertion of the Song at two different locations in the context may indicate the late addition of that Song in the history of the growth of the first chapters of Samuel since the Song did not belong to the first layer of the text. When it was inserted into the text, it was inserted in a slightly different place in some manuscripts" (Tov, *Greek and Hebrew Bible*, 435).

lowly and abases the proud (1 Sam 2:3–9), culminating with anticipation of an exalted king who from Hannah's perspective could only be a future king (1 Sam 2:10).[2] Within the context of the Former Prophets, the prayer thus takes up the refrain of the conclusion to Judges (Judg 17:6; 18:1; 19:1; 21:25; cf. Deut 12:8), which identifies the absence of a king as the reason for the persistent problems during the period of the judges, and introduces the hope of the ideal anointed king as the central theme of the book of Samuel. This hope is not in the mere establishment of a monarchy (see Judg 9; 1 Sam 8). Rather, Hannah appears as a model reader of the poems of the Pentateuch (see earlier discussion, especially on Num 24:7) whose hope is in the coming of a messianic king.[3] Her prayer also works in concert with other major poetic units in the book of Samuel (2 Sam 1:17–27; 22:1–51; 23:1–7) to guide the reader through the narratives to the covenant with David (2 Sam 7) and the expectation of a Davidic king who is yet to come.

The LXX features a considerable expansion in 1 Sam 2:10 (1 Kgdms 2:10) as well as a mixed message about Hannah's hope for a king:

> The Lord will make his adversary weak; the Lord is holy. Let not the clever boast in his cleverness, and let not the mighty boast in his might, and let not the wealthy boast in his wealth, but let him who boasts boast in this: to understand and know the Lord and to execute justice and righteousness in the midst of the land. The Lord ascended to the heavens and thundered. He will judge earth's ends and gives strength to our kings and will exalt the horn of his anointed. (NETS)

The expansion is a version of the text of Jer 9:23–24, and its inclusion was likely motivated by its similarity in content to 1 Sam 2:1a, 3a, 4, 7, 9b.[4] The LXX most probably preserves here a witness to a more original Hebrew text of Jer 9:23–24 than the text attested by either MT or LXX Jeremiah.[5] The next to last clause of the translation ("and gives strength to our kings") employs the present tense and the plural "our kings" (i.e., the people's kings) as opposed to the MT's singular "his king" (i.e., the LORD's king). This

---

2. "A sober criticism, while not asserting categorically that the Song cannot be by Hannah, will recognize that its specific character and contents point to an occasion of a different kind as that upon which it was composed" (Driver, Notes on the Hebrew Text and the Topography of the Books of Samuel, 28).

3. See Sailhamer, Meaning of the Pentateuch, 254.

4. Ps 75 shows an awareness of this expanded version of Hannah's prayer (see Ps 75:3–5, 7, 10 and 1 Sam 2:3, 7b, 8b, 9a, 10 [LXX]).

5. See Seeligmann, *Gesammelte Studien*, 454–55; Tov, *Greek and Hebrew Bible*, 448–52.

seems to refer to a current monarchy, which would admittedly be strange from the perspective of Hannah.[6] On the other hand, the last clause of the translation ("and will exalt the horn of his anointed") uses the future tense and refers to the LORD's anointed king just like the MT. Thus, the LXX's distinction between the present kings and the future anointed one is at the very least open to a messianic interpretation.

Tg. Jon. presents Hannah's prayer in its entirety as a prophecy of things to come.[7] She prophesies in the expansion of 1 Sam 2:1 that her son Samuel is about to be a prophet over Israel (see 1 Sam 3:20). Samuel's grandson Heman and his fourteen sons will sing praise in the sanctuary with their brothers the Levites (see 1 Chr 6:33; 15:17; 25:5; 2 Chr 5:12). Hannah also prophesies about the deliverance from the Philistines in the days of Samuel and the revenge against the Philistines who will bring the ark of the covenant on a new cart (see 1 Sam 4–7). She goes on to prophesy about Sennacherib the king of Assyria, Nebuchadnezzar the king of Babylon, the kingdoms of Greece, and the sons of Haman in the time of Mordecai and Esther (Tg. Jon. 1 Sam 2:2–5). It is only at the conclusion of Hannah's prophecy (Tg. Jon. 1 Sam 2:10) that she speaks of the defeat of the final enemy (Gog) and the magnification of the messianic king:

> The Lord will shatter the enemies who rise up to do harm to his people. Against them from the sky with a loud sound the Lord will blast. He will exact just vengeance from Gog and the armies of violent peoples who come with him from the ends of the earth. And he will give strength to his king, and he will magnify the kingdom of his Messiah.

The reference to the defeat of Gog in the last days (Num 24:7 [SP, LXX]; Ezek 38–39; Rev 20:8), which the Targums of the Pentateuch have already featured prominently in their messianic renderings (see the earlier discussion of Exod 40:9–11; Num 11:26; 24:17, 20), establishes a context that requires the king at the end of the verse to be the Messiah (and not just another anointed king).[8]

---

6. In other words, this is different from anticipation of a future monarchy or dynasty. It also differs from passages that speak of a plurality of people who will reign with the Messiah in his future kingdom (Isa 32:1; Jer 3:15; 23:4–6; Dan 7:13–14, 27; Rev 5:10; 20:6).

7. See Harrington, "Apocalypse of Hannah," 147–52.

8. "In the apocalyptic context developed by the Tg, the anointed one is the eschatological Messiah" (Harrington and Saldarini, *Targum Jonathan*, 106.

Tg. Jon.'s messianic rendering of 1 Sam 2:10 has its basis first of all in the relationship between 1 Sam 2:10b ("And he will give strength to his king [למלכו], and he will exalt [וְיָרֵם] the horn of his anointed one") and Num 24:7b1 ("and his king [מלכו] will be higher [וְיָרֵם] than Agag [SP, LXX: Gog]"). It is also supported by several innerbiblical and early postbiblical interpretations of 1 Sam 2:10 (Ezek 29:21; Pss. 89:24; 112:9; 132:17; 148:14 [LXX]; Luke 1:69; 4Q491c). For instance, MT Ps 148:14a1 says, "And he exalted (וַיָּרֶם) a horn for his people," but the LXX reflects a text that says, "And he will exalt (= וְיָרֵם) a horn for his people." The early nature of the messianic exegetical tradition for 1 Sam 2:10 represented by Tg. Jon. is also evidenced by the influence of Hannah's prayer on Mary's Magnificat in Luke 1:46–55.[9] Mary appears to recognize in the coming birth of her child a kind of fulfillment of Hannah's prophetic words (see also Zechariah's words in Luke 1:69).

1 Sam 2:35

Immediately following Hannah's prayer is an account of the failure of Eli's two sons, Hophni and Phineas (1 Sam 2:11–26), and a prophetic announcement that the privilege of the priesthood will pass from the house of Eli (from the line of Aaron's son Ithamar) to the house of a faithful priest (presumably from the line of Aaron's other son Eleazar) (1 Sam 2:27–36; see also 1 Sam 3). This immediately calls to mind the possibility of either Samuel (1 Sam 3:20; 1 Chr 6:13) or Zadok (1 Kgs 2:35) as a candidate for the faithful priest. The language of 1 Sam 2:35, however, speaks of one whom the LORD will raise up (והקימתי) as a faithful (נאמן) priest who will do according to what is in the LORD's heart/mind (בלבבי); the LORD will build for him an enduring house (ובניתי לו בית נאמן), and he will walk before the LORD's anointed one (לפני משיחי) all the days. This language only applies to the king elsewhere in the book of Samuel (see 1 Sam 10:1; 13:14; 16:7, 22b; 2 Sam 7:11, 12, 16; see also 1 Chr 17:11, 14). Thus, the innerbiblical interpretation of the covenant with David in Zech 6:12–13 (cf. 2 Sam 7:13) understands the coming king to be one who will not only rule on his throne but also be a priest on his throne (contra LXX),[10] which is illustrated by the

---

9. See Shepherd, *Text in the Middle*, 118–19; Wright, *New Testament and the People*, 378–84.

10. Tg. Jon.'s version of the covenant with David in 2 Sam 7 is not explicitly messianic, but its version of Zech 6:12–13, which is based in part upon 2 Sam 7:13, is explicitly

image of Joshua the high priest with a royal crown on his head (Zech 6:11). Because one individual will occupy both offices, there will be no conflict between the two.

The messianic nature of Tg. Jon.'s version of 1 Sam 2:35 is manifest in its reference to the faithful priest's enduring "kingdom": "And I will raise up before me a faithful priest who according to my Word and according to my will he will do, and I will establish for him an enduring kingdom, and he will serve before my Messiah all the days." Where the MT and the LXX have "enduring house," the Targum has "enduring kingdom." This is a rather odd way to speak of the priest's house, but it works well with the idea that the faithful priest is also the king. The priest will thus serve before the Messiah not in the sense that he will be a separate entity but in the sense that he will be one and the same person. The concept of the priest-king is developed in the biblical depictions of Melchizedek (Gen 14:18–20; Ps 110; see also 11QMelch), Abraham, (Gen 22:2; 23:6 [LXX]), Moses (Exod 6:14–27; Deut 33:5), and perhaps also Samuel (1 Sam 2:18; 7:15). This concept has a major influence on the understanding of Jesus in the NT documents, particularly Heb 7 (see also Matt 22:41–46; Mark 12:35–37; Luke 20:41–44). On the other hand, the sectarian documents of the Qumran community reveal a conception of two Messiahs (the Messiahs of Aaron and Israel; 4QD[a] 10 I, 12; 1QS IX, 11; 1QSa II, 11–22),[11] which accommodates the biblical notion of a priestly function for the Messiah but avoids the conclusion that a single Messiah would be both priest and king.

2 Sam 22:1–51; 23:1–7

Much the same way that the Targums of the Pentateuch targeted the major poetic units for their messianic exegesis, so Tg. Jon. focuses its attention on the large poems in the book of Samuel for the same purpose. This has already been seen at the beginning of the book with the prayer of Hannah

messianic. Targum tradition may have left 2 Sam 7 untouched due to its manifestly messianic character. In other words, the thought may have been that the reader required no further guidance in this regard (see Shepherd, *Text in the Middle*, 122–29). It seems less likely that the absence of explicit messianism in the Targum of 2 Sam 7 is the result of an attempt to counteract Christian exegesis of the passage (see Levey, *Messiah*, 36). Such an effort to combat Christian exegesis is generally not a feature of the Targums elsewhere. Indeed, when it comes to messianic exegesis, the Targums tend to agree with Christian exegesis as much as or more than rabbinic literature in general.

11. See Schiffman, *Reclaiming the Dead Sea Scrolls*, 317–28.

(1 Sam 2:1–10), which introduces the main theme of the LORD's anointed king. Now at the conclusion of the book two poems are juxtaposed, David's song (2 Sam 22:1–51) and David's last words (2 Sam 23:1–7), which serve to reiterate that the hope of the covenant with David (2 Sam 7) is still intact despite the failures of David narrated in 2 Sam 9–20.[12] The Targums thus show a remarkable early awareness of the use of poems as a compositional technique to help readers understand the narratives that they accompany.

The Targum presents David in 2 Sam 22:29 as a prophet to whom the LORD has shown the world that is about to come for the righteous (cf. 2 Sam 23:1–2; Neh 12:24; 2 Chr 8:14; Acts 2:30). This sets up his prophecy about the Messiah in 2 Sam 22:32:

> Then, because of the miracle and the redemption that you will perform for your Messiah and for the remnant of your people who are left, all the peoples, nations, and tongues will praise and say, "There is no God but the Lord," for there is none apart from you. And your people will say, "There is no one strong except our God."[13]

The Hebrew text of 2 Sam 22:32 ("For who is God apart from the LORD, and who is a rock apart from our God?") is a clear echo of the words at the beginning of Hannah's prayer (1 Sam 2:2), and this can hardly be a coincidence given the other connections between the two poems (see 1 Sam 2:1 and 2 Sam 22:3; 1 Sam 2:7–8 and 2 Sam 22:28; 1 Sam 2:10 and 2 Sam 22:51). The Targum's language of divine redemption or deliverance for the Messiah has parallels in the Pentateuch (Num 24:7–8) and the Prophets (Hab 3:13; Zech 9:9). Likewise, the inclusion of the nations in the messianic salvation of the people of God is a prominent feature of other messianic prophecies (see, e.g., Gen 49:10; Isa 11:10; 42:6; 49:6; Dan 7:13–14). The conclusion to the Hebrew text of 2 Sam 22 in verse 51 takes up the language of the covenant with David and speaks of the LORD's deliverances of his king and his covenant loyalty to his anointed one, both to David and to his seed forever (cf. 2 Sam 7:12–16; 1 Chr 17:11–14). The messianic interpretation of 2 Sam 22 in Tg. Jon. finds confirmation in the reproduction of the poem in the

---

12. It is generally recognized that chapters 21–24 are an appendix that forms a chiastic structure: A) Famine (2 Sam 21:1–16), B) Warriors (2 Sam 21:17–22), C) Poem (2 Sam 22:1–51), C1) Poem (2 Sam 23:1–7), B1) Warriors (2 Sam 23:8–39), A1) Plague (2 Sam 24).

13. This expansion also occurs in Tg. Jon. Hab 3:18 and Tg. Psalm 18:32 (Eng., 18:31).

Psalter (Ps 18), which is paired with a Torah psalm (Ps 19).[14] The two other Torah psalms in the Psalter (Pss 1 and 119) are also paired with messianic psalms (Pss 2 and 118; see Matt 21:9, 42; 23:39; Mark 11:9–10; 12:10–11; Luke 13:35; 19:38; 20:17; John 12:13; Acts 4:11, 25–26; 13:33; Heb 1:5; 5:5; 1 Pet 2:7).

David is also depicted as a prophet in the Targum of 2 Sam 23:1:

> And these are the words of David's prophecy that he prophesied about the end of the world, concerning the days of comfort that are about to come. David the son of Jesse said, and the utterance of the man who was anointed for a kingdom, Messiah [or, anointed] by the Word of the God of Jacob, and it is good to number with your palate the sweetness of the praises of Israel.[15]

This depiction of David is prompted by the double occurrence of נאם ("prophetic utterance") in the Hebrew text of 2 Sam 23:1 and by the reference to the Spirit of the LORD (i.e., the Spirit of prophecy) by whom David claims to have spoken in 2 Sam 23:2 (cf. Num 11:29; Mic 3:8; 2 Chr 15:1; 20:14; 24:20). It is also motivated by the content of the poem, particularly verse 3. Thus, David's last words are words about the last days. While it is clear from the Targum's rendering of 2 Sam 23:3 that it understands David ultimately to be speaking about another, the Messiah, it is not immediately evident whether the Targum of 2 Sam 23:1 has in view one individual (David) or two (David and the Messiah).[16]

Witnesses to the Hebrew text of 2 Sam 23:1b also differ on the number of individuals referenced. The MT seems only to have David in view: "The prophetic utterance of David the son of Jesse and the prophetic utterance of the man who was raised on high (הֻקַם עָל),[17] the anointed (משיח) of the God of Jacob and the pleasant one of the songs of Israel." 4QSam[a], however, appears to continue the thought of 2 Sam 22:51. The first and last parts refer to David, but the second and third parts refer to David's seed (understood

14. See Mays, "Place of Torah Psalms," 3–12.

15. "These words are not merely a lyrical expansion of that promise [in 2 Sam 7], but a prophetic declaration uttered by David at the close of his life and by divine inspiration, concerning the true King of the kingdom of God" (Keil, *Books of Samuel*, 694).

16. See Levey's translation: "said the man who was anointed to the Messianic kingship by the Memra of the God of Jacob" (Levey, *Messiah*, 40).

17. The Syriac renders עָל ("on high") as if it were עֹל ("yoke"). The Latin Vulgate translates this same word as if it were עַל ("concerning"): "said the man to whom it was appointed concerning the Christ (de christo) of the God of Jacob" (cf. Luther; see Marsh, *Martin Luther on Reading the Bible*, 162–92).

in an individual sense rather than a collective sense): "The prophetic utterance of David the son of Jesse, and the prophetic utterance about the man whom God raises up (הקים אל), the Messiah (משיח) of the God of Jacob, and the pleasant one of the songs of Israel." The *hiphil* of קום with God as subject signals a connection to the words of the covenant with David (2 Sam 7:12) and other prophecies about the messianic king (e.g., Jer 23:5; 30:9; Ezek 34:23). The LXX, which translates נאם ("prophetic utterance") as if it were נאמן ("faithful"), appears to follow a source text similar though not identical to 4QSam[a]: "Faithful is David the son of Jesse, and faithful is the man whom the Lord raises up (= הקים) as the anointed/Christ/Messiah of the God of Jacob, and beautiful are Israel's psalms."

Whereas modern interpreters tend not to understand 2 Sam 23:3–5 in a messianic sense,[18] Tg. Jon. renders verse 3 in such a way that the reader can easily see that the ruler to which David refers in the first part of 3b is God, while the one to which he refers in the second part is the Messiah:[19] "David said, 'The God of Israel spoke to me, the Mighty One of Israel who rules over humanity, the one who judges the truth, he said to appoint for me a king, he is the Messiah who is about to rise up and rule in the fear of the Lord.'" The language of this rendering is reminiscent of Dan 4:17, which says that the Most High is ruler (שליט) over the kingdom of mankind and he gives it to whomever he pleases (see Dan 7:13–14, 27). The phrase "in the fear of the Lord" in both the Hebrew text and the Targum has an important connection to the presentation of the Messiah in Isa 11:1–3 (also, for מושל ["ruler"] as a messianic title, see Jer 30:21; Mic 5:2). The LXX takes 2 Sam 23:3b in a slightly different direction: "Speak a parable [= מָשָׁל]. How might you [pl.] strengthen fear of God by a man (ἐν ἀνθρώπῳ)?" This translation may be related to the use of ἄνθρωπος ("man") as a messianic title elsewhere in the LXX (see the earlier discussion of Num 24:7, 17; see also Isa 19:20).

The description of the messianic ruler continues in the Hebrew text of 2 Sam 23:4, which compares the king to the light of a cloudless morning when the sun rises. This has several points of contact with other messianic prophecies elsewhere in the Hebrew Bible (see Num 24:17; Isa 9:2; 42:6; 49:6; Mal 4:2). The text goes on to say that the brightness of this light brings forth growth from the ground after the rain (cf. Ezek 34:23, 26; Hos 6:3;

---

18. E.g., McCarter, *2 Samuel*, 476–86.

19. It is arguable that the Hebrew text refers to the Messiah in both parts (see Jer 23:5; Zech 9:9).

Pss 72:5–7; 110:3). The early versions (LXX, Syr., Vulg.) do not feature an explicit messianic interpretation of this text, but Tg. Jon. understands the light of the Messiah to benefit the righteous whose glory will be as radiant as the morning light (cf. Dan 12:3; Matt 13:43), and like the sun, which will be 343 times brighter (7 x 7 x 7; see Isa 30:26; cf. Isa 60:19–20; Zech 14:6–7; Rev 21:22—22:5).

The Hebrew text of 2 Sam 23:5a is ambiguous as to whether it is a statement ("For not so is my house with God.") or a question ("For not so is my house with God?"). The former works well if David has been speaking about the Messiah up to this point. That is, David's house is not currently the house of the Messiah. The latter works well if David has been speaking only about his rule and dynasty thus far. That is, the question would be a rhetorical question that assumes an affirmative response. Both the LXX and the Syriac are equally ambiguous about this. Printed editions of the LXX punctuate the text with a question mark, and this is followed by the NETS version. Brenton's translation of the LXX, however, renders the text as a statement: "For my house *is* not so with the Mighty One." The Latin Vulgate, as rendered by the Douay-Rheims Bible, translates the text as a statement, but it is expressing the sentiment of 2 Sam 7:18–29 that David feels unworthy of the covenant relationship: "Neither is my house so great with God, that he should make with me an eternal covenant" (*nec tanta est domus mea apud Deum ut pactum aeternum iniret mecum*). Modern English versions are also divided about what to do with this text. The KJV, for example, takes it to mean that David's house is not currently as described in the previous verses: "Although my house *be* not so with God; yet he hath made with me an everlasting covenant" (cf. ASV). On the other hand, the ESV assumes that 2 Sam 23:5a is a question: "For does not my house stand so with God?"[20] The NET converts this into a positive statement: "My dynasty is approved by God."

Tg. Jon.'s rendering of 2 Sam 23:5a has been understood in more than one way. Harrington and Saldarini translate it as follows: "David said: 'More than this (is) my house before God.'"[21] It is difficult to see, however, in what sense David's house could possibly be more than what is described in 2 Sam 23:3–4. Levey translates, "Said David, moreover: 'My house is in

---

20. The NIV interprets כֵן not as the adverb "so" but as the adjective "right": "Is not my house right with God?"

21. Harrington and Saldarini, *Targum Jonathan*, 204.

the presence of God.'"[22] The main difference between these two translations is their understanding of the Aramaic phrase יתיר מכדון, which the former understands as part of David's discourse ("More than this"), and the latter takes in an adverbial sense ("moreover") with the introduction to David's discourse. Thus, the Targum of 2 Sam 23:5a does little to disambiguate the Hebrew source. Nevertheless, it is evident from the way the Targum renders the remainder of the verse that it ultimately looks beyond David's rule and dynasty to an enduring eschatological kingdom: "for he has made an everlasting covenant with me that my kingdom will last like the orders of creation [בראשית (Gen 1:1)] and will be preserved for the world to come." This kingdom will have no competition.

The indefinite or everlasting covenant (ברית עולם) to which 2 Sam 23:5b refers is the covenant with David in 2 Sam 7 (cf. Gen 9:16; 17:7; Exod 31:16; Isa 55:3; 61:8; Jer 32:40; Ezek 37:26). This covenant is not primarily about David but about David's seed. Masoretic manuscript witnesses differ as to whether 2 Sam 23:5b refers to David ("for an everlasting covenant has he made with me [לי]") or to his seed ("for an everlasting covenant has he made with him [לו]"). The covenant is arranged in all its parts and preserved for the future. This is because all of David's deliverance and desire will not come to fruition (lit., "he [God] will not cause those things to sprout [לא יצמיח]") in his lifetime (see KJV, ASV). Some translations (e.g., ESV, NET) render this as a question ("Will he [God] not cause those things to sprout?"),[23] which could indicate either that David's deliverance and desire will come to fruition in his lifetime or simply that God will bring these things to pass at some point. It is worthwhile to note that the negated verb לא יצמיח ("he will not cause to sprout") may have an important link to the messianic title "Sprout" or "Branch" (צמח) (see Isa 4:2; Jer 23:5; Zech 3:8; 6:12; Ps 132:17).

KINGS

1 Kgs 4:33a

At first glance, 1 Kgs 4:33a would seem to be the last place where readers might expect to find a messianic interpretation in the Targum. The Hebrew

22. Levey, *Messiah*, 41.

23. See also Lucian's recension and the Syriac, which have no representation of the negation.

text of this half verse tells of how Solomon in his great wisdom "spoke about the trees, from the cedar in Lebanon to the hyssop that goes forth in the wall." Tg. Jon. transforms this so that it speaks of how Solomon "prophesied about the kings of the house of David who were about to rule in this world and in the world of the Messiah" (cf. Isa 32:1; Jer 23:4–5; Mic 5:5–6; Dan 7:13–14, 27; Rev 5:10; 20:6). The Targum, however, is not without its reasons for doing this. Trees, and cedars in particular, are commonly used in the Bible as figures for rulers (see Judg 9:15; Isa 2:13; 14:8; Zech 11:1–2). Furthermore, the cedar is a figure for a messianic ruler in the prophecy of Ezek 17:22–24. Levey adds that Ps 72, which most Masoretic manuscripts attribute to Solomon, is, according to the Targum, a prophecy about the Messiah.[24]

ISAIAH

Isa 4:2

Outside of the Targums of the Pentateuch, the Targum of Isaiah is one of the most productive in terms of messianic renderings of passages. According to Bruce Chilton, usage of the term "Messiah" in the Targum of Isaiah is consistent with the theology of an early *meturgeman* who provided the basic framework upon which later interpreters built.[25] The first occurrence of this usage is in Isa 4:2: "At that time [MT: In that day], the Messiah of the Lord [MT: the Branch of the LORD] will be for joy [MT: beauty] and for glory, and those who do the Torah [MT: the fruit of the land] will be for greatness [MT: exaltation] and for praise [MT: renown] to the remnant of Israel." The salvation texts of Isa 2:2–5 and 4:2–6 frame three judgment passages in Isa 2:6–22; 3:1–15; 3:16—4:1. This relationship between Isa 2:2–5 and 4:2–6 may have given rise to an eschatological interpretation of the phrase "In that day" (Isa 4:2) as referring to "in the end of days" (Isa 2:2; see the earlier discussion of this phrase in connection with the poems of the Pentateuch [Gen 49:1; Num 24:14; Deut 4:30; 31:29]).[26]

---

24. Levey, *Messiah*, 42.

25. Chilton, *Glory of Israel*, 86–87.

26. "The dominant eschatological emphasis of 2:1–4 and 2:6ff. reverberates strongly in 4:2. Not just ordinary time is being extended, but God's time of eschatological judgment and salvation, which comprises one single reality without a fixed temporal sequence" (Childs, *Isaiah*, 35).

The Targum interprets the phrase "the Branch of the LORD" (צמח יהוה) to be a messianic title, and this is consistent with the way Tg. Jon. interprets צמח ("Branch") elsewhere (see Jer 23:5; Zech 3:8; 6:12; see also 4QFlor [4Q174]; 4Q252). The phrase "the fruit of the land" is then interpreted to be "those who do the Torah," presumably on the basis of Ps 1:1–3 where the text says that those who devote themselves to the Torah will be like fruit-bearing trees.[27] On the other hand, Calvin understands both the branch and the fruit to denote "an unusual and abundant supply of grace."[28] Brevard Childs, however, comments as follows:

> [O]nce the term "branch" had become a technical term for the Messiah in later prophetic literature, it is difficult to imagine this earlier, non-technical usage not accumulating a richer connotation than perhaps originally intended. Particularly does this move seem likely when one recalls that the passage has been linked intertextually with its larger Isaianic context. Had not Isa. 11:1 spoken of a "shoot" (*nēṣer*) from the stump of Jesse, which initiated the prophetic theme of the return of paradisical peace and harmony (vv. 6–9; cf. 65:21ff.)?[29]

Childs concludes that in the present literary context the branch is the Messiah, and the fruit of the land represents the return of paradise. Not to be overlooked, however, is the way in which Isa 28:5 takes up the language of both parts of Isa 4:2. "In that day," according to Isa 28:5, "the LORD of hosts will be for a crown of beauty and for a diadem of glory to the remnant of his people" (see later discussion of Tg. Jon.). This will manifest itself in the coming of a messianic king (Isa 28:16; cf. 8:14; Zech 3:9; Ps 118:22; Dan 2:34–35, 44–45; Rom 9:33; 10:11; 1 Pet 2:6).

Isa 9:6–7

Isa 9:6–7 is the first of several examples in the Targum of Isaiah where the interpretation aligns more with early Christian exegesis than with mainstream Jewish or rabbinic exegesis,[30] suggesting an early exegetical tradition that was never revised in the wake of debates between Jews

---

27. Franz Delitzsch considers "the fruit of the land" to be another messianic epithet (Delitzsch, *Isaiah*, 99).

28. Calvin, *Commentary on Isaiah*, 152.

29. Childs, *Isaiah*, 36.

30. See McKinion, *Isaiah 1–39*, 70–78. See also Luke 1:32–33.

and Christians about the meaning of the passage. Since this point is by no means a universally accepted one, it will require some demonstration. The Hebrew text of these two verses concludes a unit (Isa 6:1—9:7) and serves to identify the one whose "name" will be called "God with us" (Isa 7:14; cf. Jer 23:6; see also Matt 1:21–23) as a messianic king whose fuller description is subsequently provided in Isa 11:1–10.[31] This king's "name" will be called "Wonder, Counselor [not Wonderful Counselor], Mighty God [cf. Isa 10:21], Everlasting Father [not in a trinitarian sense], Prince of Peace" (Isa 9:6).[32] He will sit on the throne of David in fulfillment of the Davidic covenant (2 Sam 7:12–16), ruling in justice and righteousness (cf. Jer 23:5), and his kingdom will last forever (Isa 9:7; see also Dan 7:14).

The LXX translation of Isa 9:6b differs considerably from the MT; but given the general character of LXX Isaiah,[33] this difference is likely not due to the presence of a different Hebrew source text for the Greek translator. Rather, the translator himself has introduced an interpretation that is at variance with the sense of the Hebrew text: "and he will be called Messenger of Great Counsel; for I will bring peace upon the rulers, peace and health to him." The translation is still about the coming child who will sit on the throne of David, but suddenly the unique epithets "Mighty God" and "Everlasting Father" no longer apply. This leaves open the question of whether the child will be the Messiah or simply a righteous king like Hezekiah. Isac Leo Seeligmann, who considers all the epithets of the Hebrew text to constitute the "name" of the Messiah, understands the Messenger of Great Counsel in the LXX to be a messianic title (cf. Isa 52:7; Jer 32:19; Nah 1:15).[34] The translator has mistaken the Hebrew אבי ("Father") to be אביא ("I will bring"). Thus, God proclaims the Messiah as one who will announce peace and as one through whom he will bring peace (cf. Mic 5:5; Zech 9:10; Ps 72:3). On the other hand, it is entirely possible that the LXX has in view a king like Hezekiah in whose days there would be peace and stability (Isa 39:8). There is nothing about the translation that requires a messianic interpretation.

---

31. See Childs, *Isaiah*, 80–81.

32. The qal verb ויקרא (lit., "and he called") need not be re-vocalized as a niphal (as suggested in the BHS apparatus). The verb has no explicit subject and is thus indefinite (see GKC §144d). For this reason the early versions (LXX, Syr., Tg., Vulg.) render it as a passive verb.

33. See Tov, *Textual Criticism of the Hebrew Bible*, 137.

34. Seeligmann, *Septuagint Version of Isaiah*, 291.

For later Jewish tradition, the prevailing opinion is that the child of Isa 9:6–7 is not the Messiah. The referent is Hezekiah, and Hezekiah is not the Messiah. This is in marked contrast to the Christian explanation of Christ from this text as God in the flesh. According to b. Sanh. 94a, Hezekiah cannot be the Messiah due to the spelling of לסרבה with a "closed" ם rather than an "open" מ. This indicates that God intended to make Hezekiah into the Messiah, and Sennacherib into Gog and Magog, but this option was closed because of the way Hezekiah contrasted with David. If David, who recited many songs before God, was not made Messiah, how could Hezekiah, who recited no songs, be made Messiah? The text goes on to say that the earth offered a song to fill this gap, but there is no indication that this resulted in the designation of Hezekiah as the Messiah. The Talmud later cites the view of Hillel that there would be no future Messiah because "they consumed him in the time of Hezekiah" (b. Sanh. 98b, 99a), which perhaps means that the time of his coming was consummated, although it is not clear whether this means Hezekiah was the Messiah. This view of Hillel is then immediately contradicted in b. Sanh. 99a where reference is made to the messianic prophecy of Zech 9:9, which came well after the time of Hezekiah.

The understanding of the official Babylonian Talmud is perpetuated in the influential medieval commentary of Rashi who explicitly refutes the Christian interpretation of Isa 9:6–7.[35] According to Rashi, Christians (and all early versions, including the LXX and Tg. Jon.!) have erred because they have taken ויקרא to mean "and he will be called" rather than "and he called." This has led to the misunderstanding that Christ will be called all the appellations of Isa 9:6 by the people. Rashi's view is that the "names" of Isa 9:6 are God's names, and it was God who, as the wonderful counselor and everlasting father, called Hezekiah "prince of peace." Despite his knowledge of the Targum of this passage, which considers the prince of peace to be the Messiah, Rashi does not go so far as to say that Hezekiah was the Messiah. Even Redak, who believes the prophecy ultimately looks forward to the reinstatement of the Davidic kingdom in the messianic era (Isa 9:7), limits the prophecy of Isa 9:6 to Hezekiah and does not consider him to be the Messiah.

Tg. Jon.'s rendering of Isa 9:6–7 has been understood in more than one way. On the one hand, it is clearly messianic, which is at odds with mainstream Jewish interpretation but in agreement with Christian

35. Rosenberg, *Mikraoth Gedoloth: Isaiah*, 1:87–88.

interpretation. It does not limit the prophecy to Hezekiah. On the other hand, it is not clear from the Targum whether the epithets "Mighty God" and "Everlasting Father" apply to God (as in Jewish tradition) or to the Messiah (as in Christian tradition). Below are three published translations of verse 6b. The first two are in agreement that the epithets apply to God, although they disagree about the extent of the Messiah's name, but the last translation is somewhat ambiguous about the epithets.

> Levey: and his name has been called by the One who gives wonderful counsel, the Mighty God, He who lives forever: 'Messiah,' in whose day peace shall abound for us.[36]

> Chilton: and his name will be called *before the* Wonderful Counselor, *the* Mighty God, existing forever, *"The messiah in whose days* peace *will increase upon us."*[37]

> Eldon Clem: And his name has been called from before the One Who Causes Wonderful Counsel, God the Warrior, the Eternally Existing One—the Messiah who will increase peace upon us in his days.[38]

Since Clem does not use quotation marks, it is not clear whether "God the Warrior [= Mighty God], the Eternally Existing One [= Everlasting Father]" is in apposition to "the One Who Causes Wonderful Counsel" or simply the beginning of the Messiah's name, yet this reflects well the ambiguity of the Aramaic text itself. It is entirely possible to render the Targum as follows: "and his name is called before the one who makes counsel wonderful: 'Mighty God, One Who Lives Forever, the Messiah in Whose Days Peace Will Increase upon Us.'" Regardless of the way in which this is understood, it is clear that the Targum interprets the prince of peace to be the Messiah, not Hezekiah.[39] This is reiterated in its rendering of Isa 9:7 where the text says that the greatness of those who do the Torah in the messianic kingdom will be great—a clear link back to the Targum's messianic rendering of Isa 4:2 (see also Isa 2:2–5). Thus, while the Targum is not necessarily perfectly aligned with Christian tradition (note also that it does not call the Messiah "Wonder, Counselor"), its messianic interpretation is closer to that tradition than it is to the predominant Jewish one.

---

36. Levey, *Messiah*, 45. See also Isa 28:29.

37. Chilton, *Isaiah Targum*, 21.

38. Accordance.

39. See Strack and Billerbeck, *Commentary on the New Testament*, 386.

Isa 10:27

The Hebrew text of Isa 10:24–27 urges the people of Zion not to be afraid of Assyria, the enemy who strikes them with the rod and who lifts up his staff against them "in the manner of Egypt," for in a little while the LORD's indignation against his own people will come to an end, and he will turn his attention to the destruction of the enemy (see Isa 10:5–19). He will arouse against him a scourge, "like the striking of Midian at the rock of Oreb" (see Judg 7:25; Isa 9:4), and he will lift his staff over the sea, "in the manner of Egypt" (see Exod 14:26). Tg. Jon. interprets this second occurrence of the phrase "in the manner of Egypt" to mean "as the tyranny of Pharaoh passed from you at the sea, and mighty deeds will be performed for you as in the manner of Egypt." In that day, the enemy's burden will be removed from the people's shoulder, and his yoke from their neck. The yoke will be destroyed because of שמן. The Targum interprets שמן to be the "oil" of anointing (1 Sam 16:13) and thus understands the text to mean that the nations will be shattered before the Messiah.

Levey comments, "This passage is significant because it draws a parallel between the deliverance from Egypt and the deliverance which is to be effected by the Messiah, the re-enactment of the original drama of liberation."[40] A comparison may be made here to the prophecy of Num 24:7–9 (cf. Num 23:22, 24), which also speaks of a new, messianic exodus (see also Isa 11:11, 16; 12:2 [cf. Exod 15:2; Ps 118:14]). There are several factors in the context of Isa 10 that encourage an eschatological and messianic reading of the text. First, Isa 10:20–23 speaks of remnant that will return to Mighty God (cf. Isa 7:3; 9:6), for the Lord is performing "a complete destruction and that which is determined" (כלה ונחרצה) in the midst of all the land (cf. Isa 28:22). This distinctive language reappears later at the end of the eschatological and messianic prophecy of Dan 9:24–27. Second, the image of the removal of the "yoke" (על) in Isa 10:27 resurfaces in Jer 30:8–9 (cf. Hos 3:5; see also Isa 9:4), which is another passage that Tg. Jon. interprets messianically. Third, the text of Isa 10:27–34, which defies historical identification (cf. Mic 1:8–16),[41] leads directly into the extended messianic prophecy of Isa 11:1–10.

---

40. Levey, *Messiah*, 47.
41. See Childs, *Isaiah*, 96–97.

Isa 11:1–10

Isa 11 is certainly one text for which readers would expect to find a messianic rendering in the Targum. The opening verse of this chapter traces the ancestral lineage or family tree of the Messiah back to David's father Jesse: "And a branch (חטר) will go forth from the stem of Jesse, and a sprout (נצר) from his roots will bear fruit" (cf. Dan 11:7; see also T. Jud. 24:4–6). The Hebrew words translated "branch" and "sprout" here are not the same as the word translated "Branch" in Isa 4:2 (צמח), but they do fall into the same semantic field (see also Isa 53:2; 60:21). Tg. Jon. translates the text as follows: "And a king will go forth from the sons of Jesse, and the Messiah from the sons of his sons will be anointed [or, raised]." The Targum simply removes the metaphor and identifies the referent as a messianic king from the descendants of Jesse.

The extant text of Tg. Jon. for Isa 11:1 preserves a messianic interpretation that goes back at least as early as the Dead Sea Scrolls and the Gospel according to Matthew. 4Q161 (4QpIsa^a) is a fragmentary *pesher* ("interpretation") or commentary for Isaiah. It understands Isa 10:33–34 to be a reference to the Kittim (see the earlier discussion of Num 24:24). Then, after citing Isa 11:1–5, it says: "[The interpretation of the word is about the Branch] of David who is about to stand in the e[nd of days]" (see Isa 2:2; 4:2). The text goes on to say that this messianic figure will defeat his enemy and rule over the peoples and "Magog" (see Ezek 38–39; Rev 20:8). 4Q285 (4QSM) also provides a messianic interpretation of Isa 10:34—11:1: "And a branch will go forth from the stem of Jesse . . . the Branch of David. And they will be judged . . . and the Ruler of the Congregation, the Bra[nch of David] will kill him" (cf. CD 7:18–21).[42] Matthew's messianic interpretation of Isa 11:1 is more subtle. In his account of the return of Jesus' family from Egypt to live in Nazareth, Matthew says that this happened so that what had been spoken by the prophets—that he would be called a Nazarene—might be fulfilled (Matt 2:23). Given the fact that such a prediction does not occur in the prophets, and given the early church testimony to the Semitic origins of Matthew's Gospel, it is likely that the Greek text reflects a play on words between נצר ("sprout") from Isa 11:1 and the word נצרי ("Nazarene").[43] In other words, by referring to the prophets to explain why Jesus became a "Nazarene" (נצרי), Matthew identifies Jesus the Messiah as

---

42. See also Priestly Blessings for the Last Days 5:20–29.

43. See Shepherd, "Semitic Wordplay," 52–56.

the "sprout" (נצר) from Isa 11:1 (see also Matt 1:1, 22–23; 3:3; 4:14–16; 8:17; 12:15–21; b. Sanh. 43a).

According to Isa 11:2–3a, the Spirit of the LORD will rest upon the Messiah (cf. Isa 42:1; 61:1), endowing him with all the qualities set forth in the prologue to the book of Proverbs (Prov 1:1–7; cf. Deut 34:9; 2 Sam 23:2; 1 En. 49; 1Q28b 5:25; 4Q444; Pss. Sol. 17:37; 18:7; b. Sanh. 93b). The importance of this for the authors of the Synoptic Gospels can be seen in their accounts of Jesus' baptism (Matt 3:16; Mark 1:10; Luke 3:22) and in their efforts to show the superiority of Jesus' wisdom to that of Solomon (Matt 12:42; Luke 11:31). The Messiah of Isa 11:3b–9 will bring forth justice, righteousness, and peace just as the Messiah of Isa 9:6–7 (see also Isa 42:1–4; 65:25).[44] The image of the Messiah slaying the wicked in Isa 11:4b (cf. 49:2) is an important feature of the depiction of the warrior Christ in the book of Revelation (Rev 1:16; 2:12, 16; 19:15; see also 2 Thess 2:8; Pss. Sol. 17:24, 29, 35). The Targum as it appears in Codex Reuchlinianus identifies the wicked in Isa 11:4b as "Armilus" (i.e., "Romulus"), which is a cipher for Rome. Levey notes that Rome takes the place of Gog in late rabbinic legend.[45]

The second occurrence of משיחא ("Messiah") in the Targum of Isa 11 comes in verse 6. It will be in the days of Israel's Messiah that the land will enjoy the peace envisioned by Isa 6:6–9 (cf. Isa 2:4; 65:25; Hab 2:14). Peace is a common feature of prophetic depictions of the Messiah and his kingdom (e.g., Isa 9:6–7; Ezek 34:25; Mic 5:5a; Ps 72:3). According to Isa 11:10a, the nations in that future day will seek the root of Jesse who stands as a banner for peoples (cf. 11:1).[46] Tg. Jon. interprets this to mean that kingdoms will heed the descendant of Jesse who is about to stand as a sign for the peoples (cf. Gen 49:10; Isa 42:4, 6; 49:6; 66:19; Ps 72:10–11; Dan 7:13–14). This first of all indicates that the Lord will lift a banner (i.e., the Messiah; cf. Num 21:8) to the nations and gather the banished of Israel and the scattered of Judah in order to reunite them (Isa 11:11–14; cf. Jer 3:18; Ezek 37:15–28; Zech 9:13; 10:6). It also means that the nations themselves will be drawn to the Messiah (see Isa 66:18–24; cf. Jer 3:17; John 3:14; 12:32; Rom 15:12).

---

44. Note how Isa 65:25 not only revisits the imagery of Isa 11:6–9 but also incorporates language from Gen 3:14–15 (see also Isa 27:1). See Shepherd, *Text in the Middle*, 14–16.

45. Levey, *Messiah*, 52.

46. The phrase "the root of David" is a messianic title in Rev 5:5; 22:16. See also Gen. Rab. 97.

Isaiah 11:15–16 employs new exodus imagery to depict the messianic deliverance (cf. Num 24:7–9; Tg. Jon. Isa 10:26–27). This is immediately followed by a song of praise (Isa 12) that cites from the poetic celebration of the original exodus in Exod 15: "For my strength and song is Yah the LORD, and he has become my salvation" (Isa 12:2b; cf. Exod 15:2a).[47] Isaiah 12:2b thus bridges the gap between Exod 15:2a and Ps 118:14,[48] which is part of a psalm that looks forward to a new, messianic "exodus" or deliverance and serves as the basis for the New Testament authors' understanding of the leaders' rejection of Jesus (Ps 118:22; see Matt 21:33–46) and his so-called triumphal entry (Ps 118:25–26; cf. Zech 9:9–10; Ps 24:7–10; see Matt 21:1–11; John 12:12–19).

Isa 14:29

At the end of a lengthy oracle concerning Babylon in Isa 13:1—14:23 are two short passages devoted to Assyria (Isa 14:24–27) and Philistia (Isa 14:28–32). The latter passage features an oracle from the year of King Ahaz's death (ca. 715 BCE) that warns the people of Philistia not to rejoice that the rod of the one who struck them is broken, "for from a serpent's root will go forth an adder, and its fruit will be a flying fiery serpent" (Isa 14:28–29). Tg. Jon. connects the serpent's root in this text with the root of Jesse in Isa 11:1, 10: "for from the descendants of Jesse the Messiah will go forth, and his works will be among you like a dismembering [Antwerp Polyglot: flying] serpent." This rendering bears a relationship to the story about the bronze serpent in Num 21:4–9 where those who look upon the serpent in faith live and do not die from the serpent bites. According to 2 Kgs 18:4, the bronze serpent eventually became the object of forbidden worship, but in John 3:14–15 the serpent raised by Moses in the wilderness is analogous to the raising of the Son of Man as an object of faith (see John 8:28; 12:32, 34; see also 1 Cor 10:9; cf. Isa 11:10; 66:19). The one who believes in the Son will not perish but have everlasting life (John 3:16). Other features of Isa 14:28–32 that may have prompted the Targum's messianic interpretation of verse 29 include the references to those who lie down in security (Isa 14:30a; cf. Jer 23:5–6; Ezek 34:23, 25, 27–28) and to the establishment of Zion, the City of David (Isa 14:32; cf. 2:3).

---

47. Exod 15 goes on to speak of the eternal kingship of the LORD (Exod 15:18).

48. See Shepherd, *Text in the Middle*, 62–64.

Isa 16:1–5

The oracle concerning Moab in Isa 15–16 shares a substantial amount of material with Jer 48. This relationship is usually explained in terms of Jeremiah's dependence upon Isaiah rather than Isaiah's dependence upon Jeremiah or mutual dependence upon a common source.[49] The absence of the potentially messianic text of Isa 16:1–5 in Jer 48, however, has always been a curiously unexplained aspect of this dependence, especially given Jeremiah's messianic interests elsewhere (e.g., Jer 23:5–6; 30:9). George Gray suggests that the text is "an interpolated Messianic passage which has re-acted on the interpretation of v.[4a, b], turning what was an address to Şion (v.[1]) into an address to Moab."[50] He also notes that the passage by itself "would suggest familiar features of the Messianic age."

Tg. Jon. interprets the sending of a ram to the ruler of the land in Isa 16:1 to be the bringing of tribute to the Messiah of Israel (cf. Ps 72:10). The LXX, on the other hand, translates, "I will send as it were creeping animals on the land" (= שלוח כרמש לארץ). The Syriac reads בר ("son") instead of כר ("ram"): "Send to the son of the ruler of the land." The Latin Vulgate, however, highlights the ram in particular as a lamb and renders, "Send the lamb, O Lord, the ruler of the land/earth" (cf. John 1:29). Levey thinks that the messianism of the Latin Vulgate here may be based on the Targum.[51]

The Hebrew text of Isa 16:5 says that a throne will be established in covenant loyalty. This language comes from the covenant with David (2 Sam 7:15–16; 1 Chr 17:13–14) and is reiterated in multiple messianic prophecies (see, e.g., Isa 9:6–7; Zech 6:12–13). Thus, Tg. Jon. understands it to mean that the throne of the Messiah of Israel will be established in goodness. The Hebrew text of the verse goes on to say that one who judges and seeks justice and who is swift or skilled in righteousness will sit on the throne in faithfulness in the tent of David. Again, these are hallmarks of messianic prophecies elsewhere in the book of Isaiah (e.g., Isa 9:6–7; 11:3–5; 42:1–4) and beyond (e.g., Jer 23:5–6; Ps 72:1–4). The Targum says that the Messiah will sit on the throne in truth in the city of David as a judge, seeking judgment/justice and doing truth/righteousness. Its rendering of "the tent of David" as "the city of David" may be under the influence of the messianic prophecy in Amos 9:11, which speaks of the restoration of

---

49. See Parke-Taylor, *Formation of Jeremiah*, 128–31.

50. Gray, *Critical and Exegetical Commentary*, 289.

51. Levey, *Messiah*, 57.

the Davidic kingdom (see Tg. Jon.) in terms of the raising up of the fallen "booth" of David (cf. Isa 1:8; 4:6).

Isa 28:5

Levey considers the messianic rendering of Isa 28:5 in Tg. Jon. to be inexplicable,[52] but a comparison of the Hebrew and Aramaic texts of Isa 28:5 with those of Isa 4:2 reveals that the Targum's messianic interpretation of Isa 28:5 is motivated by its interpretation of similar language in Isa 4:2:

> Isa 4:2 (Hebrew): In that day, the Branch of the LORD will be for beauty and for glory, and the fruit of the land will be for exaltation and for renown to the remnant of Israel.

> Isa 4:2 (Aramaic): At that time, the Messiah of the Lord will be for joy and for glory, and those who do the Torah will be for greatness and for praise to the remnant of Israel.

> Isa 28:5 (Hebrew): In that day, the LORD of hosts will be for a crown of beauty and for a diadem of glory to the remnant of his people.

> Isa 28:5 (Aramaic): At that time, the Messiah of the Lord of hosts will be for a crown of joy and for a diadem of praise to the remnant of his people.

The Targum's sensitivity to the shared used of this language in texts separated by a great distance from one another like this is remarkable. The Hebrew text of Isa 28:7 goes on to say that the LORD will be for a spirit of justice, one of the key features of the messianic kingdom (Isa 4:4; 9:6–7; 11:3–5; 42:1–4). Furthermore, the latter half of the chapter contrasts the corrupt leaders with a "stone" (Tg. Jon.: "king") with whom justice and righteousness will come (Isa 28:16–17; see 8:14; Zech 3:9; Ps 118:22; Dan 2:34–35, 44–45). This stone is the Messiah according to the apostles Paul (Rom 9:33) and Peter (1 Pet 2:6).[53]

Isa 42:1–7

The first of Isaiah's servant songs in 42:1–4 or 42:1–7 raises the question of the identity of the servant. Normally a servant of the LORD in the Bible is

52. Levey, *Messiah*, 58.
53. See Shepherd, *Text in the Middle*, 139.

an individual (e.g., Moses, Joshua, David), but in Isaiah there are several clear instances where the servant of the LORD is the nation of Israel (e.g., Isa 41:8; 43:10). Thus, mainstream Jewish interpretation has historically understood the servant of the songs (Isa 42:1–4 or 1–7; 49:1–6 or 49:1–9; 50:4–11; 52:13—53:12) to be Israel. On the other hand, there is no a priori reason why the term "servant" always has to refer to the same entity. Furthermore, the servant in these songs seems to be an individual who acts on behalf of Israel. Not only do the songs share a good deal of material with one another, but also they have many links back to the description of the Davidic Messiah in Isa 9:6–7 and 11:1–10.[54] Thus, mainstream Christian interpretation has historically understood the servant in these songs to be the Messiah.

The immediately preceding context of Isa 41:25–29 refers to the arousal of Cyrus from the northeast (Isa 41:25–26; see also Isa 41:2; 44:28; 45:1). Then the LORD says that he will give to Jerusalem a "bearer of good news" (מבשר) (Isa 41:27). When the LORD looks among his people, there is no such man, there is no "counselor" (Isa 41:28–29; cf. Isa 9:6). Therefore, he presents his servant in Isa 42:1 as the bearer of good news (cf. Isa 61:1). The book of Isaiah continues to develop the use of the language in Isa 41:27–28 to help the reader understand who the bearer of good news is. Isa 52:7 speaks of how beautiful on the mountains are the feet of a "bearer of good news" (מבשר), and this leads directly into the fourth servant song (Isa 52:13—53:12). This text is quoted in the messianic prophecy of Nah 1:15 (see also 11QMelch [11Q13]) and in Rom 10:15, which extends the good news bearing mission of Christ to the apostles and the early church (cf. Isa 42:6; 49:6; Acts 13:47). Isaiah 59:16 takes up the wording of Isa 41:28 to say that the LORD sees that there is no man and is appalled that there is no one intervening. Therefore, his arm delivers for him, and his righteousness supports him. Isaiah 63:3, 5 reapplies this to the Messiah (see Gen 49:11–12; Isa 63:1–2; Rev 14:20; 19:13).

The Hebrew text of Isa 42:1a presents the bearer of good news as the LORD's chosen servant. The LXX represents mainstream Jewish interpretation and identifies this servant as the nation of Jacob/Israel. Several witnesses to Tg. Jon., however, identify the servant as the Messiah. This split in the early Jewish understanding of the servant is even more remarkable when it is considered that the earliest Christian interpretation of Isa 42:1–4 is also messianic. Matthew 12:15–21 gives a brief account of Jesus warning

54. Shepherd, *Text in the Middle*, 138.

the crowds not to make him known, which is then said to have happened in order that what was spoken by Isaiah in 42:1–4 might be fulfilled (cf. b. Ber. 56b). In particular, Isa 42:2 speaks of how the Messiah will not come with great fanfare. The most straightforward understanding of Matthew's citation is that he has interpreted Isa 42:1–4 to be messianic and has explained Jesus as the Messiah revealed in that text. It is less convincing to say that Matthew has interpreted the servant in Isa 42:1–4 to be Israel and then reapplied the language to Jesus as the new Israel. While the concept of Jesus as the new or true Israel is popular among modern New Testament scholars, it is not one that is ever expressed clearly in the biblical text.[55] Thus, once again the Targum bears witness to an early exegetical tradition that goes back at least as early as the first century CE and aligns more closely with mainstream Christian exegesis than with the dominant Jewish interpretation.

The Targum's messianic interpretation of the servant in Isa 42:1 has much to commend it from the context of the passage. The text of verse 1 says that the servant has the Spirit of the LORD upon him. This is exactly what is said of the Davidic Messiah in Isa 11:2 (see also Isa 61:1; cf. Matt 3:16; Mark 1:10; Luke 3:22; 4:18). Isa 42:1 also says that the servant will bring forth justice to the nations. This is one of the most recognizable marks of the Davidic Messiah and his kingdom according to Isa 9:7; 11:3–5, 10. The Targum has thus shown remarkable sensitivity to the larger context of the book and its seemingly deliberate effort to link the Davidic Messiah and the servant of the LORD. The emerging portrait of the Messiah in the book of Isaiah is a rather well-rounded one of a reigning warrior king who defeats his enemies and a lowly figure who acts on behalf of the righteous remnant to vindicate them.

The descriptions of the servant in Isa 42 and 49 have much in common. In both texts the servant is "a covenant for a people" and "a light to the nations" (Isa 42:6; 49:6, 8; see 9:2; 55:3; 61:8; cf. Luke 2:32; Acts 13:47; see also 1 En. 48:4). In both texts the servant sets the prisoners free (Isa 42:7; 49:9; see also 61:1). Why then does the Targum not explicitly call the servant in Isa 49 the Messiah? The answer seems to be the presence of the

---

55. This concept is most commonly invoked in expositions of John 15:1–17, yet John's presentation of Jesus as the true or faithful vine is not intended to depict the replacement of Israel but the redemption of Israel. The primary source for this imagery is the book of Isaiah (Isa 5:1–7; 27:2–6) in which the transformation of Israel from a fruitless people to a people bearing the fruit of righteousness comes through the work of the Messiah (Isa 53:11; 61:3). Thus, the picture of John 15 is that of one who makes the branches of the vine(yard) fruitful.

word "Israel" in the Targum's Hebrew source text for Isa 49:3. This reading identifies the servant as the nation of Israel, but such an identification is highly problematic within the context of the passage. The servant in Isa 49:5–6 is one who acts on behalf of Israel. Thus, the servant cannot at the same time be Israel. It appears that an early scribe inserted the word "Israel" in Isa 49:3 on the basis of texts like Isa 41:8, but he did not pay attention to the context. There is one Masoretic manuscript that does not have the word "Israel" in Isa 49:3. It appears best on the basis of the evidence to accept this shorter reading as the original one.[56]

Isa 52:13—53:12

There is no explicit identification of the servant of the LORD in the Targum of Isa 50:4–11, which is the third servant song. This is somewhat puzzling given the closeness of this passage to the fourth servant song in Isa 52:13—53:12 where the Targum interprets the servant to be a messianic figure. Isaiah 50:4–11 also appears to be influential for John's depiction of Jesus as one who only says or does what he hears from the Father (Isa 50:4–5; cf. John 5:19, 30; 6:38; 7:16; 8:28, 38; 12:49; 14:10; see also Pss. Sol. 17:32) and for Luke's depiction of Jesus as one who is resolved to go to the place of suffering (Isa 50:7; cf. Luke 9:51). The Hebrew texts of Isa 50:4–11 and 52:13—53:12 both focus on the suffering of the servant, but it is the latter of these two that goes into more detail about the purpose of the servant's suffering. This may very well explain why the Targum has not devoted much attention to Isa 50:4–11. The Targum has essentially left the identity of the servant in the third song for the reader to decide, but great energy has been expended on the crafting of its rendering of the fourth song in order to manage the perceived problem in the Hebrew text of a suffering Messiah. Rather than attempting to accomplish this feat twice in Isa 50:4–11 and 52:13—53:12, the Targum has put all its eggs in one basket, so to speak, with its efforts to rework Isa 52:13—53:12.

Tg. Jon.'s rendering of the fourth servant song (Isa 52:13—53:12) finds itself between the two worlds of Christian tradition and Jewish tradition. On the one hand, the Targum agrees with Christian tradition when it identifies the servant as an individual messianic figure: "Look, my servant the Messiah will prosper" (Tg. Jon. Isa 52:13a; cf. Matt 8:14–17; Luke 22:37;

---

56. See von Rad, *Old Testament Theology*, 252.

John 12:38; Acts 8:26–40; Rom 10:16; 15:21; 1 Pet 2:18–25).[57] On the other hand, the Targum agrees with Jewish tradition in that it paraphrases the song in such a way that the Messiah does not suffer. As noted in the prior discussion of Exod 40:9–11, there was a conception in early Judaism of a suffering Messiah the son of Ephraim, but the Targum makes no appeal to this in its rendering of Isa 52:13—53:12. There was simply no room for the idea that the Davidic Messiah might suffer and die. For early Christians, however, the connections between the prophecies of the Davidic Messiah (Isa 9:6–7; 11:1–10) and the servant songs were too strong to ignore, and the concept of a Messiah who would both suffer and reign became fundamental to their messianic theology. Chilton summarizes well the nature of the shared exegetical tradition between the Targum and Christianity:

> In a word, the hopes of the primitive meturgeman centered on a messiah as he looked forward to recovery from the disaster of 70. The gospel of Jesus was not yet of sufficient concern to make him alter his interpretation for apologetic reasons, and it is permissible to infer that, in his messianic understanding of the Isaiah servant, the meturgeman attests a primitive exegesis common to Judaism and Christianity.[58]

After the Targum introduces the servant as the Messiah in Isa 52:13–15 (cf. Rom 15:21), it does not depict the Messiah in Isa 53:1–3 as one "despised and forsaken of men" the way that the Hebrew text has it (cf. John 12:38; Rom 10:16).[59] Rather, it says that "the glory of all the kingdoms" will become an object of scorn and cease. Rashi comments that Israel is the one who is despised and rejected by men.[60] Where the Hebrew text of Isa 53:4–6 presents the messianic servant as one who suffers on behalf of the people, bearing their sicknesses and pains as well as the punishment for their transgressions and iniquities (see 1 Pet 2:24–25), the Targum merely has the Messiah seeking pardon for the people's sins as an intercessor (cf. Isa 53:12; Rom 8:34; Heb 7:25), and it is the will of God to forgive the people because of him. According to the Targum, it is not the Messiah

---

57. See also Elliott, *Isaiah 40–66*, 154–73. Yalqut Shimoni to Isa 52:13 also identifies the servant as the Messiah (see also b. Sanh. 98b on Isa 53:4), but this is not the dominant tradition within Judaism. Rashi represents the prevailing standard opinion in his commentary when he identifies the servant as the righteous people of Jacob/Israel (see Rosenberg, *Mikraoth Gedoloth: Isaiah*, 2:422).

58. Chilton, *Glory of Israel*, 94.

59. See also the language shared between Isa 53:2 and 4:2; 11:1, 10.

60. Rosenberg, *Mikraoth Gedoloth: Isaiah*, 2:424.

who is considered smitten by God but the people (cf. Rashi). Furthermore, the Targum highlights not the substitutionary role of the Messiah in Isa 53:5 but his role in rebuilding the temple (see 2 Sam 7:13; Zech 6:12–13). Matthew, on the other hand, cites Isa 53:4 to explain the healing ministry of Jesus (Matt 8:14–17).

The Hebrew text of Isa 53:7–8 speaks of the servant in terms of a silent lamb being led to the slaughter (see Exod 12:3, 6–7; John 1:29; see also Luke 23:9) and in terms of one who is cut off from the land of the living for the transgression of the people. Luke's account of the encounter between Philip and the Ethiopian in Acts 8:26–40 explicitly identifies the servant in this text as Jesus (see Acts 8:32–35). The Targum, however, says that the messianic servant will deliver the strong of the peoples like a lamb to the sacrifice. He will remove the rule of the peoples from the land of Israel, and the punishment for the sins of Israel will come to the peoples. According to the Hebrew text of Isa 53:9, the servant is with a rich man in his death despite the fact that his grave is assigned with wicked men (see Matt 27:57–61; Mark 15:42–47; Luke 23:50–56; John 19:38–42). This is because the servant has neither done anything wrong nor said anything wrong, contrary to the belief of those in Isa 53:4b who think that the servant is suffering due to divine judgment against him for wrongdoing. The Targum transforms Isa 53:9 to say that the Messiah will deliver the wicked to Gehenna, but Peter takes it to mean that Christ committed no sin when he bore the people's sin in his body and thus set the example for how to suffer righteously as a Christian (1 Pet 2:21–24).

The last section of the song (Isa 53:10–12) turns to the satisfaction that the suffering of the servant brings to the LORD. It is the LORD's will to crush the servant in order to accomplish his purpose. If the servant will give himself as a "guilt offering" (אשם; see Lev 5), he will see "seed" (see Isa 6:13; 44:3; 54:3; 59:21; 61:9; 65:9, 23; 66:22), he will prolong days, and the good pleasure of the LORD will prosper in his hand (Isa 53:10). This speaks of the faithful remnant of the people of God who will exist because of the servant's offering of himself as their substitute (see again Isa 53:4–6). It also anticipates the servant's resurrection from the dead (see Isa 53:9; cf. 1 Cor 15). Tg. Jon. takes the text of Isa 53:10 in a slightly different direction to say that it is the LORD's will to refine and to purify the remnant of his people. They will see the kingdom of their Messiah. They will have many children and live long lives, and they will practice the Torah. According to Ibn Ezra, Isa 53:10 refers not only to the generation that will return to God's Torah

when the Messiah comes but also to the nations who will return to the
Torah (see Isa 2:1–5; 42:4).

1QIsa[a, b] and the LXX supply an object, "light" (אור), for the first clause
of Isa 53:11: "Because of the toil of his life he will see light" (cf. NIV; see
NETS: "from the pain of his soul, to show him light"). This alters the sense
of the text considerably because it removes the possibility that God might
be the subject of the verb ("he will see"). The addition essentially requires
the text to mean that the servant will see the light at the end of the tunnel,
so to speak. That is, there is something for him beyond his death (cf. Ps
56:13). Of course, this is already clear from Isa 53:10, 12. The Hebrew text
of 1QIsa[a] in general is a non-aligned text (i.e., neither MT-like nor LXX-
like) and it is written in what Emanuel Tov has called the "Qumran Scribal
Practice," which among other things features extensive use of the *matres
lectionis* or vowel letters.[61] This observation is significant. Isac Leo Seeligmann argued that the reading "light" in this scroll, while satisfying the felt
need for an object with a verb that normally has an object, is not original
but is rather a secondary reading produced by the dualistic worldview of
the members of the Qumran sect who referred to themselves as "the sons of
light" (see the War Scroll and the Rule of the Community).[62] 1QIsa[b], on the
other hand, is in general a MT-like text (not proto-MT), yet it also includes
this reading (see also 4QIsa[d]). The LXX has thus followed a Hebrew text in
which this reading was already present, or, as is often the case elsewhere in
LXX Isaiah, the translator had a text close to the MT without "light" and
chose to supply this object for reasons that similarly motivated the Hebrew
scribes of the Qumran scrolls.[63]

61. Tov, *Textual Criticism of the Hebrew Bible*, 100–104. It is apparent from the scroll
that two different scribes produced the two halves of the book (Isa 1–33 and 34–66). The
scribe responsible for the second half of the book "left out more sections than scribe A,
which were filled in subsequently by himself or a different hand, in small letters, between
the lines and in the margin" (idem, *Scribal Practices and Approaches Reflected in the Texts
Found in the Judean Desert*, 21).

62. Seeligmann, *Gesammelte Studien*, 401–19. Contrary to Seeligmann, Eugene Ulrich
argues that the addition of the object "light" is not a sectarian variant (Ulrich, "Absence
of 'Sectarian Variants,'" 184). The general lack of sectarian variants among the biblical
scrolls from Qumran is likely due to the fact that many of the scrolls were not copied on
site but were brought there from other locations.

63. The differences between MT and LXX Isaiah are generally thought to be due to
the translator's technique rather than the presence of a different Hebrew source text
(see Tov, *Textual Criticism*, 137), although there are exceptions to this (see Seeligmann,
Septuagint Version of Isaiah). Hebrew scribes and Greek translators often do the same
kinds of things with texts, and it can be difficult to tell whether the variation begins with

The MT of the first clause of Isa 53:11, which does not supply an object, most plausibly assumes God to be the subject of the verb. The first and last clauses of Isa 53:10 have "the LORD" as their subject, and the servant has to be reintroduced as the subject in the second half of Isa 53:11. This understanding leads to the conclusion that God looks upon the suffering of the servant and is satisfied with what he has accomplished on behalf of the people. The work of the righteous servant (cf. 1 John 2:1) paves the way for the justification of "the many" (cf. Isa 53:12; 54:1; Mark 10:45) who believe that the servant has born the punishment for their iniquities (Isa 53:1, 11). Tg. Jon.'s version of Isa 53:11, however, focuses more on the Messiah's deliverance of the people from being in servitude to other peoples. The people of Israel are the ones who will "see" the vengeance against their enemies and be "satisfied" with the plunder of the enemy kings. The Messiah will declare the innocent to be so by his wisdom in order to bring "many" into submission to the Torah, and he will intercede for them concerning their sins (cf. Tg. Jon. Isa 53:4, 10).

Along with the image of the exalted servant in the first verse of the song (Isa 52:13; cf. 6:1; 57:15), the picture of the servant as a victorious warrior king enjoying the spoils of battle at the beginning of the last verse of the song (Isa 53:12) is exactly the way the Targum depicts the Messiah throughout the song. For Tg. Jon., the servant is an exalted ruler who defeats his (and Israel's) enemies, but he is not a suffering servant. The closest that the Targum comes to an admission that the servant in the Hebrew text is at least potentially a suffering figure occurs in its rendering of the latter part of Isa 53:12. The MT says that the servant divides the plunder because he pours out his life to death and is numbered with transgressors yet bears the sin of many and intercedes for transgressors (see again Isa 53:4–6; see also 1 Pet 2:24). According to the Targum, this means that the servant hands over his life to death and subjects the rebels to the Torah, yet he seeks (pardon) for many sins, and for the rebellious it is forgiven because of him.[64] Due to the general avoidance of the servant's suffering throughout the Targum's version of the song, interpreters have concluded

---

the Hebrew Vorlage or with the work of the translator (see Screnock, "New Approach," 229–57). Seeligmann suggests the possibility that the teachers of Qumran somehow influenced Alexandrian Judaism and the Bible translators produced there (Seeligmann, *Gesammelte Studien*, 415).

64. Rashi, Ibn Ezra, and Redak all understand Isa 53:12 to mean that Israel bears the sins of the nations and prays for their welfare; as a result, the nations enjoy peace (Rosenberg, *Mikraoth Gedoloth: Isaiah*, 2:429).

that the servant's handing over of his life to death in the Targum of this verse can only mean that he is willing to suffer martyrdom to accomplish his mission.[65] It must be admitted, however, that this interpretation of the Targum is not entirely clear.[66]

Isaiah 52:13—53:12 is the last passage of the book that the Targum interprets messianically, although there are certainly other opportunities for messianic interpretation. For instance, Isa 61:1–9 shares material with earlier messianic prophecies and with the servant songs (Isa 11:1; 42:1, 7; 49:9), yet the absence of the term "servant" (עבד) in the Hebrew text has likely discouraged an explicitly messianic rendering. Nevertheless, Luke's account of Jesus reading this text in the synagogue at Nazareth appears to depend upon a very important detail from the Targum (Luke 4:16–30). The Targum identifies the speaker in Isa 61 as "the prophet" (Tg. Jon. Isa 61:1; cf. Tg. Jon. Isa 50:4–5). When Jesus finishes his reading of Isa 61:1–2a1 (see m. Meg. 4:4; see also Isa 58:6), he tells the audience that this Scripture is today fulfilled in their hearing. The people apparently take this to mean that the very reading of the text is a kind of fulfillment of the text (cf. b. Menah. 110a). It is only when Jesus identifies himself with the prophetic voice in the text ("No prophet is welcome in his hometown") that the crowd turns against him.

Isaiah 63:1–6 is another passage where readers might expect to find a messianic rendering in the Targum. The Hebrew text depends upon the latter part of the messianic prophecy in Gen 49:8–12, which the Targums of the Pentateuch unanimously interpret messianically (see earlier discussion). According to Gen 49:11b, the coming king from the tribe of Judah washes his clothing in wine, which both the Palestinian Targum tradition and Isa 63:1–6 take to be an image of the bloodstained garments of the warrior Messiah. This interpretation then resurfaces in the depiction of Christ in the book of Revelation (Rev 14:20; 19:15).

---

65. See Levey, *Messiah*, 66; see also Chilton, *Isaiah Targum*, 105.
66. See Chilton, *Glory of Israel*, 94.

JEREMIAH

Jer 23:5–6

The messianism of the book of Jeremiah begins with Jer 3:15 and 4:2,[67] but the first messianic rendering in Tg. Jon.'s version of the book comes in Jer 23:5a, which is part of a passage that takes up the language of Jer 3:14–18 and 4:2. Chapters 21 and 22 of Jeremiah highlight the failure of the sons of Josiah to live up to the standards of justice and righteousness set by their father (see 2 Kgs 22–23). The announcement of judgment for the sons of Josiah comes in Jer 23:1–4 where it is said that the LORD is about to "visit" (פקד) upon these "shepherds" the evil of their deeds because they have not "attended to" (פקד) the flock (Jer 23:2). The Targum rightly understands this to mean that the leaders (i.e., the kings) have not fulfilled their responsibility to the people (cf. Jer 2:8). The LORD himself will gather the remnant of his people and return them to their land where they will be fruitful and multiply (Jer 23:3). This anticipates a restoration of the lost blessing of life and dominion in the land of the covenant (see Gen 1:26–28; Jer 3:16). Thus, Jer 23:4 looks forward to the LORD's raising up of multiple shepherds/kings. According to Jer 3:15, these shepherds will be in accordance with God's heart just like David (1 Sam 13:14). The juxtaposition of Jer 23:4 with 23:5–6 suggests that the Messiah will reign supreme, but the people of God will reign with him (cf. Isa 32:1; Mic 5:2–6; Dan 7:13–14, 27; Rev 5:9–10).

The Hebrew text of Jer 23:5a ("Look, days are coming," the prophetic utterance of the LORD, "and I will raise up for David a righteous Branch") looks forward to the eschatological fulfillment of the covenant with David (see 2 Sam 7:12; 23:1; Jer 30:8; Ezek 34:23). The use of the messianic title "Branch" depends upon Isa 4:2 and 11:1, two texts that Tg. Jon. interprets messianically (see earlier discussion). Jer 23:5a in turn influences another prophet, Zechariah, in his depiction of the Messiah (Zech 3:8; 6:12–13; see also 4QFlor [4Q174]; 4Q252), which also receives a messianic interpretation from Tg. Jon. (see subsequent discussion). According to Tg. Jon., the "righteous Branch" of Jer 23:5a is none other than "a Messiah of righteousness" (or, "a righteous Messiah"; cf. Syr.: "the radiance of righteousness"; see also MT Jer 33:15). The LXX renders this same phrase as "a righteous sunrise/dawn" (cf. LXX Zech 3:8; 6:12). The use of ἀνατολή ("sunrise/dawn") in the Greek text links the prophecy to LXX Num 24:17, which speaks of

---

67. See Shepherd, *Commentary on Jeremiah*, 96–97, 108–12.

a messianic star that "will rise" (ἀνατελεῖ) from Jacob (cf. Mal 4:2; Matt 2:1–12; 2 Pet 1:19; Rev 22:16; see also Luke 1:78).

The messianic king will reign and act wisely (Jer 23:5b; cf. Josh 1:8; Isa 52:13). In contrast to the sons of Josiah, the Messiah will perform justice and righteousness (cf. Isa 9:7; 11:3–5; Ps 72:1–2; see also Jer 4:2). The Targum interprets this to mean that the Messiah will prosper and enact true justice and merit. In his days, Judah will be delivered, and Israel will dwell in security (Jer 23:6a; cf. 3:17–18), and the "name" or "reputation" of the Messiah will be "the LORD our righteousness" (Jer 23:6b; LXX: "Iosedek"). This is not a name in the proper sense of the term but a description of the Messiah himself (cf. Isa 7:14; Matt 1:21–23; see also Lam. Rab. 1:51; b. B. Bat. 75b). The Messiah is the LORD in the flesh (cf. Isa 9:6). The Targum paraphrases this "name": "Acts of merit will be done for us before the Lord in his days" (or, "May acts of merit be done for us before the Lord in his days").

Jeremiah 23:7–8 is a doublet of the material found in 16:14–15.[68] The LXX has these two verses at the end of the chapter after Jer 23:40. The content announces that days are coming when the people will no longer refer to the LORD in their oaths as the one who brought them out of the land of Egypt (i.e., the original exodus). Rather, they will refer to him as the one who brought them out of the land of the north (i.e., the new exodus). In other words, the new act of deliverance will supersede the old one and become the new standard or paradigm of deliverance (cf. Isa 43:18–19). The precise nuance of this depends upon the location of this unit in the text. Its placement in Jer 16:14–15 and at the end of chapter 23 in LXX Jer sets it within contexts of judgment where the emphasis is on the harsher judgment to be endured in the land of the north as compared to what the people experienced in the land of Egypt. The MT's placement of these verses after the messianic prophecy in Jer 23:5–6 highlights the greater deliverance from the land of the north in the new exodus and connects it to the messianic hope (cf. Num 24:7–9; Isa 11:16).

The messianism of Jer 23:1–8 as interpreted by the Targum finds its way into the New Testament via the exposition of the Jeremiah passage by the prophet Ezekiel in chapter 34 of his book. Ezekiel 34 adopts much of the specific language from Jeremiah to provide an extended version of the contrast between the bad shepherds or kings and the LORD as the good

---

68. See Parke-Taylor, *Formation of Jeremiah*, 72–79.

shepherd or king (cf. Ps 23).[69] The kingship of the LORD manifests itself primarily in the raising up of a messianic shepherd ("my servant David") according to Ezek 34:23 (cf. 2 Sam 7:12; 23:1; Jer 23:5; 30:9; Ezek 37:24; Hos 3:5). It will be during the reign of this king that the people will enjoy the security envisioned by Jer 23:5–6. Ezekiel's text directly influences John's presentation of Jesus as the good shepherd (John 10:7–21; see also Heb. 13:20; 1 Pet 5:4).[70] For John, explanation of Jesus from this passage is key to his overall purpose in writing (John 20:30–31).[71]

Jer 30:8–9, 21

The text of Jer 30:8–9 stands near the beginning of the so-called Book of Comfort or Book of Consolation (see Jer 30:2–3; cf. Deut 30:3). The eschatological context for the prophecy is set by the opening words found in Jer 30:5–7, which refer to the coming day in terms applied elsewhere to the Day of the LORD: "great is that day" (cf. Isa 13:6, 9; Joel 2:11, 31; Zeph 1:14; Mal 4:5; "there is none like it" (cf. Joel 2:2; Dan 12:1); and "it is a time of distress" (cf. Nah 1:7; Zeph 1:15; Dan 12:1).[72] The wording of Jer 30:8 differs considerably between the MT and the Hebrew *Vorlage* of the LXX:

> MT: "In that day," the prophetic utterance of the LORD of hosts, "I will break his yoke from upon your neck, and your bonds I will tear off, and strangers will never again serve by him."

> LXX *Vorlage*: "In that day," the prophetic utterance of the LORD, "I will break a yoke from upon their neck, and their bonds I will tear off, and they will never again serve strangers."

The MT refers to "his yoke," for which the antecedent of the pronoun "his" is likely Nebuchadnezzar (see Jer 27–28). The LXX *Vorlage*, however,

---

69. "Ezekiel seems to have had Jeremiah's oracle before him and presented his 'Shepherd Address' as an exposition of his contemporary's prophecy" (Block, *Book of Ezekiel: Chapters 25–48*, 275–76).

70. "Basically it would seem that Ezekiel's portrait of God (or the Messiah) as the ideal shepherd, in contrast to the wicked shepherds who plunder the flock and allow sheep to be lost, served as the model for Jesus' portrait of himself as the ideal shepherd, in contrast to the Pharisees, who are thieves who rob the sheep and hirelings who allow the sheep to be scattered" (Brown, *Gospel according to John I–XII*, 398). See also Peterson, *John's Use of Ezekiel*.

71. See Carson, "Syntactical and Text-Critical Observations," 693–714.

72. See also Jer 30:24b (cf. 23:20b; 48:47; 49:39).

does not have the pronoun ("a yoke") and thus leaves open the possibility that the text speaks of deliverance from an eschatological foe (see Jer 25:9 [LXX]; Ezek 38:14–17). Tg. Jon., despite the fact that it translates a proto-MT source, interprets the yoke not to be the yoke of Nebuchadnezzar in particular but "the yoke of the peoples" (cf. Ezek 38:1–9).

Rather than serving strangers, the people will serve the LORD their God and "David their king" whom the LORD will raise up for them (cf. 2 Sam 7:12; 23:1; Jer 23:5; Ezek 34:23; 37:24–25; Hos 3:5).[73] The Targum understands this contextually not to be a reference to the historical David but a reference to "the Messiah, the son of David, their king." The same interpretation appears in b. Sanh. 98b:

> R. Judah says that Rav says: The Holy One, Blessed be He, is about to establish another David for them, as it is said, "And they will serve the LORD their God and David their king whom I will raise up for them" (Jer 30:9). "He raised up," is not said, but, "I will raise up." R. Pappa said to Abaye: But it is written, "And my servant David will be their prince forever (Ezek 37:25)." "Like an emperor and a viceroy."[74]

This text speaks of "another David" (דוד אחר) who is not from the past but still to come in the future. It is interesting to note that the similar prophecy in Ezek 37:25 does not receive a messianic interpretation. The Targum of Ezek 37:25 likewise does not provide an explicitly messianic rendering.

The text of MT Jer 30:10–11 does not appear in the Hebrew source text of the LXX. It is a doublet of the material found in both the MT and the LXX of Jer 46:27–28 (LXX 26:26–27). Nevertheless, the secondary addition of these two verses in the Book of Comfort certainly fits the context. The text revisits the words spoken to Jeremiah in Jer 1:8, 17 and reapplies them to the people of God. Thus, just like the prophet, the people need not fear or be dismayed, for the LORD is present with them to deliver them. The current state of the people is that of a metaphorical battered and bruised body (Jer 30:12–17; cf. Isa 1:6; Mic 1:9). These "wounds" are self-inflicted due to the people's breaking of the covenant, but the LORD will heal the people and restore them and rebuild them so that there will be cause for celebration (Jer 30:18–20).

---

73. LXX: "And they will work for the Lord their God, and David their king I will raise up for them."

74. See also Redak in Rosenberg, *Mikraoth Gedoloth: Jeremiah*, 2:239.

Key to this future restoration is the coming of the Messiah as anticipated by Jer 30:21, but the messianism of Jer 30:21 is more subtle than that
of Jer 30:9 and requires sensitivity to the details of its intertextual links.
Here again there are substantial differences between the MT and the LXX,
and Tg. Jon. agrees partly with one and partly with the other:

> MT: "And his majestic one will be from him, and his ruler from his
> midst will go forth; and I will draw him near, and he will approach
> me. For who is the one who would pledge his heart to draw near to
> me?" the prophetic utterance of the LORD.

> LXX: "And his majestic ones will be over them, and his ruler from
> him will go forth; and I will gather them, and they will return to
> me. For who is the one who would pledge his heart to draw near
> to me?" says the Lord.

> Tg. Jon.: "And their king will be anointed from them, and their
> Messiah from among them will be revealed; and I will draw them
> near, and they will eagerly follow my worship. For who is the one
> whose heart desires to draw near to my worship?" says the Lord.

The first clause of the MT speaks of an individual, "his majestic one," who
will come from "him" (i.e., Jacob; see Jer 30:18; cf. Num 24:17). Tg. Jon.
interprets this "majestic one" to be "their king" who will be anointed from
"them" (i.e., the people of Jacob). On the other hand, the LXX speaks of a
plurality, "his majestic ones," who will be over "them" (i.e., the people; cf.
Isa 32:1; Jer 3:15; 23:4; Mic 5:5–6). Both the MT and the LXX, however,
refer in the next clause to a singular ruler ("his ruler") who will go forth
either "from his midst" (MT) or "from him" (LXX; cf. Deut 17:15b; 18:15,
18). There is likely literary dependence here upon the messianic prophecy
in Mic 5:2: "from you for me he will go forth [Tg. Jon.: before me the Messiah will go forth] to be a ruler (מושל) over Israel" (see also 2 Sam 23:3; Isa
11:1). Thus, the Targum understands the ruler to be "their Messiah" who
will be revealed "from among them."[75]

The LXX and the Targum depart from the MT in the latter part of
Jer 30:21. According to the MT, the LORD says: "and I will draw him near,
and he will approach me. For who is the one who would pledge his heart to
draw near to me?" This presumably refers to the approach of the messianic
ruler from the previous clause. The text bears a strong resemblance to the
vision of the Son of Man in Dan 7:13b: "and up to the Ancient of Days he
came, and before him they drew him near (הקרבוהי)." Daniel's dependence

---

75. See b. Sanh. 98b; Redak in Rosenberg, *Mikraoth Gedoloth: Jeremiah*, 2:242.

upon Jeremiah is evident from Dan 9:2, and Daniel's text (7:13b) in turn becomes the source of Jesus' favorite way to refer to himself in the Gospels ("the Son of Man").[76] As illustrated by the story of Uzziah (2 Chr 26:16–21), it is normally the prerogative of priests rather than kings to enter the LORD's presence (see Exod 28:35, 43; Ezek 44:13, 15; see also Pss 15:1; 24:3), but the Messiah will be both king and priest according to the order of Melchizedek (see Zech 6:12–13; Ps 110; Heb 7). Thus, the nature of the question ("For who is the one who would pledge his heart to draw near to me?") is essentially rhetorical. Who in his right mind would take his life into his own hands to draw near to the LORD unless he were the Messiah? On the other hand, both the LXX and the Targum interpret the antecedent of the singular ("him" and "he") in this latter part of Jer 30:21 to be Jacob (i.e., the people of Jacob): LXX: "and I will gather them, and they will return to me"; Tg. Jon.: "and I will draw them near, and they will eagerly follow my worship." What then is the meaning of the question about who would pledge his heart to draw near to the LORD? The Targum interprets it as follows: "For who is the one whose heart desires to draw near to my worship?" In other words, the history of Israel has shown that the people are not going to take the initiative to draw near to the LORD. They require the LORD to bring them back so that they can return (see Jer 31:18b; Lam 5:21).

Jer 33:12–13

In the first edition of the book of Jeremiah represented by the LXX,[77] the Book of Comfort, which now includes chapters 32 and 33 in addition to chapters 30 and 31, concludes with a prophecy about the transformation of the desolate land into pastures for shepherds and their flocks (Jer 33:12–13). As discussed later, the text of Jer 33:14–26 is an addition in the second edition of the book (MT) and does not appear in the LXX or its Hebrew *Vorlage*. While Jer 33:12–13 may simply be a prophecy about the restoration of pastoral life in the land, the use of shepherd imagery elsewhere in the book strongly suggests that there may be more to it than that. A shepherd is commonly a metaphor for a king in the book of Jeremiah (e.g., Jer 2:8; 3:15; 6:3; 10:21), particularly in the messianic prophecy of Jer 23:1–6 (cf. Ezek 34). Thus, where Jer 33:13b says, "again will the sheep pass according to the hands of one counting" (cf. Lev 27:32; Ezek 20:37), the

76. See Shepherd, "Daniel 7:13," 99–111.

77. See Tov, *Textual Criticism*, 286–93.

Targum renders it to mean: "again will the people follow the words of the Messiah" (cf. John 10:27).[78]

Jer 33:14–26

Jer 33:14–26 is the longest continuous passage that does not appear in the LXX or its Hebrew source (cf. MT Jer 39:4–13 [> LXX]). LXX Jeremiah is approximately one-sixth shorter than MT Jeremiah and generally bears witness to an earlier, more original Hebrew edition of the book. LXX Jeremiah also features a different arrangement of the book. This is most notable in the placement of the nations corpus (Jer 46–51) in a different order after Jer 25:13, but there are also smaller units that appear in a different arrangement (e.g., Jer 10:5–9; 31:35–37). The generally faithful translation technique of the Greek translator strongly suggests that these differences are due to the Hebrew source text and not to the work of the translator himself.[79] Furthermore, the discovery of Hebrew fragments of the book of Jeremiah among the Dead Sea Scrolls (4QJer[b, d]) that agree with the LXX in shortness and arrangement also points to the existence of a Hebrew text of the book that differed substantially from that of the MT. Given the systematic nature of the various editorial and exegetical additions to the book now found in the MT, it appears highly unlikely that the LXX and the MT simply represent two stages in an otherwise unattested series of stages of growth or that they are two snapshots in the history of transmission of a book that grew and changed by scribal accretion over many years with the MT essentially representing the end of the process of development.[80] The first edition of the book is a complete, coherent work that is open to the kind of eschatological interpretation of the enemy from the north (see LXX Jer 25:9) and the prophecy of seventy years (see LXX Jer 25:11) found in Ezek 38:14–17 and Dan 9:24–27. The second edition of the book (MT) features a distinct layer of revision from beginning to end that fundamentally historicizes the book's prophecy in such a way that the focus is entirely upon Babylon and the seventy years of captivity (MT Jer 25:9, 11).

---

78. Rashi: "Israel will come and go under the hands of a king who walks at their head" (Rosenberg, *Mikraoth Gedoloth: Jeremiah*, 2:273; cf. Mic 2:12–13).

79. Contra Fischer, *Jeremiah Studies*.

80. For an example of this view of a "rolling corpus," see William McKane's two-volume commentary on the book of Jeremiah in the International Critical Commentary series.

According to Eugene Ulrich, the general phenomena now known as variant literary editions are consistent with this evidence: "The witnesses that have survived attest to the continuation of this process of faithful transmission occasionally punctuated by evolutionary leaps to a new, revised, and expanded edition of biblical books."[81]

The content of MT Jer 33:14–26 indicates that the design of the addition is to use the language of the covenants with Noah, Abraham, and David to promote the idea of a covenant with the Levites. The subordinate role of the Levites to the priesthood of Aaron was always a source of tension (see, e.g., Num 16). This text seeks to rectify that situation by elevating the Levites to the same status as that of the Aaronic priesthood. It was not the responsibility of the Levites to offer burnt offerings and sacrifices (see Num 3; Ezek 43:19; 44:15; 1 Chr 6:33–34; 23:28), yet MT Jer 33:18 suggests that it was. There was no covenant with the Levites, only a covenant with Aaron and his sons (see Lev 2:13; Num 18:19; 25:10–13; Deut 33:9; 1 Sam 2:35; Mal 2:4; Neh 13:29), yet MT Jer 33:21 suggests that there was a covenant with the Levites.

The text of MT Jer 33:14–16 reuses that of Jer 23:5–6 in a very subtle way to introduce the addition. MT Jer 33:14 begins like Jer 23:5 ("Look, days are coming," the prophetic utterance of the LORD, "and I will raise up"), but then there is an expansion in the remainder of the verse through the beginning of 33:15. This separates the verb ("and I will raise up") from "for David" in 33:15 (cf. Jer 23:5) and dissolves the link to the language of the covenant with David in 2 Sam 7:12 ("and I will raise up your seed after you"; cf. 2 Sam 23:1; Jer 30:9; Ezek 34:23). MT Jer 33:15 uses a different verb ("I will cause to sprout") and changes the object from "a righteous Branch" (Jer 23:5) to "a branch of righteousness." It is possible that the phrase "a branch of righteousness" means "a righteous Branch," but the remainder of the verse and verse 16 show that righteousness itself is likely in view. If this is correct, then the subject of the following clause ("and he will do justice and righteousness in the land") is indefinite: "and justice and righteousness will be done in the land." This is in marked contrast to Jer 23:5 where the messianic king who reigns and acts wisely is the one who performs justice and righteousness. Whereas Jer 23:6a speaks of the deliverance and security of Judah and Israel "in his days" (i.e., in the days of the messianic king), MT Jer 33:16a says that Judah and Jerusalem will be delivered and secure "in those days." It becomes evident from what follows that the change from

---

81. Ulrich, *Dead Sea Scrolls*, 108.

"Israel" to "Jerusalem" is not because Jerusalem is the royal city but because it is the city of the temple and the priesthood. According to Jer 23:6b, the "name" or description of the Messiah will be "the LORD our righteousness" (cf. Isa 7:14). According to Jer 33:16b, this is not the name of the Messiah. Rather, it is what the city of Jerusalem will be called (cf. Ezek 48:35).

Tg. Jon. follows a proto-MT source for its translation of the book of Jeremiah. Therefore, the text of Jer 33:14–26 is in its Hebrew *Vorlage*. The Targum renders the phrase "a branch of righteousness" messianically as it does all the other "Branch" texts (Isa 4:2; Jer 23:5; Zech 6:12); it also repeats the verb ("I will raise up") from Jer 23:5 and 33:14: "I will raise up for David a Messiah of righteousness." The phrase "a Messiah of righteousness" is the same one that the Targum uses for "a righteous Branch" in Jer 23:5. Thus, the Targum is remarkably unaffected by the changes in the Hebrew text here, despite the fact that it faithfully renders the change in focus to the city of Jerusalem in Jer 33:16. It is as if the mere presence of the term "branch" and its usage in other prophetic texts were enough to yield a messianic interpretation.

EZEKIEL

The term "Messiah" never appears in the Targum of Ezekiel despite the fact that the Hebrew text of the book lends itself to explicitly messianic renderings at a number of points (e.g., Ezek 17:22–24; 21:27; 34:23–24; 37:24–25). In particular, the expectation of a future king called "my servant, David" (Ezek 34:23–24; 37:24–25) is lacking the kind of overt messianic designation that similar expectations receive elsewhere in Tg. Jon. (see Tg. Jer 30:9; Hos 3:5). Furthermore, the Targum makes no mention of the Messiah in the chapters devoted to the eschatological enemy "Gog" (Ezek 38–39), an enemy who figures prominently in the messianic interpretations of the Pentateuchal Targums.

Levey concludes from this that the Targum of Ezekiel is for whatever reason eschatological but non-messianic and thus the product of authorship different from that of the rest of Tg. Jon.[82] It has been observed, however, that while use of the term "Messiah" is the most consistent feature of messianic renderings in the Targums, it is not a necessary feature (see, e.g., Tg. Neof. Gen 1:1; see also Deut 33:5). Thus, given the absence of any clear reason why the Targum of Ezekiel would be uniquely non-messianic

82. Levey, *Messiah*, 86–87.

among the Latter Prophets in Tg. Jon., it is advisable to look for other indicators of messianism.

Ezek 17:22–24

The text of Ezek 17 begins with a "riddle" (חידה) and a "proverb" (משל) (Ezek 17:2). According to this parable, a great eagle came to Lebanon and took "the top of the cedar" (Ezek 17:3–4). The eagle then replaced the top of the cedar with "the seed of the land," which became a vine (Ezek 17:5–6). The interpretation provided in Ezek 17:12–14 indicates that this symbolizes how the king of Babylon, Nebuchadnezzar (the great eagle), came to Jerusalem (Lebanon) and took its king, Jehoiachin (the top of the cedar). He then replaced Jehoiachin with a member of the royal family ("the royal seed"), Zedekiah (the seed of the land), to be ruler over a lowly kingdom (the vine). The parable goes on to say that another great eagle came, and the vine turned toward it (Ezek 17:7–8). This symbolizes how Zedekiah rebelled against Nebuchadnezzar and sent messengers to Egypt to appeal to Pharaoh Hophra for aid (Ezek 17:15). In the end, however, the parable says that the vine will wither (Ezek 17:9–10), symbolizing how Pharaoh will not be able to help Zedekiah (Ezek 17:16–21).

The conclusion of the chapter adds bonus material to the parable (Ezek 17:22–24) after both the parable and its interpretation have ended. The LORD says that he will take from "the top of the cedar" and plant it on a high mountain in Israel, presumably Mount Zion (see Isa 2:2–3).[83] It will bear fruit and become a majestic cedar, and all the flying creatures will live under it in the shade of its branches (cf. Ezek 31:6; Dan 4:11–12; Matt 13:32). All the trees will know that the LORD is the one who makes the high tree low and the low tree high; he makes the moist tree dry and the dry tree bud (cf. Isa 53:2). Later in Ezek 29:21, the LORD says, "In that day, I will cause to sprout (אצמיח) a horn for the house of Israel" (cf. LXX; see also 1 Sam 2:10; Ps 132:17). The shared language of taking from the top of the cedar in Ezek 17:3 and 17:22 indicates that the one whom the LORD will plant on a high mountain in Israel is a Davidic king. Since the parable and its interpretation acknowledge the end of the Davidic dynasty

---

83. According to Johan Lust, the reading καὶ κρεμάσω αὐτόν ("and I will hang him") at the end of verse 22 in the majority of LXX manuscripts is due to Christian reworking: "It fits into a series of quotations of the fathers who applied these texts to the death of Christ 'hanging' on the wood of the cross" ("Iezekiel/Ezechiel/Ezekiel," 581).

with Zedekiah, the last king of Judah, this king must be a future one. The kingdom of this future king will be a great one (see 2 Sam 7:13, 16; Dan 2:34–35, 44–45; 1 Chr 17:12, 14). It is difficult at this point not to think of the eschatological Messiah and his everlasting kingdom, especially when the tree imagery is compared with other messianic prophecies (see Isa 4:2; 11:1, 10; Jer 23:5; Zech 3:8; 6:12; see also Tg. Ps 80:16 [Eng., 80:15]).

Tg. Jon. translates Ezek 17:22 in such a way that the meaning of the metaphor is clear for the reader: "And I will draw near from the kingdom of the house of David one who is compared with a high cedar, and I will raise him up from the sons of his sons—a youth. I will exalt/anoint and raise him up like a high and elevated mountain." According to the Targum, the LORD will raise up this descendant of David on the mountain of the Holy One of Israel (Tg. Ezek 17:23). He will gather armies and form supporting troops (or, build fortresses) and become a strong king. All the righteous will depend upon him, and all the humble will dwell in the shade of his kingdom (see Tg. Hos 14:8). Thus, all the kings of the peoples will know that the LORD is the one who makes the strong kingdom low and the weak kingdom strong (Tg. Ezek 17:24; cf. Dan 4:17). What king and kingdom could this be after Zedekiah other than the eschatological Messiah and his kingdom? The Targum does not appear to have in view a historical descendant of David like Zerubbabel who never reigned on the throne. It is true that the Targum does not use the term "Messiah" here, but it is fair to ask whether such a designation is really necessary after the previous explanation of the symbolism. At the very least, the Targum's rendering of Ezek 17:22–24 cannot be called non-messianic or anti-messianic. Despite the absence of the term "Messiah," the Targum does not seem to be deliberately avoiding or altering the messianic sense of the passage.

The most influential Jewish and Christian voices from the history of interpretation largely confirm what the average reader of the Hebrew text of Ezek 17:22–24 and its Targum would suspect, although the precise nature of the messianic exegesis varies from interpreter to interpreter. For instance, Jerome (cf. Vulg.) says that the high tree made low and the low tree made high both refer to the passion of Christ who humbled himself in the incarnation and was exalted in the resurrection.[84] Rashi also understands the one taken from the top of the cedar in Ezek 17:22 to be "King Messiah."[85]

---

84. Stevenson and Glerup, *Ezekiel, Daniel*, 75–76. See also Calvin, *Commentaries on the First Twenty Chapters*, 207–13; Keil, *Ezekiel*, 140–41.

85. See also Kara and Mezudath David in Rosenberg, *Mikraoth Gedoloth: Ezekiel*,

On the other hand, Redak interprets this same figure to be Zerubbabel, but he acknowledges that the Targum's interpretation of the text is messianic.[86] Even modern interpreters concede the messianic sense of the passage. Daniel Block comments, "In this context *rak*, 'shoot,' serves as a harbinger of the messianic figure who will be presented in greater detail in later salvation oracles."[87]

Ezek 21:24–27

The Hebrew text of Ezek 21:24–27 is an address to King Zedekiah, the wicked "prince" (i.e., son of Josiah) of Israel whose day of punishment for his iniquity has arrived (Ezek 21:25]). The LORD says to remove the turban and to take off the crown and adds, "This not this [NET: Things must change]. Make high the low, and make low the high" (Ezek 21:26; cf. Ezek 17:24). He then says that he will make "it" (i.e., the turban/crown) into a "ruin" (עוה), which is given three times in the MT but twice in the LXX (Ezek 21:27a). The most challenging part of the passage is its conclusion in Ezek 21:27b: "Also this, he is not [גם זאת לא היה], until the one to whom the judgment belongs comes, and I will give it." This text appears to cite from Gen 49:10b ("until the one to whom it belongs comes"):[88]

> According to Steiner, Ezek 21:32b interprets עד in Gen 49:10 to mean "until" in the sense of cessation rather than culmination: "Also this will not happen until the one to whom the judgment belongs comes (עד בא אשר לו המשפט), and I will give it." This reading understands the debated שילה in Gen 49:10b to mean "to whom tribute belongs": "until the one to whom tribute belongs comes (עד כי יבא שילה), and to him will be obedience of peoples." In context Steiner takes Ezek 21:32b to refer to Nebuchadnezzar who brings the Davidic dynasty to its end. His reading assumes that the demonstrative זאת ("this," fem.) refers either to the "ruin" (עוה) or to the general situation of the removal of the crown (Ezek 21:31).

1:134.

86. Rosenberg, *Mikraoth Gedoloth: Ezekiel*, 1:134–35.

87. Block, *Book of Ezekiel: Chapters 1–24*, 550.

88. See again Steiner, "Four Inner-Biblical Interpretations," 33–60. See also Mic 1:15 (LXX) and 7:12.

It is also possible that זאת refers to עטרה ("crown," fem.) in Ezek 21:31. The sense would then be that there will be no crown (i.e., no king) until the rightful king arrives. This is attractive because the present king in Ezek 21:30 is the "prince" (נשיא). His ultimate replacement according to Ezek 34:23–24 is the messianic "prince." According to this reading of Gen 49:10b, שילה means "to whom it (i.e., the kingship) belongs" (cf. *Tg. Onk.*). The "obedience of peoples," not just Israel, will be his (Gen 27:29; Isa 11:10; 42:6; 49:6; 55:4; Dan 7:14). Such an understanding of Ezek 21:32b fits well with Steiner's observation later in the article about the similarities between Ezek 21:32 and Zech 9:9, even suggesting that Zechariah might be dependent upon Ezekiel.[89]

Given the unanimous messianic interpretation of Gen 49:10 among the Pentateuchal Targums, it is reasonable to expect a messianic rendering of Ezek 21:27 in Tg. Jon., but this is in fact not what the reader finds in the Targum. In the Targum of Ezek 21:26, the Lord says that he will remove the turban of Seraiah the high priest (see 2 Kgs 25:18–21; Jer 52:24–27) and cause the crown of Zedekiah the king to cease. Neither will be established in his position, and they both will go into exile. Gedaliah the son of Ahikam, to whom it does not belong, will receive it (see 2 Kgs 25:22); and as for Zedekiah, to whom it belongs, it will pass from him. In the Targum of Ezek 21:27, the Lord goes on to say that he will exact payment from them (i.e., Seraiah and Zedekiah) in accordance with their sins. Furthermore, the situation will not be established for Gedaliah until the Lord brings upon him the vengeance of Ishmael the son of Nethaniah and delivers him into his hand (see 2 Kgs 25:23–26). This is quite obviously a paraphrase that historicizes the prophecy on the basis of the story in Jer 41. It does not necessarily follow, however, that the paraphrase is motivated by a desire to hide or obscure the messianism of the text. The Hebrew text itself is somewhat more cryptic than other messianic passages in the book, and it depends upon the reader's ability to make the connection to Gen 49:10b. This is normally the kind of intertextual link that the Targum would detect, but in this case it goes unnoticed.

Ezek 34:23–24; 37:24–25

As noted previously in the section on Jeremiah, Ezek 34 is an extended exposition of Jer 23:1–6. The bad shepherds of Ezek 34:1–10 are the sons of

89. Shepherd, *Text in the Middle*, 48.

Josiah who have failed to live up to the standards of justice and righteousness established by their father (see Jer 21:1—23:4). The LORD pledges to be the good shepherd (Ezek 34:11–16), but the practical manifestation of this will be in the coming of the Davidic Messiah:

> "And I will raise up over them one/a shepherd [רעה אחד; LXX: another shepherd (= רעה אחר)], and he will shepherd them, my servant David. He is the one who will shepherd them [> LXX], and he is the one who will become their shepherd. And as for me, the LORD, I will be their God, and my servant [my servant > LXX] David will be prince in their midst. I, the LORD, have spoken [> Syr.]" (Ezek 34:23–24; cf. Jer 23:5; Mic 5:4; see also Pss. Sol. 17:40).

The people will live "in security" during the days of this shepherd (Ezek 34:25–31; cf. Jer 23:6). Tg. Jon. identifies the shepherd in Ezek 34:23 to be a leader who will provide for the people. He will be a "king" in their midst (Tg. Jon. Ezek 34:24). The Targum does not say anything more than this despite the fact that Jer 23:5 and other similar messianic prophecies (Jer 30:9; Hos 3:5) receive explicitly messianic interpretations in Tg. Jon. The Hebrew text and the modest rendering of the Targum are self-evidently eschatological and messianic without any further embellishment. The Targum does not make the text non-messianic. It only refrains from making the text more explicitly messianic than it already is.

The same applies to Ezek 37:24–25, which speaks of "my servant David" as "king" (LXX: "ruler") and "one/a shepherd" (Ezek 37:24). David, the LORD's servant, will be the people's "prince" forever (Ezek 37:25; cf. 2 Sam 7:13). Tg. Jon. understands this to mean that the Lord's servant David will be a king and a "leader." He will be the people's "king" forever. B. Sanh. 98b (see the earlier discussion of Jer 30:9) pairs Jer 30:9 ("And they will serve the LORD their God and David their king whom I will raise up for them") and Ezek 37:25 ("and my servant David will be their prince forever"). It interprets "David their king" in Jer 30:9 to be the future Messiah (cf. Tg. Jon.; see also Hos 3:5), but it interprets "my servant David" in Ezek 37:25 to be the historical David. Both will reign in the future, and the relationship between the two will be like that between an emperor (the Messiah) and a viceroy (the historical David). This seems to imply a resurrection of the historical David. Whatever may be said for the Talmud's reading of the text here, it is clear that this interpretation is not represented in the Targum of Ezek 37:24–25. The Targum may be read as a messianic prophecy just as well as the Hebrew text may be.

The absence of any messianic renderings in Tg. Jon.'s version of the chapters devoted to Gog (Ezek 38–39) is especially puzzling due to the propensity of the Targums in general to incorporate Gog into their messianic interpretations elsewhere. Nevertheless, this may be compared to the absence of Christ in the passage about Gog in the book of Revelation (Rev 20:7–10; but see Rev 17:14; 19:19). For an explanation of this absence, there is no need to look any further than the fact that the Messiah is not a feature of the Hebrew text of Ezek 38–39. The only text of the Hebrew Bible that speaks directly about the Messiah's victory over Gog is the Samaritan Pentateuch and the LXX *Vorlage* of Num 24:7b. As noted earlier, the Targums work primarily from the proto-MT.

The final vision of the new temple in Ezek 40–48 features multiple references to a נשיא ("prince").[90] The prince in view here is likely the messianic prince of Ezek 34:24 and 37:25. This is apparently a way to link the prophecy about the future sanctuary with the words of the covenant with David: "He is the one who will build a house for my name" (2 Sam 7:13a; cf. Zech 6:12–13). Tg. Jon., however, makes no attempt to connect the prince of Ezek 40–48 with the prince of Ezek 34:24 and 37:25. Whereas the Targum translates נשיא with מלך ("king") in Ezek 34:24 and 37:25 (see also Ezek 30:13), it translates the same word in Ezek 40–48 with רב ("leader"), which is the way the Targum normally translates נשיא elsewhere in the book.[91]

THE BOOK OF THE TWELVE

Hos 3:5; 14:7

Tg. Jon.'s messianic interpretation of Hos 3:5 is anticipated by its rendering of Hosea 1:11: "And the sons of Judah and the sons of Israel will be gathered together, and they will appoint for themselves one head from the house of David, and they will go up from the land of their exile, for great will be the day of their gathering [MT: the day of Jezreel]." The text looks forward to a reunification of Judah and Israel (cf. Jer 3:18). The people will appoint for themselves "one head," an allusion to Num 14:4. The Targum interprets this one head to be one "from the house of David."[92] The people will go up

---

90. See Ezek 44:3; 45:7–9, 16–17, 22; 46:2, 4, 8, 10, 12, 16–18; 48:21–22.

91. See Ezek 7:27; 12:10, 12; 19:1; 21:12, 25; 22:6; 26:16; 27:21; 32:29; 38:2–3; 39:1, 18.

92. Rashi says that the one head is "David their king" (see Hos 3:5), and Redak identifies him as "the King Messiah" (Rosenberg, *Mikraoth Gedoloth: The Twelve Prophets*, 1:8).

from "the land of their exile" in a kind of new exodus (see Hos 2:14–15; cf. Isa 11:16),[93] for great will be the day of "their gathering." The Targum interprets the day of "Jezreel" ("God sows") to be the day of the people's gathering when God sows them in their land (see Hos 1:4; 2:22–23; cf. Jer 31:27; Zech 13:9).

Hos 3:4–5 stands apart from the material in Hos 3:1–3 to explain the meaning of the prophet's words in Hos 3:3 and to look beyond the anticipated judgment to the hope of the restoration of the people of God in the last days (cf. 2 Chr 15:3–4). The content of Hos 3:4–5 comes not from the eighth-century prophet Hosea but from the prophetic composer of the Book of the Twelve (Hos–Mal).[94] These verses set forth the program of the Twelve,[95] and the composer of the Twelve develops the message of this program in the subsequent compositional seams of the Twelve that lie between the individual books.[96]

The calling card of the composer of the Twelve is citation from the book of Jeremiah.[97] The text of Hos 3:5 ("Afterward, the children of Israel will return and seek the LORD their God and David their king, and they will fear to the LORD and to his goodness in the end of days") is a citation of the messianic prophecy in Jer 30:9: "And they will serve the LORD their God and David their king whom I will raise up for them" (LXX: "And they will work for the Lord their God, and David their king I will raise up for them"). As noted previously, Tg. Jon. interprets Jer 30:9 messianically and identifies "David their king" as "the Messiah, the son of David, their king" (see again b. Sanh. 98b). The Targum is thus consistent with itself when it identifies "David their king" in Hos 3:5 as "the Messiah, the son of David, their king" (cf. Pss. Sol. 17:21). The Targum of Hos 3:5 says that the children of Israel will return and seek the "fear/worship" of Lord their God

93. See also b. Pesaḥ. 88a.

94. Note that the text does not speak merely of Hosea's audience, the northern kingdom of Israel, nor is it part of the Judean redaction of the book. Rather, the text envisions a return under a new David to the kind of unified kingdom that the people enjoyed under the historical David.

95. "We should understand 3:4–5 as a programmatic introduction to the theme of Israel's messianic hope. This hope runs throughout the Minor Prophets" (Sailhamer, *NIV Compact Bible Commentary*, 414).

96. For an overview of the composition of the Twelve, see Shepherd, *Commentary on the Book of the Twelve*, 23–36.

97. Shepherd, *Commentary on the Book of the Twelve*, 23–36. Such citation occurs in each of the seams of the Twelve.

and "obey" the Messiah, the son of David, their king (cf. Gen 49:10b). They will eagerly pursue the worship of the Lord, and great will be his goodness that will come to them "in the end of days." It has already been noted that the phrase "in the end of days" appears prominently in connection with the messianic poems of the Pentateuch (see the discussion of Gen 49:1, 8–12; Num 24:7–9, 14, 17).

The Targum of Hosea not only begins with a messianic rendering (Hos 3:5) but also ends with one (Hos 14:7). The Hebrew text of Hos 14:4–7 speaks of future healing (i.e., restoration) for the people. The LORD will be "like dew" to the people, and they will flourish (Hos 14:5–6). This imagery calls to mind eschatological and messianic prophecies elsewhere in the Hebrew Bible (see 2 Sam 23:4; Isa 26:19; 27:6; Ezek 34:26; Hos 6:3–4; Ps 72:6–7). Hosea 14:7a says that those who live "in his shadow" will return, which the Targum interprets to mean that the people will be gathered from their captivities and will dwell "in the shade of their Messiah" (cf. Isa 4:2, 6). The Hebrew text says that the people "will revive" (יחיו) grain and sprout like the grapevine (cf. Isa 27:6). The Targum interprets this to mean that "the dead will live" and enjoy the goodness that will increase in the land (cf. Isa 26:19; Dan 12:2). This reference to the resurrection must be understood in light of the Targum's rendering of an earlier passage in Hosea. According to the Hebrew text of Hos 6:2, the hope is that the LORD "will make us alive" (יחיֵנו) after two days, and on the third day cause us to rise, "and we will live" (ונחיה) before him (cf. Gen 22:4–5; Heb 11:17–19; see also Matt 16:21; Col 1:18). Tg. Jon. renders this as follows: "He will make us alive in the days of comfort, which are about to come in the day of the resurrection of the dead. He will raise us, and we will live before him." Perhaps a similar understanding of Hos 6:2 and 14:7 has exerted an influence on the apostle Paul's citation of Hos 13:14 in his chapter on the resurrection (1 Cor 15:55).

After the book of Hosea, Tg. Jon. does not have any messianic renderings in the Book of the Twelve until the book of Micah. This leaves Joel, Amos, Obadiah, and Jonah in between Hosea and Micah without any explicit messianic interpretations. Certainly one passage where readers of the Targum might expect to find a messianic interpretation is Amos 9:11–15. This passage looks forward to a day when the LORD will raise up the fallen "booth" (LXX, Syr.: "tent") of David and rebuild it "like days of old" (cf. Isa 1:26; Jer 33:7, 11; Zech 12:7; see also Isa 44:26; 49:17 [1QIsaᵃ]; 58:12; Jer 30:18; 31:4). Tg. Jon. interprets the fallen "booth" of David to be the fallen "kingdom" of David. According to the Targum, the restored kingdom of

David will rule over all the kingdoms. This certainly has messianic impli-
cations, but it is as close as the text of the Targum comes to an explicitly
messianic rendering. Other early Jewish sources are more direct. 4QFlor
(4Q174) cites Amos 9:11 in connection with the words of the covenant
with David (2 Sam 7:12–14) and the prophecy of the messianic Branch of
David (Isa 4:2; Jer 23:5–6; Zech 3:8; 6:12–13; see also 4Q252). The Babylonian Talmud (b. Sanh. 96b, 97a) derives a messianic title from the phrase
"the fallen booth of David": "the son of the fallen one." The citation of Amos
9:11–12 by James at the Jerusalem Council (Acts 15:16–17) presupposes
that the restored booth of David is the kingdom of Christ.[98]

Mic 4:8; 5:2

The two passages in Micah that receive explicitly messianic renderings in
Tg. Jon. are not the only two that early Jewish and Christian interpreters
considered messianic. MT Mic 1:15 says, "Again (עֹד) the (dis)possessor
will I bring to you, O inhabitant of Mareshah. To Adullam the glory of
Israel will come" (cf. Deut 33:7; see also Mic 4:8; 7:12), but the LXX ("until
I bring the heirs to you") reflects עַד ("until") instead of עֹד ("Again"): "until
(עַד) I bring to you the (dis)possessor"—a possible allusion to the messianic
prophecy in Gen 49:10b ("until [עַד] the one to whom it belongs comes, and
to him will belong obedience of peoples"). The prophecy of Mic 2:12–13
speaks of a shepherd king who leads the people out like a flock through the
gate (cf. Jer 23:1–6; Ezek 34:23; 37:24; Mic 5:4; John 10:9; Pss. Sol. 17:40;
see also Isa 52:12; Mic 7:15), "and the LORD is at their head." The MT is
somewhat ambiguous about whether there are two leaders ("their king" and
"the LORD") or one ("their king," that is, "the LORD") (cf. Mic 4:7; Zeph
3:14–15; Zech 2:10; 9:9–10),[99] but the Targum makes a clear distinction
between "their king" and "the LORD," although it makes no explicit identification of the king (cf. Gen. Rab. 48:10; Lev. Rab. 32:8; Qoh. Rab. 4:1).
According to the Targum, the king will lead the people at their head and
destroy their enemy, and the Word of the Lord will be their support. The

---

98. The citation of Amos 9:12 in Acts 15:17 comes from the LXX as found in Codex
Alexandrinus: "in order that the remnant of mankind [= אדם] may seek [= ידרשו] the
Lord [= את]." This may be compared to MT Amos 9:12: "in order that they may possess
[יירשו] the remnant of Edom [אדום]." See Shepherd, *Commentary on Book of the Twelve*,
200–205.

99. See Horbury, *Jewish Messianism*, 37–46.

Fragmentary Targum for Exod 12:42 (see previously) identifies this king in Mic 2:13 as "King Messiah."[100] Lastly, the rabbinic literature interprets Mic 7:6 to be a description of relationships in the days of the Messiah (b. Sanh. 97a; m. Sotah 9:15; b. Sotah 49b; Song Rab. 2:13). This interpretation is not reflected in the Targum, but it finds a parallel in the Gospel according to Matthew (Matt 10:34–39; see also Luke 12:49–53).

The first explicitly messianic rendering of the Targum of Micah occurs in Mic 4:8. The eschatological prophecy of Mic 4:6–7 (cf. Mic 4:1–5; Zeph 3:19) anticipates that the LORD will be shepherd/king forever on Mount Zion (Mic 4:7b; cf. Exod 15:18; Ezek 34:11–16),[101] and then the text of Mic 4:8 adds: "And as for you, Migdal-eder [Tower of Flock], fortified hill of Daughter Zion, to you the former dominion will come and enter, a kingdom [LXX adds: out of Babylon] for Daughter Jerusalem." Tg. Jon. interprets "Migdal-eder" ("Tower of Flock") to be the Messiah of Israel. That is, the Messiah is the tower, a symbol of strength, and the people of Israel are the flock (cf. Mic 2:12–13; 5:4). The beginning of Mic 4:8 ("And as for you, Migdal-eder") is comparable to that of the messianic prophecy in Mic 5:2: "And as for you, Bethlehem Ephrathah." The only other reference to Migdal-eder in the Hebrew Bible occurs in Gen 35:21 where its location is given in proximity to Ephrathah, that is, Bethlehem (Gen 35:19; see also Luke 2:4, 8; m. Sheqal. 7:4).[102] According to the Hebrew text of Mic 4:8, it is to Zion/Jerusalem that the former dominion/kingdom will come (see Mic 4:1; cf. Isa 1:26; Jer 33:7, 11; Zech 12:7 [LXX]). The Targum, however, says that the kingdom is about to come to the Messiah of Israel "who is hidden from before [or, because of] the sins of the assembly of Zion" (cf. Tg. Jon. Zech 4:7; 6:12; see also Isa 49:2; 1 En. 48:6; 62:7; 4 Ezra 13:26), and the former dominion will come to the kingdom of the assembly of Jerusalem (see Gen 49:10; Deut 33:7; Mic 1:15; 7:12; see also Dan 7:13–14). This either means that the Messiah is kept from the sins of the people until he receives

100. Rashi says that the one who goes up before the people in Mic 2:13 is "their savior" (Rosenberg, *Mikraoth Gedoloth: The Twelve Prophets*, 2:209). Others suggest that the reference is to Elijah the prophet as in Mal 4:5–6 (Rosenberg, *Mikraoth Gedoloth: The Twelve Prophets*, 2:209).

101. Tg. Jon.: "The kingdom of the Lord will be revealed to them on Mount Zion from now to eternity."

102. As noted previously, Tg. Ps.-J. renders Gen 35:21 in an explicitly messianic fashion based on the interpretation of Mic 4:8 found in Tg. Jon.: "And Jacob journeyed and pitched his tent beyond the tower of Eder, the place where King Messiah will be revealed [or: will reveal himself] in the end of days."

the kingdom, or it means that the Messiah's reception of the kingdom is prevented by the sins of the people until a certain time. The text of the Targum thus interprets Mic 4:8 to envision a return to the unified kingdom of David and Solomon under the headship of the Davidic Messiah (see 1 Kgs 4:25; Mic 4:4; Zech 3:10; see also Hos 3:5).

The messianic interpretation of Mic 5:2 is very ancient in both Jewish and Christian interpretation. When Herod asks the Jewish chief priests and scribes about the birthplace of the Messiah in Matt 2:4, their immediate response is "in Bethlehem of Judea" on the basis of the prophecy in Mic 5:2 (Matt 2:5–6; see also John 7:42). The LORD addresses Bethlehem Ephrathah in Mic 5:2 as one too small or too insignificant to be counted among the tribes of Judah, despite the fact that Bethlehem is known as the hometown of David (1 Sam 16:1; 17:12; Ps 132:6; Ruth 4:11; see also Gen 35:19, 21; Mic 4:8). This sets up the irony that a ruler will emerge from such a small or insignificant place.[103] The anticipation of this ruler's emergence is ultimately what makes Bethlehem significant, which leads to the rendering of Mic 5:2 as it appears in Matt 2:6: "And as for you, Bethlehem, in the land of Judah, by no means least are you among the rulers of Judah." The Hebrew text of Mic 5:2 says that one will go forth from Bethlehem for the LORD to be a "ruler" (מושל) over Israel whose origins or activities are from long ago, from days of old (see Hab 1:12; Prov 8:22; John 1:1; see also Mic 4:8; 7:14, 20). Tg. Jon. understands this to mean that the Messiah will go forth from Bethlehem before the Lord to exercise dominion over Israel, he whose name has been mentioned since long ago, since days of old (see Tg. Jon. Zech 4:7).[104]

The LORD announces in Mic 5:3 that he will give the people over to their enemies until time when she who is in labor gives birth (see Mic 1:15; 4:8–10; see also Isa 7:14). At that time, the remnant of the Messiah's brothers (i.e., the Judeans) will return to or in addition to the sons of Israel (i.e., the northern kingdom). The Targum essentially leaves this verse uninterpreted, but the Talmud understands it to mean that the Messiah will not come until the wicked kingdom of Rome has spread over the entire world for nine months (i.e., the time from conception to the birth of a child).[105] When the

---

103. Rashi: "the Messiah, son of David, and so Scripture says (Ps. 118:22): 'The stone the builders had rejected became a cornerstone'" (Rosenberg, *Mikraoth Gedoloth: The Twelve Prophets*, 2:219).

104. Since before creation, according to 1 En. 48:3; b. Ned. 39b; b. Pesaḥ. 54a; Rashi (citing Ps 72:17) in Rosenberg, *Mikraoth Gedoloth: The Twelve Prophets*, 2:220.

105. See b. Yoma 10a; b. Sanh. 98b. See also Rashi and Redak in Rosenberg, *Mikraoth*

Messiah comes, he will stand (LXX adds: "and see") and "shepherd" in the strength of the LORD, in the majesty of the name of the LORD his God (Mic 5:4a; see again Ezek 34:23; 37:24; Mic 2:12–13; 4:8).[106] The Targum renders this to say that the Messiah will rise up and "rule" in the strength of the Lord, in the greatness of the name of the Lord his God. According to MT Mic 5:4b, the people will "live" (וְיָשְׁבוּ), for at that time the Messiah will be great to the ends of the earth (cf. Zech 9:9–10; Ps 72:8). The Syriac and the Latin Vulgate say that the people will "return" (= וְיָשֻׁבוּ or וְשָׁבוּ), and this is the basic sense reflected in Tg. Jon.: "and they will be gathered from among their exiles, for at that time his name will be great to the ends of the earth." The Messiah himself will be the people's peace (Mic 5:5a; see Isa 9:6; 11:6–8; Mic 4:3; Nah 1:15; Zech 9:10; Ps 72:3, 7; Eph 2:14).[107]

The text of Mic 5:5b–6a addresses what will happen if the peace of the messianic kingdom is threatened by a foreign enemy like Assyria: "we will establish against him seven shepherds and eight installed kings of mankind, and they will shepherd [Tg. Jon.: judge] the land of Assyria by the sword, and the land of Nimrod in her gates." The Targum offers no suggestion for the identity of the seven shepherds and eight kings, but the Talmud (b. Sukk. 52b) suggests the following:

> Who are the seven shepherds? David in the middle, Adam, Seth, and Methuselah on his right, Abraham, Jacob, and Moses, on his left. And who are the eight kings among men? Jesse, Saul, Samuel, Amos, Zephaniah, Zedekiah, the Messiah, and Elijah.

The number seven likely symbolizes completeness (see BDB, 988). Since numbers do not have synonyms, the next number above seven (eight) is simply a feature of the parallelism (cf. Prov 30:15–33; see also GKC §134s). The plurality of shepherd-kings may be identified with the saints who will reign with Christ in his kingdom (see Isa 32:1; Jer 3:15; 23:4–6; Obad 21; Dan 7:13–14, 27; Rev 5:10; 20:6; 22:5). This interpretation of the text fits with what the reader finds in Mic 5:6b: "And he will rescue from Assyria when he comes into our land and when he treads on our border." The shift to a singular verb with a singular subject most likely indicates that the Messiah of Mic 5:2–4 is in view. Tg. Jon. preserves this shift to a singular verb, but it makes no attempt to identify the subject of the verb. Redak, on the

Gedoloth: The Twelve Prophets, 2:220.

106. See Redak in Rosenberg, _Mikraoth Gedoloth: The Twelve Prophets_, 2:220.

107 See Shepherd, _Commentary on Book of the Twelve_, 265.

other hand, comments, "King Messiah will rescue us when he destroys the land of Assyria and Babylon with his installed kings and his leaders, so that never again will an enemy go forth from that land who will enter our land and tread on our border."[108]

Nahum and Habakkuk

There are several potentially messianic passages in Nahum and Habakkuk that the Targum opts not to make explicitly messianic. Nahum 1:15 points to the feet of "one bearing good news" (מבשר) on the mountains, someone who proclaims peace (cf. Isa 9:6; Mic 5:5a; Zech 9:10; Ps 72:3, 7). This likely has a connection to the messianic good news bearer in Isa 41:27; 52:7 (see also Rom 10:15).[109] Tg. Jon., however, leaves the herald of Nah 1:15 unidentified.

In the context of a discussion about when the Messiah will come, b. Sanh. 97b cites Hab 2:3, where the prophet is instructed to wait patiently for the appointed time of the prophetic vision of the end (cf. Dan 12:5–13; see also 1QpHab).[110] Tg. Jon. does not have a messianic interpretation of this verse, but the epistle to the Hebrews features a rendering of Hab 2:3 that appears to have in view the coming of an individual rather than the fulfillment of a prophetic vision in general. According to MT Hab 2:3b, the prophetic vision "will surely come" (בֹא יָבֹא; LXX: ἐρχόμενος ἥξει) it will not delay. Hebrews 10:37, however, says that "the one who is coming will come" (ὁ ἐρχόμενος ἥξει = הַבָּא יָבֹא) and not delay. Within the larger context of Habakkuk, this coming individual can only be the anointed king of Hab 3:13.

Hab 3:13 occurs in the context of a theophany in Hab 3:3–15 that describes God's future judgment of the wicked and deliverance of the righteous in terms of familiar images drawn from the biblical narratives in Genesis through Kings (e.g., exodus, conquest, etc.). The first half of this verse says, "You go forth for the deliverance of your people, to deliver your anointed one" (cf. Num 24:8; Zech 9:9). The second half of the verse then ties this to the biblical theme of striking the head of the enemy known from

108. Rosenberg, *Mikraoth Gedoloth: The Twelve Prophets*, 2:222.

109. See the earlier discussion of the messianic servant of the LORD in Isa 42:1–7.

110. See Fishbane, *Biblical Interpretation in Ancient Israel*, 492–93. Augustine: "Of what else than the advent of Christ, who was to come, is Habakkuk understood to say" (Ferreiro, *Twelve Prophets*, 191).

other messianic poems (see Gen 3:15; Num 24:17; Pss 68:21; 110:5–6). The Latin Vulgate, which understands the text messianically, interprets the object marker (את) in Hab 3:13a as if it were the preposition "with": "You go forth for the salvation of your people, for salvation with your Christ." Tg. Jon. renders Hab 3:3–15 as if it were a rehearsal of the biblical narrative rather than an eschatological vision. Thus, the deliverance of the anointed one in Hab 3:13 is simply the deliverance of an unidentified historical king. Rashi suggests that the text refers to the deliverance of Saul and David.[111] A few Masoretic manuscripts and witnesses to the LXX (minus Vaticanus and Sinaiticus) have "your anointed ones" in Hab 3:13 instead of "your anointed one."[112] It is possible that this is intended to form a parallel with "your people," but it is more likely that it is another historicized version of the text intended to refer to multiple historical kings delivered by God. On the other hand, Redak goes against the grain of the general trend of Jewish exegetical tradition and interprets the anointed one in Hab 3:13 to be the "Messiah, the son of David."[113]

The only text of Habakkuk that Tg. Jon. renders messianically is not necessarily one that the reader would anticipate. According to the Hebrew text of Hab 3:18, the prophet resolves to exult in the LORD, to rejoice in the God of his salvation in spite of the dire circumstances described in Hab 3:17. The Targum, however, interprets Hab 3:17 to be a series of metaphors for the downfalls of Babylon, Media, Greece, and Rome. Thus, it is messianic deliverance that serves as the basis for the prophet's exultation in Hab 3:18: "Then, because of the miracle and the redemption that you will perform for your Messiah and for the remnant of your people who are left, they will praise, saying, 'The prophet says, "I will rejoice in the Word of the Lord, I will exult in the God who performs my redemption."'" This messianic expansion also occurs in the Targums of 2 Sam 22:32 and Ps 18:31. It is possible that this messianic interpretation of Hab 3:18 became known to Jerome via his Jewish teachers. His translation of this verse in the Latin Vulgate is explicitly messianic and Christian: "I will rejoice in the Lord, I will exult in God my Jesus." This translation takes ישעי ("my salvation") as if it were the name יֵשׁוּעַ or יֵשַׁע ("Jesus") plus a first common singular pronominal suffix.

---

111. Rosenberg, *Mikraoth Gedoloth: The Twelve Prophets*, 2:279.

112. LXX Barberini, a variant Greek translation of Hab 3, has "your chosen ones."

113. Rosenberg, *Mikraoth Gedoloth: The Twelve Prophets*, 2:279. See also Roberts, *Nahum, Habakkuk, and Zephaniah*, 156.

Zechariah

The two books preceding Zechariah in the order of the Twelve—Zephaniah and Haggai—have no messianic renderings in Tg. Jon. Nevertheless, these books have passages that interpreters have historically understood to be messianic (e.g., Zeph 3:14–15; Hag 2:6–9, 20–23).[114] Furthermore, these same passages connect with key messianic texts in Zechariah (Zech 3:8; 6:12–13; 9:9–10), some of which receive messianic interpretations in the Targum. The first text that the Targum renders messianically in Zechariah is Zech 3:8. Here the LORD addresses Joshua the high priest and his companions, the "men of wonder" (i.e., the prophets; see Isa 8:18; 20:3; Ezek 12:6, 11; see also 5:1–2), and says that he is about to bring his servant "Branch" (LXX: "sunrise/dawn"; cf. LXX Num 24:17). This takes up the language of the prophecy in Hag 2:23, which identifies Zerubbabel as the LORD's servant, and applies it to one who is yet to come (cf. Isa 42:1; see also GKC §116p), thus making Zerubbabel a prefiguration of the coming one. Tg. Jon. identifies the "Branch" (צמח) in Zech 3:8b as "the Messiah" in accordance with its rendering of this messianic title elsewhere (Isa 4:2; Jer 23:5; Zech 6:12; see also 4Q252). Indeed, the Targum appears to be sensitive to the fact that these texts are all intertextually related. Zechariah 3:8 and 6:12 depend upon Jer 23:5, and Jer 23:5 depends upon Isa 4:2 (and Isa 11:1, 10). The Targum adds to the end of Zech 3:8: "and he will be revealed" (see 4 Ezra 7:28; cf. Tg. Jon. Mic 4:8).

The text of Zech 3:9a then shifts to the metaphor of the messianic stone over which the eyes of the LORD providentially watch (see Isa 8:14; 28:16; Ps 118:22; Dan 2:34–35, 44–45; Matt 21:42–44; Rom 9:33; 1 Pet 2:6–8).[115] The LORD says that he is about to engrave the engraving of this stone (Zech 3:9b)—an allusion to the engraving of the names of the sons of Israel on the two stones of the priestly garment (Exod 28:9, 11, 21, 36; 39:6, 9, 30). This anticipates the presentation of the Messiah in Zech 6:12–13 as one who is both king and priest. By means of this new king-priest the LORD will remove the iniquity of the land represented by the filthy (excrement-covered)

---

114. For Zeph 3:14–15, see Horbury, *Jewish Messianism*, 37–43. See also the citation of Hag 2:6 in Heb 12:26 and the translation of Hag 2:7a1 in the Latin Vulgate: "and the desired one of all the nations will come" (cf. 1 Sam 9:20). For Hag 2:20–23, see Abarbanel's explanation of this text as a prophecy about the war of Gog and Magog, which is followed by the coming of the Messiah (Rosenberg, *Mikraoth Gedoloth: The Twelve Prophets*, 2:316).

115. See Keil, *Minor Prophets*, 531. See also Rev 4:6, 8.

garments of the high priest Joshua (Zech 3:3–4). The conclusion to the prophecy in Zech 3:10 changes imagery once again and looks forward to the day when the people will call one another to come under a grapevine and under a fig tree. This image comes from the depiction of the peace and prosperity enjoyed during Solomon's reign in 1 Kgs 4:25. It has likely been mediated to Zechariah via Mic 4:4, which envisions a return to the golden age of David and Solomon in the messianic kingdom (see also Mic 4:8).

The stone imagery of Zech 3:9 is the link to the Targum's next messianic rendering in Zech 4:7. The vision of the menorah in Zech 4:1–5 does not receive its interpretation until Zech 4:10–14. Between these two texts is the word of the LORD to Zerubbabel: "Not by might and not by strength but by my Spirit" (Zech 4:6; cf. 1 Sam 2:9b–10; Hag 2:5b). Then follows the question in Zech 4:7a: "Who are you, O great mountain? Before Zerubbabel you will become a level place" (cf. Matt 17:20).[116] Tg. Jon. interprets the great mountain to be a "foolish kingdom."[117] Levey notes an alternative rabbinic interpretation that understands the great mountain to be the Messiah: "What are you, O great mountain, (Zech. 4:7), this is the King Messiah, and why does he call him 'great mountain?' For he is greater than the Patriarchs."[118] On the other hand, the Targum introduces its messianic interpretation in the second half of the verse. The Hebrew text of Zech 4:7b says, "And he will bring forth the chief stone with noises/shouts of 'Grace, grace' to it" (see Zech 12:10).[119] The Targum renders, "And he will reveal his Messiah whose name has been said since long ago, and he will rule over all the kingdoms" (see Tg. Jon. Mic 5:2; b. Pesaḥ. 54a; 1 En. 48:3; see also Tg. Jon. Isa 53:8; Pss. Sol. 17:32; b. Ber. 34b). Thus, the chief stone is not merely the chief cornerstone of the Second Temple structure but the messianic stone as in Ps 118:22 (see Matt 21:42).

The hands of Zerubbabel laid the foundation of the second temple (see Ezra 3:10), but the hands of the Messiah will complete the greater temple (Zech 4:9; see 2 Sam 7:13; Hag 2:9; Zech 6:12–13; see also Ezek 40–48; Rev 21:22).[120] Those who "despise a day of small things"—that is, those who see

116. Or: "Who are you, O great mountain, before Zerubbabel? You will become a level place."

117. As noted previously, Zerubbabel prefigures the Messiah (Hag 2:23; Zech 3:8; 6:12).

118. Levey, *Messiah*, 98. See also Dan 2:34–35, 44–45 (cf. Isa 2:2; Mic 4:1).

119. LXX: "And I will bring forth the stone of inheritance, equality of grace, grace for it."

120. "Thus from the tribe of Judah were descended Solomon, who built the first

the disappointment of the Second Temple (Hag 2:3; Ezra 3:12)—will rejoice when they see "the separated stone" in Zerubbabel's hand (Zech 4:10a). The phrase "the separated stone" is typically translated as "plummet," "plumb line," or "tin tablet," but such translations obscure the use of "stone" (אבן) in the Hebrew text and its connection to Zech 3:9 and 4:7. The stone in Zerubbabel's hand is symbolic of the Messiah and his kingdom, which is separated from the kingdoms of the world (see Dan 7). Just as the seven eyes of God watch over the messianic stone in Zech 3:9, so the seven lamps of the menorah represent the eyes of the LORD roaming through all the land (Zech 4:10b; cf. 2 Chr 16:9; see also Ps 33:18; Rev 5:6). When the prophet inquires about the meaning of the two olive trees (Zech 4:11), the response is that they are "the two anointed ones who are standing at the service of the Lord of all the land" (Zech 4:14; cf. Rev 11:4). This anticipates the prophecy of Zech 6:12–13, which looks forward to a single messianic figure who will hold the two anointed offices of king and priest.

Zech 6:12 is the last in a series of biblical texts (Isa 4:2; Jer 23:5; Zech 3:8) to use the messianic title "Branch" (צמח). The context of this occurrence is the sign act of the high priest Joshua who wears a royal crown in order to symbolize the one man who will be both a king and a priest (Zech 6:9–11). It is clear from Zech 6:12a that the presentation of this man is "to" Joshua and not "about" him. It is also clear from what follows that the man is not Zerubbabel.[121] The man is the messianic "man" known from other biblical prophecies (see Num 24:7, 17 [LXX]; 2 Sam 23:1 [LXX, 4QSam^a]; 2 Sam 23:3 [LXX]; Isa 19:20 [LXX]; Dan 7:13; see also John 19:5; 1 Tim 2:5). Tg. Jon. remains consistent with its rendering of צמח ("Branch") elsewhere when it identifies the צמח in Zech 6:12 as "the Messiah" (see also Ps 132:17; 4Q252). The "Branch" of Zech 6:12 also receives a messianic interpretation in Num. Rab. 18:21 and Lam. Rab. 1:51.[122]

Temple, and Zerubbabel who built the second Temple; and the royal Messiah, who will rebuild the Temple" (Gen. Rab. 97).

121. Contra Rashi and Redak (Rosenberg, *Mikraoth Gedoloth: The Twelve Prophets*, 2:345–46). "[I]nterpretations that identify the Shoot as Zerubbabel lack coherence on important issues (such as how the passage authenticated Zechariah as sent by Yahweh when Zerubbabel did not become king), in terms of inner-biblical exegesis they reduce the significance of the wider Davidic dynasty tradition found in other texts (Zerubbabel as a messiah, rather than the Messiah), and/or limit the intention of the passage to the audience of the prophet" (Petterson, "New Form-Critical Approach," 303).

122. See also Abarbanel and Mezudath David in Rosenberg, *Mikraoth Gedoloth: The Twelve Prophets*, 2:346.

The messianic Branch will "build the temple of the LORD" in fulfillment of the covenant with David (Zech 6:12b; see 2 Sam 7:13). The Syriac omits the last clause of Zech 6:12b ("and build the temple of the LORD") but includes the first clause of Zech 6:13a ("And he is the one who will build the temple of the LORD"). On the other hand, the LXX includes the last clause of Zech 6:12b but omits the first clause of Zech 6:13a. These two shorter versions of the text probably do not reflect shorter Hebrew originals. Rather, the translators likely opted to omit one of the clauses due to the misperception that one of the two was redundant. The second clause (Zech 6:13a), however, is not a mere repetition of the first (Zech 6:12b). The clause at the beginning of Zech 6:13a features the fronted independent personal pronoun "he," which highlights the fact that the future messianic king (rather than Solomon) is the one who will build the temple in fulfillment of the Davidic covenant.

The most straightforward translation of the remainder of the Hebrew text of Zech 6:13 runs as follows: "And he is the one who will bear royal splendor and sit and rule on his throne. And he will be a priest [Tg. Jon.: high priest] on his throne, and peaceful counsel will be between the two of them." Tg. Jon. renders the text in this literal fashion, but English translators of the Hebrew text and the Targum tend to render the second occurrence of "on his throne" as "beside his throne" (i.e., "And there will be a priest beside his throne"), even though the phrase is exactly the same as the first occurrence. The tension that prompts this tendency is the seemingly irreconcilable combination of a Davidic king from the tribe of Judah and an Aaronic priest from the tribe of Levi in one person. The same tension likely motivated the LXX translator to make his own adjustment: "And the priest will be on his right."[123] The Qumran community attempted to resolve this problem with its theory of two Messiahs: the Messiah of Aaron and the Messiah of Israel (see 4QD[a] 10 I, 12; 1QS 9:11; 1QSa 2:11–22; see also T. Sim. 7:2).[124] There is, however, another solution:

---

123. Cf. 1 Sam 2:35; but see 13:14; 2 Sam 7:16. See also Shepherd, *Text in the Middle*, 25–27.

124. It is interesting to note that Tg. Song 4:5 and 7:4 mentions two Messiahs—Messiah the son of David and Messiah the son of Ephraim. Normally Messiah the son of Ephraim is invoked when it is felt necessary to distinguish the suffering Messiah from the Davidic Messiah (see the upcoming discussion of Zech 12:10), but Targum Song of Songs compares Messiah the son of David to Moses, and Messiah son of Ephraim to Aaron.

Genesis 14 and Psalm 110 have provided a category for a Davidic king who is a priest according to a different priestly order (see also Matt. 22:41–46; Acts 2:34–35; Heb. 1:13; 5:6; 7). Melchizedek, the king of Salem (i.e., Jerusalem, the city of David [Ps. 76:3 (Eng., 76:2)]), was also priest of God Most High (see Ps. 110:4; see also Ezek. 45:17). This is why the counsel of peace (or, well-being, agreement) will be between the king and the priest according to Zechariah 6:13b2 (see Mic. 5:4a [Eng., 5:5a]); Zech. 9:9–10). It is not because two different individuals will be in agreement. The agreement will exist because the two offices will be held by one messianic king/priest.[125]

Moving to the second half of Zechariah, Tg. Jon. does not render the prophecy in Zech 9:9–10 in an explicitly messianic fashion. Levey thinks that this is because the idea of an afflicted Messiah "was not acceptable to the Jewish mind" (cf. Tg. Jon. Isa 52:13—53:12; see also Gen 3:15; Isa 50:4–11; Zech 12:10; Dan 9:26).[126] It is evident, however, that early Jewish and Christian interpreters understood this passage messianically (see Matt 21:5; John 12:15; Gen. Rab. 75:6; 98:9; b. Sanh. 98a; 99a).[127] Thus, it is possible that the Targum simply translates the text in a more literal manner and allows it to speak for itself. Zechariah 9:9–10 is part of a series of texts in the Book of the Twelve designed to show that the coming of God as king is in fact the coming of the Davidic Messiah as God in the flesh (cf. Isa 9:6–7; Zech 12:10):[128]

> Shout, Daughter Zion [Tg. Jon.: congregation of Zion]! Cry out, O Israel! Be glad and exult with all your heart, Daughter Jerusalem [Tg. Jon.: congregation of Jerusalem]! The LORD has removed your judgments [Syr., Tg. Jon.: judges], he has turned away your enemy [mlt Mss; MurXII, LXX, Syr., Tg. Jon.: your enemies]. The king of Israel, the LORD, is in your midst [LXX^L Mss: The Lord will be king in your midst; Tg. Jon.: The king of Israel, the Lord, has

125. Shepherd, *Commentary on Book of the Twelve*, 428.

126. Levey, *Messiah*, 100.

127. See also Rashi in Rosenberg, *Mikraoth Gedoloth: The Twelve Prophets*, 2:362.

128. "Messianism in the Persian period has been minimized somewhat comparably in the suggestion that the lowly king of Zechariah 9:9 is God rather than a messianic king, an interpretation permitted by the vitality of the anthropomorphic depictions of the deity which have just been considered. The balance of probability seems, however, to incline the other way, in the light of the royal oracles which this passage resembles" (Horbury, *Jewish Messianism*, 43).

said to cause his Shekhinah to dwell in your midst]. You will never be afraid [2 Mss, LXX, Syr.: see] again. (Zeph 3:14–15)

Shout and be glad, Daughter Zion [Tg. Jon.: congregation of Zion]! For look, I am about to come to you [Tg. Jon.: I am about to reveal myself], and I will dwell in your midst, the prophetic utterance of the LORD. (Zech 2:10)

Rejoice greatly, Daughter Zion [Tg. Jon.: congregation of Zion]! Cry out, Daughter Jerusalem [Tg. Jon.: congregation of Jerusalem]! Look, your king, he is coming to you. Righteous and delivered [LXX, Syr., Tg. Jon., Vulg.: savior; cf. LXX Isa 19:20] is he.[129] [He is] afflicted [LXX, Syr.: gentle/meek] and riding on a donkey, and on a colt, a foal. And I [LXX, Syr.: he] will cut off chariots from Ephraim and horses from Jerusalem. And the battle bow will be removed, and he will speak peace to the nations. And his rule will be from sea to sea [Tg. Jon.: west], and from river [Tg. Jon.: Euphrates] to land's ends. (Zech 9:9–10)

The prophecy of Zech 9:9–10 envisions a coming king "riding on a donkey, and on a colt, a foal" in fulfillment of the messianic prophecy in Gen 49:10–11 ("binding to the grapevine his colt, to the choice vine his foal").[130] This king will reunite Ephraim and Judah (see Isa 11:13; Jer 3:18; Ezek 37:15–28; Zech 9:13; 10:6) and bring peace to the nations (cf. Isa 2:4; 9:6; 11:6–8; 52:7; Ezek 34:24–25; Mic 4:3; 5:5; Nah 1:15; Hag 2:9, 22; Ps 72:3). His rule will extend from the Dead Sea to the Mediterranean Sea and from the Euphrates River to land's ends (see Gen 15:18; Mic 5:4b; 7:12; Pss 22:27–28; 72:8).

---

129. See Num 24:8; 2 Sam 22:51; Hab 3:13. Note that John 12:15 combines wording from Zeph 3:15b and Zech 9:9 (cf. Matt 21:5).

130. Cf. 2 Sam 18:9; 1 Kgs 1:33. Note again that the Targums of the Pentateuch all agree that Gen 49:10 is messianic.

The final messianic rendering in Tg. Jon.'s version of Zechariah appears in Zech 10:4. The Hebrew text of this verse says, "From it/him[131] will be a corner, from it/him will be a peg, from it/him will be a battle bow. From it/him every oppressor will depart together."[132] Tg. Jon. interprets the corner to be "its/his king," and it interprets the peg to be "its/his Messiah."[133] The term פנה ("corner") is used elsewhere as a metaphor for leaders (see Judg 20:2; 1 Sam 14:38; Isa 19:13), but most notably it occurs in Ps 118:22 to refer to the messianic stone that becomes the chief cornerstone despite being rejected by the builders (see Zech 4:7; Matt 21:42). The term יתד ("peg") can also be used for a leader, most notably Eliakim who is placed over the house of the king (2 Kgs 18:18; Isa 22:23). The messianic king of Zech 10:4 will be a warrior king with a battle bow (cf. Gen 49:12; Zech 9:10, 13). The Targum's messianic interpretation of Zech 10:4 has likely been prompted in part by the description of the people in Zech 10:2 as sheep without a shepherd (cf. Num 27:17; 1 Kgs 22:17; Matt 9:36). The presence of bad shepherds/kings (Zech 10:3) shows the need for the good shepherd (cf. Jer 23:1–6; Ezek 34; John 10).[134]

While Zech 10:4 is the last of the messianic texts in Tg. Jon., it is not the last in the Palestinian Targum of the Prophets. As noted in the earlier discussion of Targum Pseudo-Jonathan Exod 40:11, Codex Reuchlinianus (1105 CE), which features parallel Hebrew and Aramaic texts of the Prophets, preserves in the margin of the Targum for Zech 12:10 a witness to a messianic Palestinian Targum:

131. Either from the house of Judah or from the LORD (see Mic 5:2).

132. The term נוגש ("oppressor") has a negative connotation in context (see Zech 9:8). It does not mean "ruler," and it does not refer to the same individual who is called a corner and a peg. Rather, the ideal king will banish the oppressor.

133. Exod. Rab. 37:1 interprets the corner to be King David on the basis of Ps 118:22, and it interprets the peg to be the high priest on the basis of Isa 22:23, although Eliakim is not called high priest in that text. Cf. Zech 6:12–13.

134. This also sets up the imagery of Zech 11:4–14; 13:7 (see Matt 26:15, 31; 27:9–10). See Shepherd, *Commentary on Book of the Twelve*, 453–59, 466–70. Tg. Jon. interprets "my shepherd" in Zech 13:7 to be "the king." Some editions of the Targum have "the king of Babylon." Thus, Rashi understands the shepherd in Zech 13:7 to be the bad shepherd or wicked king (Rosenberg, *Mikraoth Gedoloth: The Twelve Prophets*, 2:388; see Zech 11:15–17). This is contrary to the interpretation of Zech 13:7 found in Matt 26:31, which understands the shepherd to be the good shepherd whom the LORD himself strikes (cf. Isa 53:10).

> And I will let rest upon the house of David and upon the inhabit-
> ants of Jerusalem the Spirit of prophecy and true prayer. After-
> wards the Messiah the son of Ephraim will go out to wage war with
> Gog, and Gog will kill him before the gate of Jerusalem. And they
> will look at me and ask why the peoples pierced the Messiah the
> son of Ephraim, and they will mourn over him.

This Targum shares with Tg. Ps.-J. Exod 40:11 an interest in "the Messiah the son of Ephraim" and his involvement in the war with Gog (Ezek 38–39; Rev 20:8). The Messiah son of Ephraim is also known from Tg. Song 4:5 and 7:4 where he is clearly distinct from the Messiah the son of David. The Messiah's involvement in the war with Gog is known from Tg. Neof. and Frg. Tg. Num 11:26, SP and LXX Num 24:7–8, and Tg. Neof. Num 24:20. The messianic interpretation of Zech 12:10 found in the Palestinian Targum finds a close parallel in b. Sukkah 52a: "It is on account of the Messiah, the son of Joseph, who was killed" (cf. 4 Ezra 7:28–29; b. Pesaḥ. 118).[135] It is this belief in a Messiah son of Ephraim/Joseph that allows the Palestinian Targum to admit a messianic sense in its rendering of Zech 12:10 without requiring the Davidic Messiah to suffer and die. On the other hand, Robert Gordon has noted Tg. Jon.'s avoidance of the MT's "whom they pierced" in Zech 12:10 and the oddity of its failure to provide an antecedent for the pronoun "him" ("and they will mourn for him") in the second half of the verse: "One possibility is that *Tg.* was subjected to (incomplete) revision as a reaction to Christian citation of this verse as a messianic proof-text."[136]

The Hebrew text of Zech 12:10 lends itself to a messianic interpreta-
tion: "And I will pour out on the house of David and on the inhabitants of Jerusalem the Spirit of grace and supplication,[137] and they will look at me

---

135. "The origin of the messiah son of Joseph is related in Zohar Hadash, Balak (Is-raeli ed. 69a, earlier ed. 56a), where it is stated: On that day, when Abijah the son of Jeroboam died, a son was born to Abijah. That son was taken from the house of Jeroboam to the desert; and there they took one hundred and seventy men, all righteous, from the tribe of Ephraim, who were not guilty of the sin of Jeroboam. That messiah is descended from that son of Abijah. Concerning [that messiah] it is written (I Kings 14:13): 'And all of Israel shall eulogize him and bury him.' The meaning of this prophecy is concealed, in that it applies to its own time as well as the future. 'For he alone of Jeroboam shall come to a grave, for there is found in that messiah a good thing toward the Lord, the God of Israel, in the house of Jeroboam.' This is that messiah, for he is a good thing toward the Lord" (Rosenberg, *Mikraoth Gedoloth: The Twelve Prophets*, 2:384).

136. Cathcart and Gordon, *Targum of the Minor Prophets*, 218n28.

137. Cf. Ezek 39:29 (MT); Joel 2:28–29.

whom they pierced,[138] and they will mourn for him like mourning for the only son, and they will show bitterness for him like showing bitterness for the firstborn." The LORD is the speaker here. Thus, the text naturally raises the question of how the LORD can be pierced (cf. Zech 13:3; see also Ps 22:16b [LXX 21:17b]). Furthermore, the second half of the verse raises the question of why the people will mourn "for him" rather than "for me." To whom does the pronoun "him" refer? The expectation is that the people will mourn for the one who is pierced, but the use of the third-person pronoun presses the reader to identify the one who is pierced with one from "the house of David." In other words, the LORD can be pierced because he comes in the flesh as the Davidic Messiah (see Zech 12:8b: "and the house of David will be like God, like the angel of the LORD before them"; cf. Isa 9:6; see also the previous comments on Zech 9:9). Thus, Zech 12:10 ranks among other biblical texts that appear to speak of a suffering Messiah (Gen 3:15; Isa 50:4–11; 52:13—53:12; Ps 22; Dan 9:26). This is precisely the way John cites Zech 12:10 with reference to the piercing of Jesus' side on the cross: "they will look at him whom they pierced" (John 19:37).[139] John (or his source) changes the pronoun "me" to "him" in order to connect the two halves of the verse.

The mourning for the Messiah (Zech 12:10b) will be done by the same people who pierce the Messiah (Zech 12:10a). Those who reject the Messiah are the very ones for whom the Messiah suffers and dies (see again Isa 53:4–6, 12). Two texts in the NT—Matt 24:30 and Rev 1:7—refer to this mourning and pair it with the messianic prophecy of the coming of the Son of Man in Dan 7:13. Commentators typically explain this mourning as a response to coming judgment, but this does not fit the original context of Zech 12:10–14. Furthermore, mourning would be a rather strange response to coming judgment. Fear would be more appropriate. It seems more likely that the mourning is that of those who have recognized the death of the Messiah on their behalf. They are mourning the death of their

138. The presence of the object marker in this clause ("and they will look at me אֵת whom they pierced") may be explained in at least two different ways. One option is that it marks the following relative clause ("whom they pierced") as a comment on the pronoun "me" (cf. Mic 3:8a; MT Hag 2:5a). Another option is that the letters א and ת (the first and last letters of the Hebrew alphabet) stand for the LORD as the beginning and the end (see Isa 41:4; 44:6; 48:12; Rev 1:8, 17; 2:8; 21:6; 22:13). This is the way Codex Alexandrinus interprets the object marker in Amos 9:12 (cf. Acts 15:17).

139. See Bynum, Fourth Gospel and the Scriptures. John's citation of Zech 12:10 is paired with a citation of Exod 12:46 (John 19:36; cf. Ps 22:14, 17).

Messiah until he returns.[140] Zechariah 12:11 compares the mourning for the Messiah to that of "Hadad-Rimmon in the valley of Megiddo." Tg. Jon. understands the valley of Megiddo here to be a reference to the mourning for Josiah whom Pharaoh Necho killed in the valley of Megiddo (see 2 Chr 35:20–25). According to Horbury, the premature death of the righteous King Josiah makes him a prototype of the suffering Messiah.[141] The sacrificial, substitutionary death of the Messiah ultimately makes provision for the sin of the people (see MT and LXX Zech 13:1; see also Isa 53:4–6, 10–12).

FINAL THOUGHTS ON THE MESSIAH OF TG. JON.

Christopher Seitz has written about what he calls the "goodly fellowship of the prophets," by which he means the achievement of intertextual association among the Former and Latter Prophets of the Hebrew Bible.[142] According to Seitz, this achievement took form in reciprocal relationship to the Torah.[143] Tg. Jon. of the Prophets shows a remarkable awareness of the interconnectedness of the messianic passages in the prophetic literature and the relationship of these passages to the poems of the Pentateuch, specifically Gen 49:8–12 and Num 24:7–9, 17. For instance, the Targum consistently renders the messianic title צמח ("Branch") as "the Messiah" in the interrelated passages of Isa 4:2; Jer 23:5–6; and Zech 3:8; 6:12–13 in order to identify the Branch as the messianic king from the tribe of Judah (Gen 49:8–12) who descends from David's father Jesse in fulfillment of the covenant with David (2 Sam 7:12–16; 23:1–5; Isa 11:1, 10; Mic 5:2). Tg. Jon. also links together the references to "David their king" in Jer 30:9 and Hos 3:5 with its unique rendering "the Messiah, the son of David, their king." This Messiah comes in fulfillment of the prophecy in Num 24:7–9 to lead

140. See Matt 9:15: "And Jesus said to them, 'The guests of the bridegroom cannot mourn while the bridegroom is with them, can they? But days are coming when the bridegroom will be taken from them, and then they will fast.'"

141. Horbury, *Jewish Messianism*, 21.

142. Seitz, *Goodly Fellowship of the Prophets*, 129.

143. See also Chapman, *Law and the Prophets*. "We will see that the prophets were aware of the meaning of the Pentateuch through their own reading and study of it. As a result of that, they helped to preserve it by producing a new 'prophetic edition' of the Pentateuch based on their understanding of the Mosaic law. This is the 'canonical Pentateuch' in our Bible today. Further evidence of the 'prophetic update of the Pentateuch' is found in some early texts and versions" (Sailhamer, *Meaning of the Pentateuch*, 14).

a new exodus (Hos 2:14–15; Jer 31:2–6; see also Isa 11:16; Hos 11:1, 5, 11; Matt 2:13–15). The Targum thus serves as a reliable guide to the strategically messianic composition of the Prophets. It also bridges a gap between Jewish and Christian interpretation of the servant of the LORD with its identification of this entity as an individual messianic figure (Isa 42:1–7; 52:13—53:12).

3

The Messiah in the Writings

THE BOOK OF PSALMS[1]

Pss 2; 18; 118

THE THREE TORAH PSALMS in the Psalter (Pss 1; 19; 119) are each paired with a messianic psalm (Pss 2; 18; 118).[2] Psalms 1 and 2 both lack superscriptions and together form an introduction to the Psalter (see b. Ber. 9b–10a).[3] Because the Hebrew text of Ps 2:2b already has the term משיחו ("his anointed"), which the Targum renders literally, it is difficult to determine whether the Targum interprets Ps 2 messianically. The Talmud interprets the psalm messianically (see b. Ber. 7b; b. Abod. Zar. 3b), but medieval Jewish commentators like Rashi and Redak understand the anointed one in verse 2b to be David and thus they refer their readers to 2 Sam 5:17.[4] Early Christian citation of Ps 2 reflects messianic interpretation of verses 2, 7, and 9 (see Acts 4:25–26; 13:33; Heb 1:5; 5:5; Rev 2:27; 12:5; 19:15). The wording

1. See Edwards, *Exegesis in the Targum.*

2. See again Mays, "Place of the Torah-Psalms," 3–12.

3. See Cole, *Psalms 1 and 2.* Most witnesses to the introduction of the citation from Ps 2:7 in Acts 13:33 have "in the second psalm," but the Western text (D) has "in the first psalm." It appears that the purpose of this combination of the first two psalms is to indicate to the readership that the Psalter is a guide to the Messiah in the Torah.

4. Some witnesses to the Greek Psalter add the superscription "A Psalm of David" to the beginning of Ps 2.

of Ps 2:7 ("You are my son. Today I have fathered you.") is reminiscent of the covenant with David, which speaks not of David but of a coming son of David: "I will be his father, and he will be my son" (2 Sam 7:14; 1 Chr 17:13; cf. LXX Ps 109:3 [MT 110:3]; Prov 8:22–25; 1QSa 2:11–12; 4Q174; 4Q246; 4 Ezra 7:28; 13:32; b. Sukkah 52a; Midr. Teh. 2:9–10; see also Ps 89:26). Emanuel White suggests that the Targum's rendering of Ps 2:7 ("You are as beloved to me as a son to a father, pure as if today I created you.") is deliberately designed to avoid the literal Christian interpretation.[5]

The latter verses of Ps 2 are perhaps the most difficult to align with a non-messianic interpretation. When did God ever give David the nations as his inheritance, or the ends of the earth as his possession (Ps 2:8)? To whom of the historical sons of David did God give the nations? Yet, this is precisely what God will give to the Messiah (see, e.g., Gen 49:10; Dan 7:13–14). The citations of Ps 2:9 in Revelation (2:27; 12:5; 19:15) follow the LXX—"You will shepherd them (= תִּרְעֵם) with an iron rod, like a potter's vessel you will shatter them"—rather than the MT: "You will crush them (תְּרֹעֵם)." A messianic interpretation of Ps 2:9 also appears in Pss. Sol. 17:21–25. Furthermore, it is worth noting that the expression "Kiss the son" (נשקו בר) in Ps 2:12, which is apparently a way to say "Pay homage to the son" (cf. Gen 41:40; 1 Sam 10:1), uses the Aramaic word for "son" (בר) and may have an important connection to the Aramaic phrase "son of man" (בר אנש) in Dan 7:13. On the other hand, the LXX, the Syriac, and the Targum of Ps 2:12 all render "Kiss the son" as "Receive instruction."

The second pairing of a messianic psalm with a Torah psalm occurs in Pss 18 and 19. Psalm 18 is a reproduction of 2 Sam 22 with some key differences throughout. The messianic rendering in the Targum of Ps 18:31 is essentially the same as the one found in Tg. Jon.'s version of 2 Sam 22:32: "For, because of the miracle and the redemption that you will perform for your Messiah and for the remnant of your people who are left, all the peoples, nations, and tongues will praise and say, 'There is no God but the Lord,' for there is none apart from you. And your people will say, 'There is no one strong except our God.'"[6] Levey suggests that the Targum of Ps 18 depends upon Tg. Jon. 2 Sam 22.[7] As noted earlier, the messianic expansion of 2 Sam 22:32 and Ps 18:31 in the Targums also appears in Tg. Jon. Hab 3:18.

---

5. White, *Critical Edition of the Targum*, 116–17.

6. See the prior discussion of 2 Sam 22:32 for further comment.

7. Levey, *Messiah*, 106.

Psalm 118, which is paired with Ps 119, does not receive an explicitly messianic interpretation in the Targum, but features of the exegetical tradition represented by the Targum have had an influence on the messianic interpretation of Ps 118 in the New Testament documents.[8] The Targum of Ps 118:22–29 assigns speaking parts to various characters from the scene of David's anointing in 1 Sam 16:1–13:[9]

> 22 *The architects forsook the youth among the sons of Jesse, but he was worthy to be appointed king and ruler.* 23 "This has been from *before* the LORD," *said the architects.* "It is wonderful in our *presence*," *said the sons of Jesse.* 24 "This is the day that the LORD has made," *said the architects.* 25 "We beseech you, O LORD, make (us) prosper now," *said Jesse and his wife.* 26 "Blessed is the one who comes in the name of *the Memra of* the LORD," *said the architects.* "We bless you from the house of *the sanctuary of* the LORD," *said David.* 27 The LORD is God, and he has given us light," *said the tribes of the house of Judah.* "Bind *the lamb for the sacrifice of* the festival with *chains, until you offer it and sprinkle its blood on* the horns of the altar," *said Samuel the prophet.* 28 "You are my God, and I will give *thanks before* you; O my God, I will *praise* you," *said David.* 29 *Samuel answered, "Give praise, O Assembly of Israel,* Give thanks before the LORD, for he is good; for his goodness endures for ever.[10]

The citations of Ps 118:25–26 in the accounts of the triumphal entry of Jesus found in Matthew and Mark also include additions that mention David: "Hosanna to the son of David" (Matt 21:9) and "Blessed is the coming kingdom of our father David" (Mark 11:10).[11] Both Matthew and John identify the one who comes in the name of the LORD (Ps 118:26) with the coming Davidic Messiah in the prophecy of Zech 9:9 (Matt 21:5, 9; John 12:13, 15).[12]

---

8. See Evans, "Aramaic Psalter," 44–91. A messianic interpretation of Ps 118 is also encouraged by verse 14: "My strength and song is Yah, and he has become my salvation." This is a citation of Isa 12:2, which is a citation of the celebration of the original exodus in Exod 15:2 (see Shepherd, *Text in the Middle*, 62–64). Isa 12:2 celebrates the new exodus led by the Messiah (Isa 11:1–10, 15–16; see also Num 24:8).

9. Such assignment of speaking parts likely takes its cue from Ps 118:2–4.

10. Stec, *Targum of Psalms*, 210–11.

11. Luke 19:38 adds "the king": "Blessed is the one who comes, the king, in the name of the Lord." John 12:13 adds "the king of Israel": "Hosanna! Blessed is the one who comes in the name of the Lord, even the king of Israel."

12. That is, the triumphal entry is but a foreshadow of what Ps 118:25–26 and Zech 9:9–10 envision (see Matt 23:39; Luke 13:35).

The Hebrew text of Ps 118:22 speaks of the "stone" (אבן) that the builders rejected becoming the chief cornerstone. The Targum, on the other hand, speaks of "the youth" (טליא) among the sons of Jesse whom the architects forsook being worthy to be appointed king and ruler. This exegesis has its basis in converting אבן ("stone") to בנא or ברא ("the son").[13] Such an understanding has perhaps prompted the citation of Ps 118:22 at the conclusion of the parable of the vineyard and the tenants. According to the parable, the tenants kill "the son" (= בנא or ברא), and this illustrates the rejection of the "stone" (אבן) by the builders (Matt 21:37–39, 42; Mark 12:6–8, 10–11; Luke 20:13–15, 17; see also Acts 4:11). The stone, of course, is a familiar messianic metaphor (Isa 8:14; 28:16; Zech 3:9; 4:7, 10; Dan 2:34–35; 44–45; Rom 9:33; 1 Pet 2:6–8).

Pss 72 and 89

Perhaps the most well-known macrostructural feature of the composition of the Psalter is its division into five "books" (1–41; 42–72; 73–89; 90–106; 107–50). The conclusions to the first four books are formally marked by doxologies (41:13; 72:18–19; 89:52; 106:48), and the fifth book ends with a series of praise psalms (146–50). Lying at the seams of these five books are psalms that have been interpreted messianically since the early history of interpretation. Both Ps 40:6–8 and 41:9 at the end of book one receive a messianic interpretation in the New Testament (see John 13:18; Heb 10:5–10). Likewise, the New Testament interprets Ps 110 near the beginning of book five in a messianic sense (Matt 22:44; 26:64; Mark 12:36; 14:62; Luke 20:42–43; 22:69; Acts 2:34–35; Heb 1:13; 5:6; 7:17, 21).[14] The Targum

---

13. The definite article in Aramaic is a suffixed א.

14. The Targum does not interpret Ps 110 messianically. Where the Hebrew text of verse 1 says, "The prophetic utterance of the LORD to my Lord," the Targum renders, "The LORD said by his Word." Thus, the psalm according to the Targum is not about someone whom David calls Lord (cf. Matt 22:43, 45; Mark 12:37; Luke 20:44). Despite Tg. Jon.'s messianic interpretation of Zech 6:12–13, which envisions the Messiah not only as a king on his throne but also as a priest on his throne, the Targum of Ps 110:4 does not seek to establish that the Messiah is a priest according to the order of Melchizedek (Gen 14:18–20; see also 11QMelch): "You are appointed a leader for the world to come because of the merit that you have been a righteous king." For Heb 7, however, it is critical to demonstrate from Gen 14 and Ps 110 not only how someone from the tribe of Judah who is neither of the tribe of Levi nor of the lineage of Aaron can be a legitimate priest but also how the priestly order of Melchizedek is superior to that of Aaron.

focuses its attention on the psalms that conclude books two and four—Pss 72 and 89—for its messianic interpretation.

According to Levey, "The dominant rabbinic opinion is that this Psalm generally [i.e., Ps 72], and specific verses, are Messianic."[15] The picture of an ideal king who reigns in justice, righteousness, and peace, and to whom the kings of the nations bring tribute, and in whom all nations are blessed, fits well with other messianic prophecies (e.g., Gen 49:10; Num 24:7–9; Isa 9:6–7; 11:1–10; Jer 23:5–6). While some of the language of Ps 72 clearly derives from descriptions of Solomon and his kingdom in the biblical narratives, the overall depiction of the king could only be applied hyperbolically to Solomon or to any other historical king. Thus, the Targum does not take the superscription לשלמה to mean "to/for" or "about/concerning" Solomon, but in the ordinary sense of an indication of authorship: "By the hands of Solomon it was spoken through prophecy" (= "Of Solomon"). That is, Solomon is prophesying about someone else. Of course, this understanding of the superscription runs into a difficulty at the conclusion of the psalm where the text seems to count it among the prayers of David (Ps 72:20). A few Masoretic manuscripts do not have the superscription, and this is likely a clue that it has been added secondarily without proper attention to the note at the end of the psalm. On the other hand, a few Masoretic manuscripts and the Syriac lack the note in Ps 72:20, which may indicate that it has been added secondarily as a concluding notice for the preceding collection without regard for the superscription. A third possibility is that the superscription and the concluding notice are intended to coexist with the understanding that the psalm is a prayer of David "to/for" or "about/concerning" Solomon (see Rashi, Redak), but this is clearly not the interpretation of the Targum.

The Targum's rendering of Ps 72:1 sets the tone for the remainder of the psalm. The Hebrew text of this verse may be translated as follows: "O God, give your judgments to the king, and your righteousness to the king's son." The Targum interprets "the king" to be "King Messiah,"[16] and it interprets "the king's son" to be "the son of King David." This messianic king will bring justice, righteousness, and peace (Ps 72:2–5), and he will come down like rain on the grass (Ps 72:6–7; cf. 2 Sam 23:4; Ezek 34:26; Hos 6:3–4). His rule will extend from sea to sea and from the river to the ends of the earth (Ps 72:8; cf. Mic 5:4; Zech 9:10). The nations will submit to him, and their

---

15. Levey, *Messiah*, 118.

16. Yalqut Shimoni: "this refers to King Messiah."

kings will bring tribute to him (Ps 72:9–16; cf. Pss. Sol. 17:34; Rev 21:24, 26). The conclusion to the prayer is the request that the Messiah's name would endure forever and increase before the sun (Ps 72:17). The Targum interprets this to be a prayer that his name would be remembered forever, "and before the sun existed his name was prepared" (see b. Pesaḥ. 54a; b. Ned. 39b; b. Sanh. 98b). All the nations will be blessed in him (Ps 72:17; see Gen 22:18; 26:4; Jer 4:2; Gal 3:16).

Ps 89 concerns itself with the Davidic covenant (Ps 89:1–4) and features an extended exposition of that covenant (Ps 89:19–27).[17] In particular, the psalm takes up the conditional language of 2 Samuel 7:14b ("If he commits iniquity") and applies it to the sons of David (Ps 89:30–32). If the members of David's dynasty fail, they will suffer the consequences. On the other hand, the terms of the covenant apply unconditionally to the one son of David who will build the temple and reign over an everlasting kingdom (Ps 89:33–37). It is this distinction between the sons of David for whom the covenant relationship is conditional and the son of David for whom the relationship is unconditional that the speaker in Ps 89:38–51 fails to understand. He thinks that the terms of the covenant apply unconditionally to all the sons of David and thus wonders why he is suffering the consequences of failure to meet the covenant's conditions. The psalm as a whole seeks to correct this misunderstanding and to bring clarity to the reader.

The end of Psalm 89 speaks of the enemies who reproach the heels of the LORD's "anointed one" (Ps 89:51). It is not clear from the Hebrew text whether the speaker is referring to himself, as in Ps 89:38, or to another (i.e., the "Messiah").[18] The Targum, however, says that the enemies have scoffed at the delay of the anointed one's footprints (cf. Tg. Jon. Mic 4:8; see also Ezek 12:21–28; Ps 90:4; 2 Pet 3:8–9), which suggests that the anointed one may be a messianic figure who is yet to come. According to Gen. Rab. 42:4, the sign of the foot (i.e., the coming) of the Messiah is the fighting of the world powers with one another (cf. Matt 24). Likewise, Song Rab. 2:13 says that the sign of the Messiah's feet (i.e., his coming) is the cursing and blaspheming of one generation after another (cf. 2 Tim 3:1–9).[19] The possible allusion to Ps 89:51 in 1 Pet 2:21 says that to follow in the footprints of Christ is to follow his example of suffering for doing good.

17. See Shepherd, *Text in the Middle*, 125–28.

18. There may be a connection here to the crushing of the heel of the woman's seed in Gen 3:15.

19. "With the heels of the Messiah, impudence will increase" (b. Sotah 49b).

Pss 21; 45; 61; 80; 132

The strategic placement of messianic psalms at key junctures in the macro-structure of the Psalter's composition (see earlier discussion) has influenced the way psalms at lower levels of the text are interpreted. The sequence found in Pss 20–24 is a good example of this: prayer for the king (Ps 20), thanksgiving from the king (Ps 21), the suffering of the king (Ps 22),[20] the shepherd king (Ps 23; cf. Jer 23:1–6; Ezek 34), and the triumphal entry of the king (Ps 24; cf. Zech 9:9–10; Ps 118:22–26). The "king" in the Hebrew text of Psalm 21 is "King Messiah" in the Targum (Ps 21:1, 7).[21] According to Exod. Rab. 8:1, Ps 21:3 speaks of God placing a crown on the Messiah (see also 4Q381). Furthermore, the life requested by the king in Ps 21:4 is not merely a long life but, according to the Targum, the eternal life of the Messiah (see also b. Sukkah 52a; cf. 2 Sam 7:13, 16; Isa 9:7; Pss 89:4, 36; 110:4; Dan 7:14; 1 Chr 17:12, 14; John 12:34).

Psalm 45 employs the well-known imagery of a royal wedding for its poetic celebration of the messianic king (cf. Rev 19:7–8). According to the Targum's version of the superscription, the entire psalm is spoken through prophecy by the sons of Korah (cf. 1 Chr 25:1).[22] The Targum identifies the king in this psalm (Ps 45:1, 5, 11, 14, 15) as "King Messiah" (Tg. Ps 45:3 [Eng., 45:2]; see also Ps 45:7).[23] In the Targum of Ps 45:15, 17, he is the eternal king (cf. Tg. Ps 21:5 [Eng., 21:4]) whose name will be remembered forever (cf. Ps 72:17). Perhaps the most striking feature of the Hebrew text of this psalm occurs in verse 6a where the king is addressed as God: "Your throne, O God, is forever and ever" (cf. 2 Sam 7:13, 16; Isa 9:6–7; Pss 89:4, 36; 110:4; Dan 7:13–14; 1 Chr 17:12, 14; see also Ps 47:6–8). The Targum

---

20. This psalm is comparable to the suffering servant songs in Isa 50:4–11 and 52:13—53:12. The Targum, which agrees with mainstream Judaism's reluctance to see the Davidic Messiah as a suffering figure, does not interpret Ps 22 messianically. On the other hand, the psalm plays an important role in the New Testament's explanation of Jesus' suffering (Matt 27:46; Mark 15:34; John 19:24). The same may be said of Ps 69 (see John 2:17; 15:25; Rom 15:3), which the Targum does not interpret messianically.

21. Childs' question with reference to Ps 2 is appropriate here as well: "Indeed, at the time of the final redaction, when the institution of kingship had long been destroyed, what earthly king would have come to mind other than God's Messiah" (Childs, *Introduction to the Old Testament*, 516)? See also Yalqut Shimoni; Blaising and Harding, *Psalms 1–50*, 161–65.

22. It is generally acknowledged that the Psalter was received as a prophetic book by early Judaism, including the Qumran community, and the New Testament authors.

23. Cf. 4Q171 4:23–27.

takes this one step further and addresses the king as the LORD (i.e., Yahweh): "Your throne of glory, O LORD (יהוה), endures forever and ever" (cf. Zech 12:10; Ps 84:9, 11). While it is tempting to insist that the Targum could not possibly be saying this, it is clearly the most straightforward reading of the text. The king is the addressee in the preceding context and in the following context, and there is no indication of a change of address in verse 6. The Targum thus rules out the possibility that "God" (אלהים) in the Hebrew text of this verse is merely hyperbole or anything other than a reference to the king as deity. It is also agrees with the citation of Ps 45:6–7 in Heb 1:8–9 where the author appeals to the deity of the Son of God to make his case for the superiority of Christ to the angels.

Ps 61 is a petition psalm that concludes with three verses that the Targum interprets messianically. The Hebrew text of Ps 61:6 is a prayer that God would add days to the life of the king so that his years would continue for generations. The Targum renders this as follows: "Days in addition to the world to come may you add to the days of King Messiah, his years like the generations of this world and the generations of the world to come." The Hebrew text of Ps 61:7 continues with a request that the king would dwell forever before God (cf. Ps 21:4). The second half of the verse features the very odd word מַן, which is usually understood to be a masculine singular *piel* imperative from מנה: "Appoint (מַן) covenant loyalty and faithfulness, may they guard him." This word, which could also be analyzed as an Aramaic interrogative ("who?"), does not appear in two Masoretic manuscripts, nor is it represented in the Greek translations of Aquila and Symmachus.[24] The Targum interprets מן as if it were the preposition מִן ("from"): "May goodness and truth from (מִן) the Lord of the world guard him." The Hebrew text then says, "So will I make music to your name forever to pay my vows daily" (Ps 61:8), which the Targum renders, "Then I will praise your name forever when I pay my vows on the day of Israel's redemption and on the day that King Messiah is anointed to be king" (cf. Ps 45:7).[25]

24. Fishbane (*Biblical Interpretation in Ancient Israel*, 64) notes the proposal of Julius Fürst that מן is an acronym for מָלֵא נוּן ("full nun"), which is a comment on the orthography of the following word יִנְצְרֻהוּ ("let them guard him"), a word that would ordinarily have the letter nun assimilated to the following letter by means of a daghesh forte: יִצְּרֻהוּ.

25. The nearby Ps 68 is not messianic in the Targum, but the tradition underlying the Targum's rendering of Ps 68:18 is sometimes thought to bear a relationship to Paul's messianic citation in Eph 4:8 ("he gave gifts to the people"; see Stec, *Targum of Psalms*, 131n27). Where the Hebrew text says, "you took (לקחת) gifts among mankind," the Targum translates, "you gave (יהבתא) them as gifts to the people." This rendering is based on an exegetical technique known as הפך ("metathesis" or "transposition") whereby the

Ps 80 is another petition psalm, a prayer that God would restore the people and make his face shine upon them so that they might be delivered (Ps 80:3, 7, 19; cf. Num 6:25). The psalm recounts the story of Israel under the metaphor of a grapevine (Ps 80:8–13; cf. Isa 5:1–7; 27:2–6; Ezek 15:1–8; 19:10–14; Hos 10:1; Matt 21:33–46; John 15:1–17). Its request is that God would look again from heaven and care for this grapevine (Ps 80:14). Ps 80:15 then adds: "and the stock that your right hand has planted and the branch (בן) that you have strengthened for yourself." The term בן ("son") is an unusual choice for "branch," yet there is a precedent for this in Gen 49:22. The Targum renders בן here as "King Messiah" (LXX: "son of man"), which might seem odd at first glance, but there are a couple of reasons for this rendering. One is that the Targum may be under the influence of Tg. Jon.'s consistent messianic renderings of צמח ("branch") in the Prophets (Isa 4:2; Jer 23:5; Zech 3:8; 6:12; see also Ezek 17:22–24). Another reason is the Hebrew text's own exegesis of Ps 80:15 in 80:17: "Let your hand be upon the man of your right hand [cf. Ps 110:1], upon the son of man (בן אדם) whom you have strengthened for yourself."[26] Here the phrase בן אדם ("son of man") explains the term בן ("son/branch") not as a metaphor for the nation of Israel but as a metaphor for an individual through whom the redemption of Israel would presumably come. The phrase בן אדם ("son of man") in this context is not a technical phrase for the Messiah. It is simply a parallel for איש ("man") that means "human being" or "man/person." Nevertheless, the man in this verse may be understood as a reference to a messianic figure, as the Targum of verse 15 attests (cf. Num 24:7, 17 [LXX]; 2 Sam 23:1 [4QSamª, LXX]; Isa 19:20 [LXX]; Zech 6:12; John 19:5; 1 Tim 2:5).[27] This is not unlike the use of the Aramaic phrase בר אנש ("son of man," "human being") in Dan 7:13. The phrase in Dan 7:13 is not a technical term for the Messiah; but because the phrase is understood to have a

---

verb לקחת ("you took") is interpreted to mean חלקת ("you distributed"; see Bacher, *Exegetische Terminologie*, 56). For a fuller discussion of Psalm 68, see Shepherd, *Text in the Middle*, 109–13.

26. The LXX uses the phrase "son of man" in both verses.

27. Note Levey's comment on the Targum of verse 15: "it would appear that the Targum takes the Messiah to be the son of God" (*Messiah*, 119; see 2 Sam 7:14). He adds, "Although it sounds Christological, almost as though it had been injected by a Christian exegete, it is probably Jewish to the core, a link in the unbroken chain of Jewish Messianic tradition" (*Messiah*, 120).

messianic referent, the Gospels allude to it using the technical phrase "the Son of Man" (i.e., that son of man in Dan 7:13).[28]

Psalm 132 is one of the songs of ascents (Pss 120–134). It is the only psalm in books four and five of the Psalter that the Targum interprets messianically. Much like Ps 89, this psalm draws heavily from the account of the covenant with David in 2 Sam 7. The psalm begins with David's desire to make a place for the ark of the covenant (Ps 132:1–10; cf. 2 Sam 7:2). It is not the role of David, however, to build a sanctuary or temple for the LORD. This responsibility will fall to one of his sons (see 2 Sam 7:12–13; Zech 6:12–13). Thus, the psalm turns its attention to the application of the terms of the covenant to the sons of David (Ps 132:11–16). As in Ps 89:30–32, these terms are said to apply conditionally to the sons of David (see 2 Sam 7:14). On the other hand, the conclusion to Ps 132 speaks of an individual son of David for whom the terms of the covenant are unconditional (cf. Ps 89:33–37; see 2 Sam 7:13, 16): "There [in Zion] I will cause a horn to sprout for David, I have arranged a lamp for my anointed one [or, my Messiah]" (Ps 132:17).[29] The Targum renders this as follows: "There I will cause a glorious king to sprout for the house of David, I have arranged a lamp for my anointed one [or, my Messiah]."[30] The term for "anointed one" is the same in verses 10 and 17 of the psalm in both the Hebrew and the Aramaic. The Targum identifies the anointed one in verse 10 as Solomon, but it makes no such historical identification in verse 17. Warrant for a messianic interpretation of verse 17 comes from the distinctive terminology of the Hebrew text. The verbal root of אצמיח ("I will cause to sprout") is the one from which the messianic title צמח ("Branch") derives (see again Isa 4:2; Jer 23:5; Zech 3:8; 6:12; see also 2 Sam 23:5; Ezek 29:21). The term קרן ("horn") appears in the messianic prophecies of 1 Sam 2:10 and Ezek 29:21 (see also Luke 1:69). The language of maintaining a "lamp" comes from 1 Kgs 11:36 where the LORD says in the immediate context, "And I will afflict the seed of David because of this, only not all the days" (1 Kgs 11:39). This interprets the messianic prophecy of Gen 49:10 to mean, "A

28. See Shepherd, "Daniel 7:13."

29. The singular pronouns in Ps 132:18 refer back to this individual king: "His enemies will I clothe with shame, and upon him his crown will shine [LXX, Syr.: my consecration will blossom]."

30. Levey (*Messiah*, 124) notes the messianic interpretation of Ps 132:17 in Lev. Rab. 31:11: "R. Hanin said: By virtue of the merit of causing a lamp to burn continually (Lev. 24:2) you will be worthy to welcome the lamp of the King Messiah. What is the reason? Because it says, 'There I will make a horn to sprout for David, etc.' (Ps. 132:17)."

scepter will not depart from Judah . . . forever (עד)."[31] That is, despite the division of the kingdom and despite the ultimate demise of the Davidic monarchy, the messianic hope is still alive.

The two books normally grouped with the book of Psalms in Hebrew Bibles—Job and Proverbs—do not have any messianic renderings in their Targums. For the book of Job, there are fragments of early Aramaic translations from the Qumran caves: the literal translation of 4QtgJob and the freer translation of 11QtgJob. These both differ considerably from the later Targum of Job. The Hebrew text of the book of Job is not particularly messianic. Thus, messianic renderings in the Targum of Job are not necessarily to be expected. The Targum of Proverbs is essentially the Syriac Peshitta version of Proverbs. Since the Syriac Peshitta is generally less inclined than the Targums to produce substantial exegetical expansions and explicitly messianic renderings, it is not surprising to find a lack of messianic interpretations in the Targum of Proverbs. Nevertheless, it is to be remembered that the Hebrew text of Prov 8:22–31; 30:4 has apparently had a major influence on Targum Neofiti's messianic rendering of Gen 1:1 (see the previous discussion).

THE MEGILLOTH

The Megilloth ("scrolls") appear in the Leningrad Codex (1008 CE) after the book of Proverbs in the following order: Ruth, Song of Songs, Ecclesiastes, Lamentations, and Esther. On the other hand, the Babylonian Talmud (ca. 600 CE) separates these books among the other books of the Writings: Ruth, Psalms, Job, Proverbs, Ecclesiastes, Song of Songs, Lamentations, Daniel, Esther, Ezra, and Chronicles (b. B. Bat. 14b). Thus, it has been suggested that the order found in the Leningrad Codex is a secondary one based on the later liturgical tradition of reading these scrolls during various festivals on the Jewish calendar: Ruth (Pentecost), Song of Songs (Passover), Ecclesiastes (Tabernacles), Lamentations (Temple Destruction), and Esther (Purim). This conclusion, however, is problematic for at least two reasons. The first is that the arrangement of these books in the Leningrad Codex does not follow the chronological order of the festivals.[32] Such chronological ordering of the books only happens in later Rabbinic Bibles: Song of Songs, Ruth, Lamentations, Ecclesiastes, and Esther. The second

31. See again Steiner, "Four Inner-Biblical Interpretations."
32. See Steinberg and Stone, "Historical Formation," 50–51.

reason is that there appear to be internal, compositional factors that have led to the placement of these books together between the book of Proverbs and the book of Daniel.

For instance, these are the only five books in the Hebrew Bible whose main subject is feminine singular: Ruth, the Shulammite woman (Song 6:13), Qoheleth (a fem. sg. ptc.; Eccl 1:1; 7:27; 12:9, 10), Daughter Zion/Judah/Jerusalem (Lam 1:6, 15; 2:1, 2, 4, 5, 8, 10, 11, 13, 15, 18), and Esther. Furthermore, each of these books features verbal links to the alphabetic acrostic poem about the virtuous woman at the end of Prov (Prov 31:10–31): Ruth 3:11 (Prov 31:10, 31); Song 6:9b (Prov 31:28); Eccl 12:13 (Prov 31:30); Lam 3:22–27 (Prov 31:30); and Esther (Prov 31:10–31). The feminine subjects of the Megilloth provide real life illustrations of the virtuous woman and her fear of the LORD brand of wisdom. There is also a sustained play on the name רות ("Ruth," "female companion") that runs throughout these books and serves to unite them. The male in the Song commonly refers to the female as רעיתי ("my female companion"; Song 1:9, 15; 2:2, 10, 13; 4:1, 7; 5:2; 6:4). The book of Ecclesiastes features the homonym רעות ("striving"; Eccl 1:14, 17; 2:11, 17, 22, 26; 4:4, 6, 16; 6:9; 12:11). As for Daughter Zion/Judah/Jerusalem in the book of Lamentations, all "her male companions" (רעיה) have betrayed her. Finally, Esther proves to be a better רעות ("female companion") than Vashti (Esth 1:19). It remains to be seen, however, whether these associations among the Megilloth have had an effect on their interpretation in the Targums.

Ruth 1:1; 3:15

The reference to the famine in Ruth 1:1 prompts a relatively large expansion in the Targum that enumerates the ten great famines in the Bible from creation to the coming of King Messiah: the first in the days of Adam (Gen 3:17), the second in the days of Lamech (Gen 5:29), the third in the days of Abraham (Gen 12:10), the fourth in the days of Isaac (Gen 26:1), the fifth in the days of Jacob (Gen 43:1), the sixth in the days of Boaz during the period of the judges (Ruth 1:1),[33] the seventh in the days of David (2 Sam 21:1), the eighth in the days of Elijah (1 Kgs 17:1), the ninth in the days of Elisha (2 Kgs 6:25), and the tenth one prophesied in Amos 8:11–12—not a hunger for food or a thirst for water but for hearing the words of the LORD

---

33. The Targum identifies Boaz as Ibzan from Judg 12:8–10 (see also b. B. Bat. 91a).

(see Lam 2:9). The same enumeration of famines occurs in Gen. Rab. 25:3; 40:3; 64:2; Ruth Rab. 1:4.

The six measures of barley that Boaz gives Ruth in Ruth 3:15 become in the Targum an occasion to speak of the six most righteous men of the world destined to descend from Ruth: David, Daniel and his companions (Hananiah, Mishael, and Azariah), and King Messiah. This list also occurs in b. Sanh. 93b, but the Messiah appears after David, and the names of Daniel's companions are given. A similar list appears in Ruth Rab. 7:2, but the three friends of Daniel are counted as one (before Daniel) so that two more names—Hezekiah and Josiah—may be added to the list after David. Both Ruth Rab. 7:2 and b. Sanh. 93b indicate that each of the six men would be blessed with six blessings. For the Messiah, the blessings are the ones mentioned in Isa 11:2.

The Targum's exegesis of Ruth 3:15 has its basis primarily in the genealogy at the end of the book in Ruth 4:18–22 (cf. 1 Chr 2:5–15; Matt 1:3–6; Luke 3:32). This abbreviated genealogy traces the line of Judah from Perez to David (Tg.: David, the king of Israel; cf. Syr.). It features among others the name of Ruth's husband Boaz and thus shows Ruth to be the ancestor of David and all those of David's lineage, including the messianic son of David. According to Dan 1:3, 6, Daniel and his three friends are not only Judeans but also of royal descent (see also Tg. Neof. Gen 38:25; Num. Rab. 13:4). The prominent placement of the genealogy at the book's conclusion strongly suggests that demonstration of the link between Ruth and David (and ultimately the Davidic Messiah) may very well now be the main purpose of the book. Ruth, who embodies the wisdom of the woman in Prov 31:10–31, is the ancestor of the one who will be wisdom personified (Prov 8:22–31; see also Tg. Neof. Gen 1:1; Col 1:15–20)—not only Solomon but also one who is greater than Solomon (Matt 12:42; Luke 11:31).

Song of Songs

For most of the history of interpretation, the Song of Songs has been read allegorically in both Jewish and Christian tradition. This is presumably because of the book's graphic content and because of the difficulties that the book presents for interpreters who are seeking to fit it within the larger biblical canon. Jewish interpreters have traditionally read the book as the story of the LORD's relationship with Israel, and this is the interpretation that emerges in the Targum. On the other hand, Christian tradition has interpreted the book to be the story of Christ's relationship with the Church.[34] Popular interpretation in the modern era has turned to the model of a drama, which has a historical precedent in the presentation of Song of Songs in Codex Sinaiticus (fourth century CE) wherein speaking parts are assigned via the headings supplied in red ink. According to this approach, the book is an unfolding love story between a man and a woman.[35] The difficulty, however, is that the genre of drama is not attested in the ancient Near East. The growing consensus among modern scholars is that the book is a collection of love poetry, although these scholars do not agree on what the precise delineation of the individual poems should be. The repetitions found within the book serve to unite its diverse content and create the illusion of a single story ([1] Song 2:7; 3:5; 8:4; [2] Song 2:16; 6:3; 7:10; [3] Song 4:1–7; 6:4–9; 7:1–9).

The expansions in Tg. Song 1:8 and 1:17 both feature messianic references. In the Hebrew text of Song 1:8, the woman is urged, "If you do not know, O most beautiful among women, go forth at the heels of the flock and tend your kid goats by the tents of the shepherds." According to the Targum, the congregation of Israel (comparable to a beautiful maiden) should walk in the ways of the righteous (i.e., the heels of the flock) and teach her children (comparable to kid goats) to go to the synagogue and to the house of study, and by the merit thereof they will be supported during the exile until the LORD sends King Messiah who will lead them to their tents (i.e., the temple that David and Solomon, the shepherds of Israel, have built for them). This anticipates that the Messiah will lead the people to the temple in accordance with the prophecies in 2 Sam 7:13 and Zech 6:12–13. In Tg. Song 1:17, Solomon prophesies that the messianic temple will be even more beautiful than Solomon's temple (see Ezek 40–48; Hag 2:6–9, 20–23; Rev 21:22). Its beams will be made of cedars from the garden of Eden. Apart from the references to Solomon (Song 1:1, 5) and the shepherd imagery, there is very little exegetical basis for the Targum's messianic renderings in these two verses. The expansions are primarily motivated by the allegory that has been imposed upon the book.

34. Sailhamer (*Books of the Bible*, 39) has suggested much more recently that Solomon's love for the woman in the book depicts the Messiah's love for wisdom (see Isa 11:2; cf. Prov 1:1–7). This view has its basis in the personification of wisdom as a woman in the book of Proverbs (see Prov 1:20–33; 3:13–20; 8).

35. Interpreters disagree about whether the love relationship is between Solomon and the Shulammite or between an anonymous shepherd boy and the Shulammite (with Solomon as the intruder).

The prominent descriptions of the woman's physical features in Song 4:1–7 (4:4–7 > 4QCant[b]) and 7:1–9 (see also Song 6:4–9 [4:8—6:10 > 4QCant[a]]) are the next two passages where the Targum contains messianic interpretations. These descriptions keep the reader's focus on the woman as an example of the ideal woman from Prov 31:10–31 (see again 31:28; Song 6:9b). In the Hebrew text of Song 4:5 and 7:3, the woman's breasts are compared to two fawns, twins of a gazelle. The version of this in 4:5 adds "that graze (הרועים) among the lilies." Song Rab. 4:5 interprets the two breasts to be Moses and Aaron through whom the Torah came to Israel and provided nourishment.[36] The Targum expands upon this interpretation for its messianic rendering. According to Tg. Song 4:5, the two breasts represent two redeemers, Messiah the son of David and Messiah the son of Ephraim. These two redeemers are said to be like Moses and Aaron (the two fawns, twins of a gazelle) who shepherded (רעו) the people in the wilderness for forty years and provided them with food and water (Tg. Song 7:4 [Eng., 7:3] has a shorter version of this). Thus, the participle הרועים ("that graze") from the Hebrew text is interpreted as a reference to the shepherds or leaders of the people.[37]

The concept of two Messiahs, the son of David and the son of Ephraim, has been met in previous discussions of Tg. Ps.-J. Exod. 40:11 and the Palestinian Targum of Zech 12:10 in the margin of Codex Reuchlinianus. The son of David is the reigning Messiah, and the son of Ephraim is the suffering Messiah. The comparison of these two to Moses and Aaron is intriguing because it brings the rabbinic concept of two Messiahs (David and Ephraim) into contact with another theory of two Messiahs found in the sectarian documents of the Qumran community: the Messiah of Aaron and the Messiah of Israel (see 4QD[a] 10 I, 12; 1QS 9:11; 1QSa 2:11–22). This allows for a priestly Messiah alongside a royal one (cf. Zech 6:12–13; Ps 110:1, 4). Tg. Song 4:5 seems to suggest a comparison between the reigning Messiah the son of David (= the Messiah of Israel?) and Moses, perhaps alluding to a messianic interpretation of the prophet like Moses (see Deut 18:15, 18; 34:10; see also Frg. Tg. [Vat.] Exod 12:42; John 6:14; Acts 3:22;

---

36. There is a Christian version of this that says the two breasts are the Old and New Testaments.

37. While the Targum cannot be accepted as a legitimate interpretation of the Song, its exegesis of texts outside the Song is impressive. This exegesis supplies the Targum with material for its allegorical interpretation of the book. Thus, Targum Song of Songs is indirectly a better guide to interpretation of the book of Exodus than it is to interpretation of the Song of Songs (see Boyarin, *Intertextuality and the Reading of Midrash*, 105–16).

7:37). It also suggests a comparison between the suffering Messiah the son of Ephraim and Aaron. If the suffering Messiah is the same as the priestly Messiah, then the sacrificial and substitutionary nature of the Messiah's suffering may be in view (see again Isa 52:13—53:12).

A final series of messianic references appears in the Targum of Song 7:11—8:4. The woman's invitation in the Hebrew text of 7:12a to go early to the vineyards to see if the grapevine has budded and to see if the pomegranates are in bloom is interpreted in the Targum to be an invitation to go to the synagogue and to the house of study to search the books of the Torah to see if the time has come for the redemption of Israel from exile (cf. Acts 1:6–7). Such a comparison of Israel to a grapevine is known from elsewhere (see Ezek 15:2; 19:10; Hos 10:1; Ps 80:8, 14). According to the Targum, the invitation is to inquire of the wise men to see if the merit of the righteous (who are compared to the pomegranate) has been revealed by the Lord and to see if the end has arrived to go up to Jerusalem (see Isa 2:1–5; Mic 4:1–5). This implies that the coming of the end is somehow contingent upon the merit of the righteous (cf. Tg. Mic 4:8). Just as the woman pledges to give her love in the vineyards (Song 7:12b), so Israel will give praise to God and offer burnt offerings and sacrifices in Jerusalem (Tg.). According to the Targum of Song 7:13, when the Lord wills to redeem his people from exile, he will say to King Messiah, "Already the time of the end of the exile has been fulfilled, and the merit of the righteous is to me like the fragrance of spices,[38] and the wise men of the generation are gathered at the gates of the academy busy with the words of the scribes and with the words of the Torah. Now, arise, receive the kingdom that I have hidden for you" (cf. Tg. Mic 4:8; Tg. Zech 4:7; 6:12).[39]

In Song 8:1, the woman wishes that her lover were her brother who nursed at her mother's breasts, for then if she found him outside she could kiss him without anyone despising her. The Targum converts this into words that Israel will say to King Messiah: "Come, be to us like a brother, and let

38. The Hebrew text of Song 7:13 says that the mandrakes give fragrance.

39. The picture of wise men busy with the words of the Torah in expectation of the coming Messiah is comparable to the juxtaposition of Ps 1 (Torah psalm) and Ps 2 (messianic psalm) at the beginning of the Psalter. Blessed is the person who murmurs in the Torah day and night (Ps 1:2) in expectation of the coming Messiah revealed therein (Ps 2). Just as Joshua the wise man (Num 27:18; Deut 34:9) waits for the coming prophet like Moses (Deut 18:15, 18; 34:10) by murmuring in the Torah day and night (Josh 1:8), so the blessed person (Ps 1:1–2) waits for the coming prophet like Elijah (Mal 3:1; 4:5) by murmuring in the Torah day and night (see Sailhamer, *Introduction to Old Testament Theology*, 239–49).

us go up to Jerusalem and suck with you the tastes/understandings of the Torah as a suckling child sucks the breasts of its mother; for, all the time that I wandered outside the land, when I remembered the name of the great God and sacrificed myself for your deity,[40] even the peoples of the earth did not despise me." The woman goes on to say in Song 8:2a that she would lead her lover and bring him into the house of her mother who taught her. The Targum transforms this to say that Israel will lead King Messiah and bring him into her temple so that he might teach her to fear the Lord and to walk in his way.[41] In Song 8:2b, the woman adds that she would give her lover spiced wine to drink, from the sweet wine of her pomegranates. According to the Targum, however, Israel will partake of the feast of Leviathan (see Isa 27:1) in the temple and drink the aged wine that has been preserved from the time when the world was created, and she will partake of pomegranates and fruits that were prepared for the righteous in the garden of Eden (see b. Sanh. 99a; cf. Gen 49:12; Amos 9:13–15; John 2:1–12).

The man's left hand under the woman's head and his right hand embracing her in Song 8:3 become in the Targum an occasion to speak of the tefillin or phylacteries on the left hand and on the head of the chosen people of Israel and the fastening of a mezuzah on the upper third of the right side of the doorpost to prevent demonic powers (see Deut 6:4–9; 11:13–21; see also Exod 13:1–16). The adjuration in Song 8:4 is the last in a series of three within the book (Song 2:7; 3:5; 8:4): "I adjure you, O daughters of Jerusalem, how can you arouse or awaken love before it desires?" The Targum takes this as the words of King Messiah to the people of Israel: "Why do you incite yourselves against the peoples of the earth by going up from Jerusalem, and why are you rebelling against the armies of Gog and Magog? Wait a short time until the peoples who have gone up to wage war against Jerusalem are destroyed, and afterward the Lord of the world will remember for your sake the love of the righteous, and it will be his will to redeem you." The reference to the armies of Gog and Magog is a point of contact with other messianic prophecies in the Targums already noted. The idea of waiting a little while for the Lord to remember his people in a beneficial way after the war is common in biblical prophecy (see, e.g., Isa

---

40. Some witnesses have "his deity." The reading "your deity" would refer to the deity of the Messiah (cf. Tg. Ps 45:7 [Eng., 45:6]).

41. The Targum thus interprets the verb תלמדני not as third feminine singular ("she taught me") but as second masculine singular ("you teach me").

10:25; 25:9; 26:20; 29:17; 40:31; Hab 2:3; Hag 2:6; John 16:16–24; see also Gen 8:1).

Eccl 1:11; 7:24

The book of Ecclesiastes is a presentation of the words of Qoheleth (Eccl 1:1; 12:9–14),[42] but his words do not begin until 1:12. The cited motto of Qoheleth in 1:2 (cf. Eccl 12:8) is immediately followed by an anonymous poem about how there is nothing new under the sun (Eccl 1:3–11). It is the conclusion of this poem that the Targum interprets messianically: "There is no remembrance of the former things; furthermore, of the latter things that will come, there will be no remembrance of them with those who come later" (Eccl 1:11). The Targum understands those who come "later" (לאחרנה) to be those who come "in the days of King Messiah" (i.e., "in the end of days" [באחרית הימים]; see Gen 49:1, 8–12; Num 24:7–9, 14, 17; Deut 31:29; 33:5, 7, 20; Isa 2:2–5; Jer 30:9, 21, 24; Ezek 38:14–17; Hos 3:5; Mic 4:1–5; Dan 2:28; 10:14; see also Eccl. Rab. 1:11). Levey suggests that this interpretation is based upon Jer 23:7–8,[43] which says that the new exodus (understood messianically [Jer 23:5–6]) will eclipse the old one in such a way that it will become the new gold standard of deliverance and replace the old one in the oath formula. To this may be added the text of Isa 43:18–19a: "Do not remember former things [like the original exodus (Isa 43:16–17)], and do not think about past things. Look, I am about to do something new [i.e., a new exodus (Isa 43:19b–21)]."

The Hebrew text of Eccl 7:24 says, "That which has happened is far away and very deep. Who can discover it?" According to the Targum, all that has happened is too remote for people to know. No one can find out by his wisdom either the day of death or the day of the coming of King Messiah (cf. Tg. Ps.-J. and Frg. Tg. [Paris] Gen 49:1; Tg. Mic 4:8; Tg. Song 7:13; see also b. Pesaḥ. 54b). As noted earlier, the question of the timing of the Messiah's coming is one that also arises in the New Testament documents (see Matt 24:3, 36; Mark 13:4, 32; Luke 21:7; Acts 1:6; 1 Pet 1:10–11). The answer is that there will be no indication of the precise "times or seasons" (Acts 1:7) or chronology of events. The Day of the Lord will come like a thief in the night (1 Thess 5:2; 2 Pet 3:10; Rev 3:3; 16:15). Readers are urged to look for the abomination of desolation (Matt 24:15; Mark 13:14) and the

---

42. See Longman, *Book of Ecclesiastes*, 2–9.

43. Levey, *Messiah*, 137.

sign of the coming of the Son of Man (Matt 24:30; 13:26; Luke 21:27; Rev 1:7) from the book of Daniel (Dan 7:13; 9:27).

Lam 2:22; 4:22

The Hebrew text of Lamentations consists of four alphabetic acrostic poems (Lam 1–4) and a final twenty-two-line poem (Lam 5). These poems reflect upon the destruction of Jerusalem and its temple at the hands of the Babylonians. The message of the book is that this destruction is the righteous judgment of God for the sin of the people (Lam 1:6, 8, 12, 18; 2:1, 17). Their only hope for the future is trust in the very God who has brought this judgment upon them (Lam 3:22–27; 5:1, 19–22). Both the LXX and the Targum attribute the book to the prophet Jeremiah (LXX, Tg. Lam 1:1), and it is this connection to the prophetic literature that invites the messianic renderings found in the Targum.

The comparison to a day of "an appointed time" (מועד) in Lam 2:22 has prompted the Targumist to think of the Passover festival, which is one of the appointed times listed in Lev 23: "May you proclaim liberty to your people the house of Israel by the hand of King Messiah as you did by the hand of Moses and Aaron in the day of the Passover" (Tg. Lam 2:22a; cf. Tg. Lam 2:7b).[44] The proclamation of liberty as a messianic task is reminiscent of Isa 61:1. The comparison of the Messiah to Moses and Aaron recalls the Targum of Song 4:5 and 7:4, although there the comparison is between the two Messiahs—the son of David and the son of Ephraim—and Moses and Aaron. More specifically, the comparison to Moses' leadership in the day of the Passover is similar to the Frg. Tg.'s (Vatican) rendering of Exod 12:42 (see earlier discussion).[45] The Messiah will be a new Moses who leads a new exodus (see Jer 23:5–8; see also Num 24:7–9).[46] According to Tg. Lam. 4:22, the prophet Elijah will play the role of high priest for the Messiah as Aaron once did for Moses (cf. Tg. Ps.-J. Exod 40:9–11; Tg. Ps.-J. Deut 30:4; see

---

44. The Hebrew text speaks of the summoning of "my terrors on every side" (מגורי מסביב), which is a well-known expression from the book of Jeremiah (Jer 6:25; 20:3, 10; 46:5; 49:29; see also Ps 31:13).

45. As for the priestly Messiah, see the previous discussion of Zech 6:12–13 (and Ps 110:1, 4).

46. Comparison to Moses is a prominent feature of the book of Jeremiah (see, e.g., Jer 1:4–10; cf. Exod 4:10–13; Deut 18:15, 18; 34:10).

also Mal 3:1; 4:5).[47] The Hebrew text of Lam 4:22 says that the punishment for Daughter Zion's iniquity is complete (cf. Isa 40:2). The time of her exile has come to an end. Thus, the Targum anticipates a messianic deliverance (cf. Num. Rab. 13:7). On the other hand, God will punish the iniquity of Daughter Edom and expose her sins. Edom is considered complicit in the Babylonian invasion (see Obad 10–11), and by virtue of the similarity of the name "Edom" to "Adam" (mankind) the nation is sometimes representative of all Gentiles either good (Amos 9:12) or bad (Isa 34). The Targum contemporizes the reference to Edom so that it becomes a reference to Rome, which will suffer defeat at the hands of the Persians (cf. Num 24:24; Dan 11:30).[48]

Esth 1:1

There are two Targums for the book of Esther: Targum Rishon and Targum Sheni. Only Targum Sheni has a messianic reference, and it appears in the Targum's rendering of the very first verse of the book. The Targum identifies Ahasuerus (Xerxes) as one of ten kings who were destined to rule: the first kingdom is that of the Lord of hosts, the second is that of Nimrod, the third is that of Pharaoh, the fourth is that of Israel, the fifth is that of Nebuchadnezzar, the sixth is that of Ahasuerus (Xerxes), the seventh is that of Greece, the eighth is that of Rome, the ninth is that of the Messiah, and the tenth is that of the Lord of hosts again.

The book of Esther depends heavily upon the reader's knowledge of other biblical books for comprehension of its intricacies. For instance, the depiction of the relationship between Mordecai the descendant of Kish (Esth 2:5) and Haman the Agagite (Esth 3:1) appears to draw upon the conflict between Saul the son of Kish and King Agag in the story of 1 Sam 15. The fatal flaw in the story of 1 Sam 15 is the taking of the prohibited plunder (1 Sam 15:3, 9, 14–15, 18–23). The story of Esther seems to be designed deliberately to redeem this failure. When the people overcome their enemies, the text notes several times their refusal to take any of the plunder (Esth 9:10, 15, 16). The book of Esther also has important ties to the books of Genesis (particularly the Joseph stories) and Daniel. Both Mordecai and Daniel are presented as new Joseph figures—Judeans who obtain by the

---

47. This is not a feature of Sperber's edition of the Targum.

48. Sperber's edition does not have the reference to the Persians.

providence of God prominent positions in the court of a foreign ruler. In the book of Daniel, the providence of God extends beyond the personal situation of Daniel to the orchestration of world history, including the unfolding sequence of kings and kingdoms (Babylon, Media/Persia, Greece) culminating in the messianic kingdom and the kingdom of God (Dan 2:21; 4:17; 7:13–14, 27). It is perhaps the juxtaposition of Esther and Daniel in the Hebrew Bible (according to the Leningrad Codex) that has influenced the rendering of Esth 1:1 in Targum Sheni.[49]

CHRONICLES

There are no Targums for the books of Daniel and Ezra-Nehemiah. This is presumably due at least in part to the presence of substantial portions of Aramaic in these books (Dan 2:4b—7:28; Ezra 4:8—6:18; 7:12–26). The final book of the Hebrew Bible according to the Babylonian Talmud is the book of Chronicles (b. B. Bat. 14b; see also Matt 23:35). This book lends itself to messianic interpretation in several ways. For example, the book itself, which is largely an exegesis of Samuel-Kings, provides a messianic interpretation of the covenant with David (see 2 Sam 7:12–16; 1 Chr 17:11–14). Furthermore, the book's idealistic version of the reigns of David and Solomon minus the failures of the two kings aligns with prophetic depictions of the messianic kingdom based on highlights from the formerly unified kingdom under David and Solomon (see, e.g., 1 Kgs 4:25; Mic 4:4; Zech 3:10).

The last name of David's genealogy in 1 Chr 3 is "Anani" (1) (עֲנָנִי Chr 3:24). The Targum interprets this to be a name for "King Messiah" who is about to be revealed (cf. Tg. Zech 4:7; 6:12). This interpretation is based on the presence of the word עֲנָנֵי ("clouds of") in Dan 7:13a: "And look, with the clouds of (עֲנָנֵי) the sky one like a son of man was coming." Of course, this assumes a messianic interpretation of Dan 7:13. According to b. Sanh. 98a, if the people are worthy, the Messiah will come "with the clouds of (עֲנָנֵי) the sky" (Dan 7:13a); but if they are not worthy, he will come "afflicted (עָנִי) and riding on a donkey" (Zech 9:9b).[50]

---

49. It is worth noting that the book of Daniel (6:1) is the only other biblical book that mentions the 120 or 127 provinces of Esther 1:1. The Syriac version of Esth 1:1 has 120, while the MT and LXX have 127 (also Esth 8:9; 9:30). MT Dan 6:2 (Eng., 6:1) has 120, but the Old Greek has 127.

50. The book of Chronicles concludes with a version of the decree of Cyrus (Ezra

FINAL THOUGHTS ON THE MESSIAH OF THE TARGUMS OF THE WRITINGS

As with the Targums of the Pentateuch and the Prophets, the Targum of Psalms tends to follow the contours of the book's macrostructure for its messianic renderings. Thus, the messianism of Targum Psalms is both selective and strategic. The gateway to the Psalter, which pairs a Torah psalm (Ps 1) with a messianic psalm (Ps 2), provides the perfect opportunity for the Targum to highlight the central theme of the book, but it is not until the second pairing of a messianic psalm with a Torah psalm (Pss 18–19) that the Targum provides an explicitly messianic interpretation. The Targum's interpretation of the final pairing (Pss 118–19) represents an exegetical tradition that has influenced the messianic interpretation of Ps 118 in the New Testament. Targum Psalms also follows closely the division of the Psalter into five books. The psalms at the conclusions of books two and three (Pss 72 and 89) receive explicitly messianic renderings.

The books of the Megilloth would seem to be the least likely to receive any attention from the Targums for messianic interpretation, yet each of these five books has at least one messianic rendering in its respective Targum. Why is this the case? There is some influence from the composition of the Megilloth, in particular the genealogy concluding with David in Ruth 4:18–22, but this does not explain everything.[51] On the one hand, the messianic renderings of the Targums of the Megilloth are different from those of the Pentateuch, the Prophets, and the Psalms in that they are more allegorical than exegetical in nature. Incidentally, this helps to bring the exegetical nature of the Targums of the Pentateuch, the Prophets, and the Psalms into relief. On the other hand, the material for the messianic interpretations of the Targums of the Megilloth comes from exegesis of books

1:1–4), which is abbreviated precisely at the point where the exhortation to go up and build the temple may be taken as a summons for the Messiah to go up and build the temple in fulfillment of the covenant with David (2 Chr 36:22–23; see 1 Chr 17:12). Thus, the decree of Cyrus is not the fulfillment of Jeremiah's prophecy of seventy years (Jer 25:11) but the beginning of the countdown to its fulfillment. This is the same eschatological and messianic interpretation of Jeremiah's prophecy found in Dan 9:2, 24–27 (see Sailhamer, "Biblical Theology," 25–37).

51. It is possible that a renewed interest in messianism in the early medieval period was the impetus for these renderings. On the other hand, such a historical phenomenon might be expected to produce many more messianic renderings than the ones that appear in the Targums of the Megilloth. It seems more prudent to look for an exegetical impetus.

outside the Megilloth. Thus, the Targums of the Megilloth can be indirect guides to other texts as well as guides to potential intertextual relationships.

4

The Reception of the Messiah of the Targums

THE RECEPTION OF THE Targums during the medieval period was largely limited to Jewish scholars who could read both the Hebrew of the Bible and the Aramaic of the Targums. Two of the most important rabbinic commentators during this period were Rashi (Rabbi Solomon ben Isaac, 1040–1105 CE) and Redak (Rabbi David Kimchi, 1160–1235 CE). The biblical commentaries of these two men reveal their understanding of the Targums as guides to the meaning of the Hebrew text for those who are able to read the Hebrew text.[1] Rashi and Redak, however, represent two very different conceptions of the eschatology and messianism of the Hebrew Bible. Furthermore, their views have had a lasting effect upon Christian reception of the Hebrew Bible primarily through their influence upon the early Christian Hebraists. The present chapter is devoted to a selection of the most prominent messianic renderings in the Targums. The corresponding commentaries of Rashi and Redak for these passages will serve to highlight the contrast between the two. The latter part of the chapter will demonstrate

1. See Barr, "Which Language Did Jesus Speak?," 9–29; Rabin, "Hebrew and Aramaic," 1030–32; Tal, "Is There a Raison d'Être?," 357–78. Rashi states in his commentary to b. Meg. 21b that the Targum is for women and commoners who do not know Hebrew, yet as a Hebrew scholar he scrupulously follows the Targum in his biblical commentary. "There is clear evidence that the Rabbis viewed the targum as more than translation in any narrow sense: its purpose was to exegete and to interpret Scripture" (Alexander, "Jewish Aramaic Translations," 239).

how Rashi in particular has shaped the Christian formulation of the literal sense of the Hebrew Bible.

RASHI AND REDAK

The two texts of the Pentateuch that all extant Targums of the Pentateuch render messianically are Gen 49:10 and Num 24:17. Rashi interprets Gen 49:10b messianically and cites Targum Onqelos in support of this.[2] Likewise, Redak refers to the messianic interpretation found in Tg. Onq. and appears to accept this as correct.[3] The influence of the official rabbinic Targum of the Pentateuch is evident here in both commentaries. As for Num 24:17, Rashi accepts the interpretation of Tg. Onq. that the star from Jacob is a king, but he rejects the Targum's identification of this king as the Messiah in its rendering of the "scepter" from Israel in the parallel clause.[4] Rashi prefers to see the scepter from Israel as another reference to an unidentified king whom he subsequently identifies as David in his interpretation of the following clause (see also Ibn Ezra). He understands the striking of the temples of Moab to be a prophecy of what David does in 2 Sam 8:2. This is consistent with the way Rashi interprets Num 24:7b. The first king of Israel (Saul) will be higher than Agag (1 Sam 15; cf. Tgg. Onk., Ps.-J.), and the kingdom of Israel will be exalted because of the powerful kings David and Solomon who will succeed Saul. On the other hand, while Redak did not write a commentary on Numbers, his younger contemporary, Ramban (Rabbi Moses ben Nachman, Nachmanides, 1194–1270 CE), fully agrees with the messianic interpretation of Num 24:17 provided by the Targums. Ramban, however, concedes Rashi's interpretation of Num 24:7. Both implicitly disagree with the messianic interpretation of Num 24:7 found in Tg. Neof. and the Frg. Tg., which say that the future king will be stronger than Saul, and that the kingdom of King Messiah will be exalted.

2. The commentaries of Rashi and Redak may be accessed at https://www.sefaria.org/texts.

3. Redak's interpretation of Gen 3:15 is also worth noting here. Neither Tg. Onq. nor Rashi interpret Gen 3:15 messianically, but messianic interpretations are found in most of the Palestinian Targum witnesses. Redak says that the enmity between the serpent and humanity will not be an unchangeable condition, for it will be resolved in the messianic era according to Isa 11:8.

4. Rashi's departure from the Targum here may be a counteractive response to Christian reception of Num 24:17 (Matt 2:2; 2 Pet 1:19; Rev 22:16).

Turning to the Former Prophets, the poems at the beginning (1 Sam 2:1–10) and the end (2 Sam 23:1–7) of the books of Samuel are the most productive for messianic renderings in Tg. Jon. Rashi offers no comment on Hannah's reference to the LORD's king in the conclusion to her prayer (1 Sam 2:10). Redak, however, says that the king is the Messiah. He also says that Hannah speaks of this king by way of prophecy. Redak does not cite Tg. Jon.'s messianic interpretation of this verse, but he does implicitly agree with it. He goes on to say that Hannah's words imply that her son Samuel will anoint the first king. Rashi does not interpret the last words of David (2 Sam 23:1–7) messianically, but Redak cites Tg. Jon.'s messianic interpretation of 2 Sam 23:3 favorably.

Due to Redak's limited commentary on the Pentateuch (Genesis) and the sparsity of messianic renderings in Tg. Jon.'s version of the Former Prophets, it is difficult to establish a sufficient sample size within these two corpora to compare and contrast the reception of the messianic interpretations of the Targums in the commentaries of Rashi and Redak. Nevertheless, it is already evident that a pattern is emerging. Rashi is willing to accept the messianism of the Targums to a certain degree (Tg. Onq. Gen 49:10b), but he is also willing to go against it (Tg. Onq. Num 24:17) or ignore it (Tg. Jon. 1 Sam 2:10; 2 Sam 23:3). He is more prone to interpret potentially messianic prophecies as prophecies of events that transpired in history, such as the reign of David. Redak, on the other hand, consistently follows the Targums and shows a greater willingness to embrace their eschatology and messianism without question.

The Latter Prophets provide the best opportunity to see what separates Rashi and Redak. Both men wrote full commentaries on these books, and Tg. Jon.'s version of the Latter Prophets features an abundance of messianic renderings. It may be recalled here that Tg. Jon. interprets messianically all the passages in the Latter Prophets with the title צמח ("Branch") (Isa 4:2; Jer 23:5; Zech 3:8; 6:12). Rashi does not interpret the first of these (Isa 4:2) in a messianic fashion, although he does concede a messianic sense for the related text in Isa 11:1. According to Rashi, the "branch" in Isa 4:2 signifies the righteous and the sages upon whom the beauty of the people will depend. No longer will their beauty depend upon the finery of the women (Isa 3:16—4:1). Redak, however, comments that the "branch" in Isa 4:2 is the Messiah, and he notes the connection with Jer 23:5. He also interprets the related passage in Isa 11:1–10 messianically. Rashi has nothing to say about the occurrence of "branch" in Jer 23:5, while Redak is very clear that he understands it to be a messianic title. Both Rashi and Redak interpret the branch in Zech 3:8 and 6:12 to be Zerubbabel, although Redak adds in his commentary on Zech 3:8 that the Messiah will bring even greater salvation. Neither commentator refers explicitly to the Targum for their interpretations of these texts, but their extensive use of the Targums elsewhere makes it highly unlikely that they were unaware of it. Rashi maintains a consistent non-messianic interpretation of "branch," while Redak allows a messianic sense in Isa 4:2 and Jer 23:5. Given the dependence upon Isa 4:2 and Jer 23:5 in Zech 3:8 and 6:12, Redak's identification of the branch in Zechariah as Zerubbabel is unexpected, for it is clear that Redak does not understand Zerubbabel to be the Messiah.

As noted in the previous discussion of Isa 9:6–7, the issues surrounding the Hebrew text and the early versions (particularly the LXX and the Tg.) are complex. Nevertheless, it is clear that Tg. Jon. interprets the Hebrew text messianically and thus agrees more with Christian tradition (e.g., Matt 1:22–23) than with Jewish interpretation, which says that the child to be born is Hezekiah. It is too much of a stretch to suggest that the Targum is implicitly identifying Hezekiah as the Messiah.[5] Both Rashi and Redak interpret Isa 9:6–7 to be about Hezekiah, but they do not suggest that Hezekiah is the Messiah.[6] Their interpretation of the passage is non-messianic, although Redak does say that Isa 9:7 ultimately looks beyond the reign of Hezekiah to the reestablishment of the Davidic kingdom in the messianic era. Rashi's commentary is an explicit refutation of the Christian interpretation of the passage.[7] As mentioned earlier, he considers the "names" of Isa 9:6 to be the names of God who called Hezekiah "prince of peace." This is based on his understanding of the verb ויקרא as "and he called" rather than "and he will be called." Thus, Rashi's departure from the Targum here is rooted in his independent exegesis of the Hebrew text, but it is also motivated at least in part by anti-Christian polemics. Rashi appears willing to give up messianic interpretation of texts that speak of his own future hope

---

5. Contra Levey, *Messiah*, 45–46.

6. Rashi also interprets the one who will go forth from a serpent's root in Isa 14:29 to be Hezekiah. He does not follow Tg. Jon.'s messianic interpretation of this verse, yet it is clear from his comment on the latter part of the verse that he knows the Targum. Redak, however, parts ways with Rashi here and cites the Targum's messianic interpretation, which is based on Isa 11:1, 10.

7. He refers to Christians here as the "others" (אחרים). Elsewhere he refers to them as the "sectarians" (מינים).

if those same texts are well-known Christian proof texts. He would rather historicize the prophecy than concede ground to his opponents.[8]

Rashi and Redak could not be more different in their interpretations of the servant of the LORD in Isa 42:1. Rashi says that the servant is Jacob/Israel, which agrees with the LXX and mainstream Jewish interpretation. Redak says that the servant is the Messiah, which agrees with witnesses to Tg. Jon. and early Christian interpretation, although Redak is certainly not making an effort to align himself with Christian exegesis. When it comes to Isa 52:13—53:12, however, Rashi and Redak agree with the dominant Jewish tradition that the servant is Jacob/Israel (see also Ibn Ezra). Why does Redak agree with the Targum's identification of the servant as the Messiah in Isa 42:1 but not in 52:13? One possibility is that he could not tolerate the idea of a suffering Messiah and was unwilling to follow the Targum's method of maneuvering around this problem. Another possibility is that he was aware of Christian appropriation of Isa 52:13—53:12 and did not want to encourage this.

Rashi has no comments on the new David in Jer 30:9 and Hos 3:5 (MT: "David their king"; Tg. Jon.: "the Messiah, the son of David, their king"). Redak allows for the Targum's messianic interpretation of Jer 30:9 (see also Jer 30:21), but he does not make his view of the new David in Hos 3:5 explicit. Rashi says that the new David in the related passage of Ezek 34:23–24 is simply a "king" (cf. Tg. Jon.), but he has no comment on the new David in Ezek 37:24–25. Redak, however, says that the new David in

8. A similar tendency to historicize has already been encountered in the proto-MT. The change from "Gog" (SP, LXX) to "Agag" (MT) in Num 24:7 alters the prophecy from an eschatological and messianic one (Ezek 38–39) to a historical one (1 Sam 15). Likewise, the change from the man whom "God raises up (הקים אל)" p(4QSam^a; cf. LXX) to the man who "was raised on high (הקם על)" (MT) in 2 Sam 23:1 alters the prophecy from one about the messianic son of David to one about David himself. Of course, it could be argued that the MT has priority in these instances, which would mean that the other witnesses have changed the originally historical prophecies into eschatological and messianic prophecies. The problem with this argument is that the other witnesses are varied and do not show consistent evidence elsewhere of a tendency to de-historicize prophecies. On the other hand, the MT is well known for its efforts to provide historical referents for otherwise open-ended or potentially eschatological texts. The most outstanding example of this is MT Jeremiah. It is generally accepted that the LXX Vorlage of Jeremiah is the more original edition of the book (see Tov, *Textual Criticism*, 286–94). This first edition leaves Jeremiah's prophecies about the enemy from the north and the seventy years (Jer 25:9, 11) open to an eschatological interpretation (Ezek 38:14–17; Dan 9:2, 24–27). The second edition represented by the MT historicizes the prophecies so that the enemy from the north is Nebuchadnezzar who will take the people into captivity in Babylon for a literal period of seventy years.

Ezek 34:23–24 and 37:24–25 is the Messiah—an interpretation that is more explicit than the Targum. Lest the reader think that Redak's interpretation is always the more messianic of the two, there is at least one example where Rashi has a messianic interpretation and Redak does not. Thus far, for the texts surveyed here, Rashi has messianic interpretations only for Gen 49:10 and Isa 11:1, but in his commentary on Ezek 17:22–24 Rashi quite unexpectedly offers a messianic interpretation that essentially agrees with the Targum, even though the Targum does not employ its usual messianic terminology. Redak, on the other hand, understands Zerubbabel to be the referent of the text (cf. Zech 3:8; 6:12) despite his acknowledgment of the Targum's messianic interpretation.

Rashi and Redak both refer to Tg. Jon.'s messianic interpretation of Mic 4:8 in their commentaries. Rashi says that the term מגדל in the phrase מגדל עדר ("Tower of Flock"), which the Targum renders as "the Messiah of Israel," is an expression of a stronghold. He then indicates his disagreement with the Targum and suggests that the term refers to the temple. Rashi also comments on the phrase עפל בת ציון ("fortified hill of Daughter Zion") and says that עפל is an expression of a mighty tower. Thus, the phrase does not mean "who is hidden from before [or, because of] the sins of the assembly of Zion" as the Targum has it. Rashi suggests that the Targum's rendering is based on taking עפל as if it were אפל ("darkness"). Redak also cites the Targum for Mic 4:8, but he appears to accept its messianic interpretation of the text as authoritative. Rashi does agree implicitly with Tg. Jon.'s messianic interpretation of Mic 5:2–6, but he does not cite the Targum in support of his position. Rather, he references Pss 118:22 and 72:17 for Mic 5:2 in particular. Redak cites the Targum for his comment on Mic 5:4b that it is the name of the Messiah that will be great. The Targum is thus presumably the guiding force for Redak's messianic interpretation of all of Mic 5:2–6, although Redak is even more explicitly messianic than the Targum in his interpretation of Mic 5:6, as noted previously.

Redak cites Tg. Jon.'s messianic interpretation of Hab 3:18 in his commentary. Rashi makes no such reference. As noted above, neither Rashi nor Redak follows Tg. Jon.'s messianic interpretations of Zech 3:8 and 6:12. The same may be said of Zech 4:7 and 10:4. It is not clear why both Rashi and Redak choose not to follow any of the Targum's messianic renderings for Zechariah. It should be noted, however, that both commentators do interpret Zech 9:9–10 messianically. This text ironically does not receive an explicitly messianic interpretation in the Targum, but Rashi says that it is impossible to interpret it as anything other than a reference to the Messiah. Redak says that the king in Zech 9:9 will be delivered from Gog and Magog. He identifies this king with the servant of the LORD in Isa 42:1–4, a text that the Targum and Redak interpret messianically. Rashi and Redak also cite the messianic interpretation of Zech 12:10 found in b. Sukkah 52a. A similar interpretation appears in the Palestinian Targum for Zech 12:10 preserved in the margin of Codex Reuchlinianus.

The book of Psalms is the last book for which we have not only a substantial number of messianic renderings in the Targum but also full commentaries from both Rashi and Redak. Neither Rashi nor Redak follows the Targum's messianic interpretation of Ps 72, although Redak does acknowledge that there are those who interpret the psalm messianically. Both Rashi and Redak prefer to interpret Ps 72 as David's prayer concerning Solomon. Rashi interprets Ps 89:51 messianically, but he cites the Talmud (b. Sotah 49b) rather than the Targum to support his interpretation. Redak also does not cite the Targum for his messianic interpretation of Ps 89:51, but his interpretation nevertheless appears to be based on the Targum's rendering, which focuses not on the increase of impudence or audacity prior to the Messiah's advent (as in b. Sotah 49b) but on those who scoff at the Messiah's supposed delay and say that he will never come.

Rashi acknowledges the rabbinic interpretation (which includes the Targum) of Ps 21:1 as referring to King Messiah but he opts instead to interpret the text as referring to David. He says that he does this in order to refute the "others" (אחרים). This is the same term that Rashi uses for Christian interpreters in his commentary on Isa 9:6–7. There is, however, a key difference between Rashi's commentary on Isa 9:6–7 and his commentary on Ps 21:1. In his commentary on Isa 9:6–7, Rashi makes an exegetical argument to refute the Christian interpretation. In his commentary on Ps 21:1, however, there is no exegetical argument. Refutation of the Christians is Rashi's sole reason for choosing David as the referent of the text. Once again, Rashi seems willing not only to go against the grain of rabbinic tradition but also to accept a diminished messianism in biblical interpretation in certain cases if it helps him to contradict Christian interpretation. What makes the present instance so remarkable is that Ps 21:1 is not nearly as prominent in Christian exegesis as Isa 9:6–7.

Redak's commentary on Ps 21 is more judicious in its approach. Redak focuses his attention on the phrase לדוד in the superscription and explains that there are basically two ways to understand it with this psalm.

The first option is to interpret לדוד to mean "about David" (= על דוד), in which case the psalm is not messianic. The other option is to interpret לדוד to mean "of David" or "by David," in which case the psalm is about the Messiah. Redak acknowledges that this latter option is the one taken by the Targum. He further notes that the Messiah is called "David" in Ezek 37:25. Redak, like Rashi, also shows his awareness of Christian interpretation of Ps 21. He says that "the Nazarenes" (הנצרים) interpret the psalm to be about Jesus, and he adds that a response must be given to them in every verse. Nevertheless, Redak's desire to refute the Christians does not prevent him from entertaining the possibility of a messianic interpretation of the psalm. He simply chooses not to identify Jesus as the Messiah. On the other hand, Rashi seems to think that messianic interpretation here is the same as conceding a specifically Christian interpretation.

Rashi does not interpret Ps 45 or Ps 61:6, 8 messianically. Redak, however, says in his commentary on the superscription of Ps 45 that the psalm is about "King Messiah." He does not cite the Targum, but his interpretation is certainly in accordance with the Targum. Redak explores what Ps 61:6 would mean if it were about David, but then he identifies the king in the verse as King Messiah, which implicitly agrees with the Targum. Neither Rashi nor Redak interprets Ps 80:15 messianically, nor do they show any awareness of the Targum's messianic interpretation. Finally, Rashi does not comment on Ps 132:17,[9] but Redak interprets the verse messianically, although he does not cite the Targum in support of his position.

In summary, this survey displays a general pattern. Rashi tends not to agree with the messianic interpretation of the Targums, while Redak tends to agree. There are certainly exceptions to this pattern, but the pattern is overall a consistent one. The two commentators do not always cite the Targums in their expositions, but they cite them enough to demonstrate that they generally have the Targums in view. Rashi gives some indication that his non-messianic interpretations are to a certain extent motivated by his desire to refute Christians. Redak also wants to refute Christian interpretation (more specifically, the identification of Jesus as the Messiah), but this does not deter him from interpreting texts messianically. It remains to be seen now whether Rashi or Redak has had the greater influence on subsequent Christian exegesis through the work of the Christian Hebraists.

9. Rashi does appeal to a messianic interpretation of this verse in his commentary on Ps 43:3.

THE CHRISTIAN HEBRAISTS

By the time of the second century CE, the Christian church was increasingly less Jewish and more Gentile. This meant that the Hebrew Bible was known primarily in translation (Greek, Latin, Syriac, etc.) to most Christians, even Christian pastors and scholars. With very few exceptions, this situation prevailed until the rise of Christian Hebraism during the Renaissance and Reformation periods. Origen (ca. 185–254 CE) and Jerome (ca. 347–419 CE) were early forerunners of the Christian Hebraists. Origen sought to bring the Greek translation of the Septuagint into greater conformity with the proto-MT Hebrew known at the time. Origen himself did not know much Hebrew, but he was able to approximate the Hebrew through his use of the existing Greek versions of Aquila, Symmachus, and Theodotion who had taken up the earlier tradition of revising the Greek of the Septuagint toward the proto-MT. Origen employed the Aristarchian asterisk (for pluses) and obelos (for minuses) to mark the Septuagint in comparison to the revised Greek versions. He presented his work in the six columns of the Hexapla: (1) Hebrew text, (2) Hebrew transliterated in Greek, (3) Aquila, (4) Symmachus, (5) Septuagint, and (6) Theodotion.[10] Jerome, on the other hand, sought to do for the Latin Bible what Origen had done for the Greek Bible. The main difference between Jerome and Origen was that Jerome actually learned Hebrew from his Jewish teachers. The Old Latin had been translated not from a Hebrew original but from the Septuagint. Thus, Jerome wanted to make a new Latin translation from the Hebrew text, and this translation eventually became known as the Latin Vulgate. It never occurred to Jerome that the Septuagint may have been translated from different, in some cases superior, Hebrew texts than the one he had received (the proto-MT). He assumed that the proto-MT was the only Hebrew text that had ever existed.

Like Jerome, the early Christian Hebraists were heavily influenced by their Jewish teachers, and they received the rabbinic Hebrew text (now the MT) as the one and only Hebrew Bible. They were also influenced by

10. "I take up the contention that the main reason for the undertaking of text-critical operations in the Hexapla was Origen's concern to have a Greek text which corresponded quantitatively with the Hebrew text used by Jews and its Greek versions, and so to arm himself better for Christian-Jewish controversy" (McKane, *Selected Christian Hebraists*, 28). The transliterated text of the second column was likely borrowed from a Jewish source that had been used by non-Hebrew speaking Jews and Christians for the liturgical reading of the Hebrew text (McKane, *Selected Christian Hebraists*, 26–27).

the grammatical and exegetical resources of medieval commentators like Rashi, Ibn Ezra, and Redak. For instance, Nicholas of Lyra (1270–1349 CE) is well known for his dependence upon Rashi's commentary. Likewise, Johannes Reuchlin (1455–1522 CE), who published *On the Fundamentals of Hebrew* in 1506, was greatly indebted to the grammars of Redak (*Mikhlol*) and his father Joseph Kimchi.[11] Given the extent of this influence, it only makes sense to ask what the nature of this influence was, particularly with regard to messianic interpretation of the Hebrew Bible.

Erwin Rosenthal has provided a compelling account of the character and significance of medieval Jewish exegesis.[12] According to Rosenthal, the concept of *Hebraica veritas* ("the true meaning of the authentic word of God") from Jerome to the Reformers was the result of close contact between Christian and Jewish exegetes. Jerome came to this with the help of the haggadic interpretation (*derash*) transmitted by the Talmudic scholars of his time.[13] The Reformers, on the other hand, came to it via the literal interpretation (*peshat*) that they inherited from the medieval Jewish exegetes who had developed their hermeneutical method to guard against Karaite and Christian influence.[14] The very weapon that the Jews fashioned to combat Christian influence ironically became not only something with which medieval Christian exegetes were forced to reckon but also the preferred tool of Christian Hebraists in the sixteenth and seventeenth centuries. Medieval Jewish exegetes saw in the *peshat* or simple sense of the text the "answer" to the spiritual/mystical sense of Christian allegorical interpretation inherited from the church fathers. Christian exegetes who adopted this simple sense found themselves interpreting traditionally christological

11. "Because he adopted the structure of Latin grammar (*Institutiones grammaticae*) of the late antique grammarian Priscian (sixth century C.E.) along with the Latin grammatical categories (case; tense-scheme of past, present, future; etc.), he shaped the later development of Hebrew study for a long time. Not until the twentieth century has there been any serious discussion—and with it various proposals—about a system of categories more adequate to the Hebrew language" (Reventlow, *History of Biblical Interpretation*, 34–35). According to Reventlow, Zwingli and Luther were among the few to recognize the work's significance at the time (Reventlow, *History of Biblical Interpretation*, 35).

12. Rosenthal, "Medieval Jewish Exegesis," 264–81.

13. See Kasher, "Interpretation of Scripture," 547–94.

14. "Medieval Jewish exegesis has thus a share in the consolidation of the Reformation and of Puritanism in this country. It is based on a deeper understanding of the Hebrew language through grammatical and lexicographical studies, more systematic and rational than anything that has gone before" (Rosenthal, "Medieval Jewish Exegesis," 266). This new approach became the foundation for modern scientific study of the Hebrew Bible.

texts in a non-messianic, non-eschatological manner. The literal sense became identified with a purely historical interpretation, and a robust defense of messianic interpretation as the literal sense was often lacking.

Rosenthal traces what he calls the "proper study of Hebrew" back to Saadia Gaon (882–942 CE) who under the influence of the Arab grammarians laid the grammatical and lexicographical foundations for the great medieval commentators. For Saadia, a figurative interpretation was only permissible if the literal sense (*peshat*) was contrary to reason, established tradition, or another biblical passage. His efforts were directed against Karaism and Muslim rationalist theology.[15] The Karaites rejected the oral tradition of rabbinic Judaism and emphasized the Hebrew Bible as the sole authority in matters of faith and practice.[16] In many ways the Karaite rebellion against rabbinic tradition is comparable to the later Protestant rebellion against Catholic tradition.[17] The successors to Saadia's work were scholars such as Menahem ben Saruq, Dunash ben Labrat, and Judah ben David Hayyuj who produced important grammatical and lexicographical works. Rosenthal also mentions in this regard the importance of the Targum to these scholars for adducing word meanings. The work of the latter, Judah ben David Hayyuj, was completed by Jonah ibn Janah whose book entitled *The Book of Roots* became the source for David Kimchi's (i.e., Redak's) dictionary of the same title.

Rosenthal rightly notes that the influence of Redak on the Christian Hebraists came more from his grammatical and lexicographical work than from his commentaries. The most influential of the medieval Jewish commentators for both Jews and Christians was Rashi. Rashi certainly acknowledged and respected the traditional rabbinic interpretation of the biblical text (*derash*), but he showed a marked preference for the simple or literal sense (*peshat*), and it was his emphasis on the literal sense that made the greatest impact. For Rashi, the *peshat* was the best way to respond to christological interpretation of the Hebrew Bible. According to Rosenthal, Rashi was prepared to depart from traditional exposition in order to combat Christian interpretation. He reinterpreted messianic prophecies either as historical prophecies (e.g., to refer to David) or as eschatological prophecies so that the texts could not refer to the Second Temple period and the

15. See Polliack, "Jewish Arabic Translations," 289–309.

16. See Kahle, *Cairo Geniza*, 17–28.

17. See McKane, *Selected Christian Hebraists*, 143–44.

time of Jesus of Nazareth.[18] Since Christians believed in the eschatological return of Christ, the historicization of the prophecies proved to be more effective in the fight against christological interpretation. Thus, Rashi's non-messianic *peshat* was received by Jews and Christians as the literal, "respectable" sense of the text.[19] For Christians, this meant that another avenue such as *sensus plenior* ("fuller sense") had to be found in order to maintain a christological interpretation. For the most part it did not occur to them that the eschatological and messianic interpretations of the Targums and commentators like Redak were actually more compatible with their traditional views of the biblical text.[20]

Second only to Rashi among the medieval commentators was Abraham ibn Ezra (1089–1167 CE). In many ways ibn Ezra was ahead of his time, and he anticipated some of the views that eventually became pillars of historical criticism such as the authorship and date of the Pentateuch and the book of Isaiah. Rosenthal highlights ibn Ezra's own statement of his hermeneutical method,[21] which he contrasted with representatives of four other methods: (1) the heads of the Babylonian academies who included too much superfluous material, (2) the Karaites who neglected tradition, (3) Rashi who incorporated too much midrashic material, and

18. "If a biblical text had been interpreted by Christians with reference to Jesus as the Messiah, Rashi would argue that its true reference was not messianic, but rather 'historical.' In most cases the 'historical' sense amounted to showing that the passage in question had its simple historical reference to David, or one of the davidic kings in Judah. It did not matter to Rashi if longstanding Jewish tradition, as represented in the Targums, for example, referred the passage to the Messiah. Rashi was more willing to suffer a diminished messianic hope among Jews in his day that to concede the simple, plain meaning (*peshat*) of a passage to Christian interpretation. Thus in developing the *peshat* as a historical tool to explain the messianic texts, Rashi also had to be concerned with the fact that it was these very texts that sustained the faith and hope of medieval Jewry" (Sailhamer, *Introduction to Old Testament Theology*, 135).

19. The trajectory of Rashi's influence may be seen in the commentary of his grandson R. Samuel b. Meir (Rashbam) who even interpreted Gen 49:10 in a non-messianic sense, contrary to the Targums and his grandfather. Rashbam said that Shiloh was the name of a town near Shechem to which Rehoboam the son of Solomon would come as king of Judah.

20. It should be emphasized, however, that Redak was by no means sympathetic to Christian interpretation. On the contrary, he was very outspoken against it, but this did not stop him from claiming that the literal sense of many biblical texts was the messianic sense.

21. This method had three components: (1) linguistic explanation of every word, (2) explanation of the whole book, and (3) exposition of the "inner meaning" in accordance with the *derash* (Rosenthal, "Medieval Jewish Exegesis," 273).

(4) the Christians who allegorized everything. The preference of ibn Ezra was for the simple sense of the text—the result of scientific study of Hebrew and of reason. "For only a consistent application of the laws of the Hebrew language and of logic can lead to an understanding of the plain meaning of the text."[22] For ibn Ezra, an allegorical meaning alongside the literal one was only acceptable with the Song of Songs.

Rosenthal credits Don Isaac Abravanel (1437–1508 CE) with being the last medieval commentator of outstanding merit. Abravanel was well versed in the works of earlier Jewish and Christian exegetes. Like his medieval Jewish predecessors, he was committed to the *peshat* and did not appeal to figurative explanations unless the simple sense was contrary to reason. According to Rosenthal, it was the Jewish expulsion from Spain that prompted Abravanel to pay careful attention to messianic prophecies in the biblical text. Abravanel believed that these prophecies were not fulfilled during the time of the Second Temple as the Christians believed. Rather, they were soon to be fulfilled in order to bring Jewish suffering to an end. Since Christians believed that the first coming of Christ was the inauguration of the last days and not the exhaustive fulfillment of biblical prophecy, Abravanel's view was not entirely at odds with christological or Christian messianic interpretation.

Lastly, Rosenthal turns to the philosophical and mystical explanations of the Hebrew Bible from Jewish interpreters during the High Middle Ages. Saadia Gaon had tried to balance reason with the tradition that he received, but "his successors often set aside the plain meaning through reading Aristotelian concepts into the Bible."[23] For Maimonides (1138–1204 CE) and his philosophical interpretation of the Bible, the Bible's figurative meaning was in agreement with Aristotle. Rosenthal comments, "Philosophical speculation was considered dangerous, but in the skilful hands of Maimonides and Gersonides it appealed to those intellectuals who had fallen under the spell of Aristotelian philosophy and could thus retain their loyalty to Judaism on the intellectual plane."[24] With regard to the mystical movement, Rosenthal says that Nachmanides (Ramban, 1195–1270 CE) gave it its most profound expression in his commentary on the Torah. The *peshat* is still predominant, but the commentary is filled with mystical allusions. Rosenthal notes that Nachmanides' disciple Bahya ben Asher (1255–1340 CE) employed in his

---

22. Rosenthal, "Medieval Jewish Exegesis," 273.
23. Rosenthal, "Medieval Jewish Exegesis," 276.
24. Rosenthal, "Medieval Jewish Exegesis," 276.

commentary four methods of exegesis. These four methods corresponded to the four Christian modes of interpretation (literal, typological, allegorical, and mystical), adapted to Jewish concepts and needs. Thus, the biblical text could have more than one meaning, but the multiple meanings had to coexist, and they could not overrule the literal meaning.

Rosenthal concludes by tracing the influence of the medieval Jewish commentators through the work of the Christian Hebraist Sebastian Münster (1488–1552 CE) to the making of the Authorized Version (KJV, 1611). Münster was taught by Conrad Pellicanus (1478–1556 CE), a disciple of Reuchlin, and by his Jewish teacher Elijah Levita (1469–1549 CE). When Münster made his Latin translation of the Hebrew Bible, he consulted first of all the Targum, which he found to be clearer than the Hebrew text. He also checked the commentaries of the great medieval Jewish exegetes. Münster's work had a profound impact on the making of the King James Version, which became the standard English translation for Protestants for the next four hundred years: "Reverence for the word of God prompted the translators of the Authorized Version to apply linguistic and historical analysis to their task, in which they allowed themselves to be guided by medieval Jewish grammatical and exegetical works."[25]

Rosenthal's account demonstrates that the *peshat* received by Jews and Christians from the medieval Jewish commentators was for the most part one that differed from traditional Jewish and Christian exegesis when it came to messianic prophecies. The simple or literal sense was often redefined as the non-messianic sense,[26] and there was certainly no allowance for a specifically christological sense even where a general messianic sense was admitted. For Jews, this resulted in somewhat of a diminishing of the Bible's messianism. For Christians, it meant that the literal sense of the Hebrew Bible had to be supplemented in some way in order for it to function as Christian Scripture.[27] For later critical scholars, it meant that a christological interpretation (and often even broadly eschatological and/or messianic interpretation) could not be received as legitimate or historically accurate. Generally lacking from this was any kind of robust or concerted effort to

25. Rosenthal, "Medieval Jewish Exegesis," 279.

26. This may be seen, for example, in Calvin's commentary on Gen 3:15 in which he jettisons the messianic interpretations of ancient Jewish and Christian tradition.

27. "The peshat meaning of the text was not as transparently Christological as it had been to the earlier Reformers. There was now a need for an additional sense in which the Hebrew Bible could be related to Christ and the NT" (Sailhamer, *Introduction to Old Testament Theology*, 140).

show that christological interpretation was in many ways consistent with the earlier traditions preserved by the Targums and with the brand of *peshat* exegesis championed by commentators like Redak.

The few examples where Christian interpreters attempted to show that their understanding of the literal sense was equivalent to the messianic sense were less than stellar to say the least.[28] It is thus understandable that such efforts did not become widely influential in academic circles. One such example is Martin Luther's 1543 treatise *On the Last Words of David: 2 Samuel 23:1–7*. William Marsh observes that this treatise was "motivated by polemical interests, specifically against Jewish and rabbinic interpretations of the OT that were holding sway over Christian Hebraists."[29] Luther rightly wanted to temper uncritical use of Jewish exegetical methods, but the way in which he went about this left much to be desired. Luther believed that possession of the New Testament put Christians in a better position to understand the Old Testament than those who knew the details of the Hebrew text.[30] This left Luther open to the accusation that he was simply reading the New Testament back into the Old Testament, even if this was not exactly what he meant.[31] Luther wanted to argue for a holistic reading of the Bible (OT + NT), but it was counterproductive for him to pit knowledge of the New Testament against knowledge of the Hebrew text. If he wanted to demonstrate continuity and coherence, it would have been better for him to show the necessity of a firm grasp of the Hebrew language for an understanding of the messianic sense yielded by the grammar and syntax of the biblical text, thereby paving the way for a greater appreciation of the New Testament authors' exegetical warrant in their appeal to these texts to explain Jesus. It is not the New Testament that explains the Hebrew Bible. Rather, it is the Hebrew Bible that explains Jesus. Luther's exposition of 2 Sam 23:1–7 focused on connections to the covenant with David (2 Sam 7; 1 Chr 17) and the promise of the seed in Gen 3:15.[32] Of course, he wanted to show that the literal sense of the text was not merely about David (see, e.g., Rashi et al.). It was a messianic prophecy that came to David by the Holy

---

28. John Calvin's commentaries were probably the most sustained and successful attempt from the Reformation period, but later critical scholars like Richard Simon were quick to dismiss him as theologically prejudiced (see McKane, *Selected Christian Hebraists*, 139).

29. Marsh, *Martin Luther on Reading the Bible*, 164.

30. Marsh, *Martin Luther on Reading the Bible*, 166–67.

31. Marsh, *Martin Luther on Reading the Bible*, 182–92.

32. Marsh, *Martin Luther on Reading the Bible*, 168–73.

Spirit.[33] Luther failed to recognize that such an understanding of the text was already prepared for him in the Targum and in Redak's commentary. Furthermore, Luther barely scratched the surface of the textual, exegetical, and intertextual issues of the passage in Hebrew (see previously). Ironically, if he had addressed these more adequately and acknowledged the value of the Jewish exegetical tradition, his case for the messianic sense as the literal sense would have been more convincing and long-lasting.[34]

McKane's survey of selected Christian Hebraists (Andrew of St. Victor, William Fulke, Gregory Martin, Richard Simon, and Alexander Geddes) follows the path of influence that led to the rise of historical criticism.[35] Andrew of St. Victor (d. 1175 CE) had only a very limited knowledge of Hebrew, but his interest in Jewish exegesis mediated to him a notion of what the *peshat* or simple sense of the text was.[36] According to McKane, Andrew's pursuit of the literal sense anticipated issues that would later emerge in critical biblical scholarship and "pushed into the foreground an exegesis of the Old Testament which does not have a Christian sense."[37] McKane at-

33. Marsh, *Martin Luther on Reading the Bible*, 175–80.

34. "By paying careful attention to the compositional strategies of the biblical books themselves, we believe in them can be found many essential clues to the meaning intended by their authors—clues that point beyond their immediate historical referent to a future, messianic age" (Sailhamer, *Introduction to Old Testament Theology*, 154). "In other words, the literal meaning of Scripture (*sensus literalis*) may, in fact, be the spiritual sense (*sensus spiritualis*) intended by the author, namely, the messianic sense picked up in the NT books" (Sailhamer, *Introduction to Old Testament Theology*, 154).

35. McKane, *Selected Christian Hebraists*.

36. "The production of Jewish interpretations for texts which were alleged to have no other sense but a Christological one set the alarm bells sounding" (McKane, *Selected Christian Hebraists*, 192).

37. McKane, *Selected Christian Hebraists*, 42. "The Church had adopted the Septuagint as a Christian Bible and it was inevitable that a Christian significance should be attached to its contents. The Hebrew Bible was always difficult and sometimes impossible to reconcile with a just treatment of its historical and human dimensions, because Christological exegesis, operating in a vacuum and acquiring the advantage of timeless truth, disengages the Old Testament from its historical moorings and dehumanizes it. Moreover, such exegesis is difficult to reconcile with the fact that the Hebrew Bible belonged to Israel and to the Jews before it belonged to the Church and that thereafter it belonged to both the Synagogue and the Church" (McKane, *Selected Christian Hebraists*, 4). McKane's comments here are based on two faulty assumptions. The first is that all christological exegesis is of the same type, a kind of eisegesis that does not do justice to the literal sense of the text. The second is that the Hebrew Bible is first and foremost a "Jewish" book as if it were the product of the postbiblical religion of Judaism. The Hebrew Bible would be better characterized as the product of the prophets, and the real issue is whether this or

taches importance to Andrew's exegesis "because it enhances the humanity of Old Testament literature by interpreting it in a historical context and a human world."[38] On the other hand, Andrew could also be characterized as shortsighted and limited in his approach to the plain sense of the text.

McKane presents William Fulke (1538–89 CE) and Gregory Martin (1542–82 CE) in conversation with one another:

> When he [Fulke] urges that the Christological interpretation of the Old Testament has gone too far and counters Martin's exegesis in particular cases, he uses the tools of humanist scholarship and fashions his arguments in agreement with what he regards as biblical science. The point which he finally makes against Martin is, however, a theological one, namely, that the sense at which he has arrived, and not the Christological sense advanced by Martin, is the one intended by the Holy Ghost.[39]

Fulke was impressed by Jewish biblical scholarship and believed that Christians must yield to the knowledge of Hebrew possessed by Jewish scholars.[40] He affirmed Jerome's efforts to translate directly from the Hebrew into Latin, but the Latin Vulgate did not replace the Hebrew text, nor was it beyond improvement.[41] Fulke wanted to see production of a variety of new English translations made from the Hebrew original not in order to arrive at the perfect translation but to establish a continual process of revising the translations on the basis of the best resources available in current Hebrew scholarship.[42] Martin, on the other hand, preferred the English translations made from the Latin Vulgate, and he was concerned that new translations made from a different source would cause a loss of confidence in the reliability and authority of the old translations. In this, Martin echoed the pastoral concerns of Augustine who had expressed objection to Jerome's work due to his expectation that a new Latin translation made from the Hebrew would cause problems in churches accustomed to the Old Latin translation made from the Greek of the Septuagint.[43] Neither Fulke nor Martin sought to defend the messianic sense as the literal sense of the Hebrew text.

____

that community stood in continuity with the texts that they received.

38. McKane, *Selected Christian Hebraists*, 68.

39. McKane, *Selected Christian Hebraists*, 5.

40. McKane, *Selected Christian Hebraists*, 93.

41. McKane, *Selected Christian Hebraists*, 97.

42. McKane, *Selected Christian Hebraists*, 98–99.

43. There was also a concern on Martin's part to protect ecclesiastical authority and

In McKane's opinion, Richard Simon (1638–1712 CE) was "the most consummate scholar of the selected Hebraists."[44] Unlike the majority of his predecessors, Simon recognized that the Hebrew text known in his day (the MT) was not the only Hebrew text in antiquity. He saw that many of the differences between the MT and the LXX were not due to the work of the Greek translators but to the presence of different Hebrew source texts from which the translators were working.[45] Simon realized that his survival as a critical scholar in a confessional environment depended upon making a clear separation between biblical scholarship and traditional Catholic orthodoxy. He did not, however, seek to accept one and reject the other. Rather, he wanted to compartmentalize the two so that he could work in complete autonomy as a biblical scholar, unfettered by Christian doctrine.[46] Simon did not renounce traditional Christian interpretation of the Bible. He simply argued that such interpretation was the domain of church tradition, while biblical scholarship had its own separate work to do (i.e., the literal or historical sense).[47] "The direction in which all this points is a study

---

the traditional interpretation of the biblical text as represented by Vulgate over against the potential multiplication of interpretations among the common people: "Martin's complaint about the 'profanity' or 'secularity' of the language in the new English versions is not only or principally a linguistic or aesthetic one. It acquires its importance for him because the vocabulary which is disappearing has a technical, ecclesiastical significance, or is related in other respects to crucial aspects of biblical interpretation. Vocabulary, present in the Vulgate, which sustains Christological interpretation of Old Testament texts is a particular cause of concern to Martin, and in these cases 'profanity' in English translations is seen by him as an erosion of the Christological content of the Old Testament" (McKane, *Selected Christian Hebraists*, 80).

44. McKane, *Selected Christian Hebraists*, 7.

45. "Simon will have nothing to do with extreme views which aim to discredit either the Massoretic text or the Septuagint. We are not to say 'only the Hebrew' with the Jews, or 'only the Septuagint' with some Christians; or 'only the Vulgate'. Both the Hebrew text and the versions are to be used and judgements are to be made 'according to the rules of criticism'" (McKane, *Selected Christian Hebraists*, 125). See also Shepherd, "Is the Septuagint?," 149–64.

46. "[H]is concern is not to explain how scripture and tradition interact, but to secure autonomy for the critical study of the Hebrew Bible" (McKane, *Selected Christian Hebraists*, 146).

47. "'We must then,' he says, 'seek the truth of the Christian religion in the commentaries of the earliest Fathers on scripture rather than a literal exegesis of the Bible'" (McKane, *Selected Christian Hebraists*, 145). Simon was wary of the Jewish *peshat* as a response to Christian interpretation (McKane, *Selected Christian Hebraists*, 119), and he urged improvement upon Jewish biblical scholarship. Nevertheless, he was indirectly and unwittingly an heir of the medieval Jewish *peshat* in his insistence upon a historical

of the Hebrew Bible whose assumptions are humanist and scientific and whose goal is the ascertaining of the plain sense."[48] This kind of distinction between church and academy is now standard fare in the modern setting.[49] Faith-based interpretation is left to the church (or synagogue), and academic study of the Bible has its place in the university. Those who seek to marry faith and academic study of the Bible are relegated to the fringes of the scholarly world.

In contrast to Simon, Alexander Geddes (1737–1802 CE) did not see a place for the continuance of Christian orthodoxy, even if it was separate and distinct from biblical scholarship.[50] Geddes wanted to replace the traditions of Christian doctrine with a new version of the faith founded upon reason: "He was now nursing an elitist hope of a gathering of thoughtful Christians from all the sects to embrace a new Christianity in a temple of reason, where only religious belief recommended by reason would be demanded."[51] Like Simon, Geddes believed that Christian Hebraism needed to advance beyond what it had inherited from Jewish scholarship, but this did not take the form of addressing the problems associated with the non-messianic *peshat*.[52] Indeed, neither Geddes nor any of McKane's selected Christian Hebraists did anything to renew or instill confidence in a literal sense that was messianic or christological.[53]

---

sense of the Bible that was independent from Christian interpretation. Simon did, however, accept a dual literal sense (historical [David] and messianic [Christ]) for some texts like Gen 49:10 (McKane, *Selected Christian Hebraists*, 145).

48. McKane, *Selected Christian Hebraists*, 149.

49. "It is not difficult to discern that this is a highway along which Old Testament scholarship has in fact advanced and that Simon, in so far as he mapped out this route, showed remarkable prescience" (McKane, *Selected Christian Hebraists*, 149).

50. "In many respects the range of Geddes's critical interests is comparable with that of Simon, but he is not satisfied with the objective of critical autonomy and he invades the sphere of Christian theology with his 'rational principles' in a manner foreign to Simon" (McKane, *Selected Christian Hebraists*, 182).

51. McKane, *Selected Christian Hebraists*, 160.

52. "When specimens of his exegetical work, whether from his Critical Remarks or from his Psalms, are examined, it is evident that he has little time for Christological interpretation of Old Testament texts, even though he is aware that such a tradition of interpretation had been attached to them within the Church" (McKane, *Selected Christian Hebraists*, 184).

53. "[O]nce the assumptions and methods of a critical scholarship, essentially humanist in conception, were applied by Christian scholars to the Hebrew Bible, the antithesis of Jewish and Christian exegesis gave way to a differently organized antithesis of historical-critical exegesis and Christian exegesis" (McKane, Selected Christian Hebraists, 193).

CONCLUSION

When viewed in light of the larger history of interpretation, the immense value of the messianic renderings preserved in the Targums becomes even more apparent. Not only do they bridge the gap between ancient Jewish and Christian interpretation, but also they bear witness to a long-standing tradition of serious biblical scholarship that received the Hebrew Bible as a messianic document. They remind interpreters that it is not necessary to accept the medieval redefinition of the literal sense as the non-messianic sense, which requires either artificial Christian supplementation or capitulation to the tenets of historical criticism. It is possible after all that the messianic sense of the text may very well be the authentic literal sense.

What was needed in response to this *critica profana* was not only a *critica sacra* but also one that specifically addressed the issue of the Bible's messianism. This was provided to a certain extent by the work of the Protestant scholastics, but their work did not have a lasting effect on biblical scholarship.

Bibliography

Alexander, Philip S. "Jewish Aramaic Translations of Hebrew Scriptures." In *Mikra: Text, Translation, Reading & Interpretation of the Hebrew Bible in Ancient Judaism & Early Christianity*, edited by Martin Jan Mulder and Harry Sysling, 217–53. 1988. Reprint, Peabody, MA: Hendrickson, 2004.

———. "The King Messiah in Rabbinic Judaism." In *King and Messiah in Israel and the Ancient Near East: Proceedings of the Oxford Old Testament Seminar*, edited by John Day, 456–73. Sheffield: Sheffield Academic Press, 1998.

Anderson, Gary. "The Interpretation of Genesis 1:1 in the Targums." *CBQ* 52 (1990) 21–29.

Bacher, Wilhelm. *Die exegetische Terminologie der jüdischen Traditionsliteratur*. 1899, 1905. Reprint, Hildesheim, Germ.: Olms, 1965.

Barr, James. "Which Language Did Jesus Speak?—Some Remarks of a Semitist." *BJRL* 53 (1970) 9–29.

Blaising, Craig A., and Carmen S. Harding, eds. *Psalms 1–50*. ACCS 7. Downers Grove, IL: InterVarsity, 2008.

Block, Daniel I. *The Book of Ezekiel: Chapters 1–24*. NICOT. Grand Rapids, MI: Eerdmans, 1997.

———. *The Book of Ezekiel: Chapters 25–48*. NICOT. Grand Rapids, MI: Eerdmans, 1997.

Boyarin, Daniel. *Intertextuality and the Reading of Midrash*. Bloomington, IN: Indiana University Press, 1990.

Brady, Christian M. M. *The Rabbinic Targum of Lamentations: Vindicating God*. Leiden, The Neth.: Brill, 2003.

Brown, Raymond E. *The Gospel according to John I–XII*. AB 29. New York: Doubleday, 1966.

Buisch, Pauline Paris. "The Rest of Her Offspring: The Relationship between Revelation 12 and the Targumic Expansion of Genesis 3:15." *NovT* 60 (2018) 386–401.

Bynum, William Randolph. *The Fourth Gospel and the Scriptures: Illuminating the Form and Meaning of Scriptural Citation in John 19:37*. NovTSup 144. Leiden, The Neth.: Brill, 2012.

Calvin, John. *Commentaries on the First Book of Moses Called Genesis*. Vol. 2. Translated by John King. Calvin's Commentaries 1. N.d. Reprint, Grand Rapids, MI: Baker, 2005.

———. *Commentaries on the First Twenty Chapters of the Book of the Prophet Ezekiel*. Vol. 2. Translated by Thomas Myers. Calvin's Commentaries 12. N.d. Reprint, Grand Rapids, MI: Baker, 2005.

———. *Commentary on the Book of the Prophet Isaiah*. Vol. 1. Translated by William Pringle. Calvin's Commentaries 7. N.d. Reprint, Grand Rapids, MI: Baker, 2005.

Cargill, Robert R. "The Rule of Creative Completion: Neofiti's Use of שכלל." *AS* 10 (2012) 173–91.

Carson, D. A. "Syntactical and Text-Critical Observations on John 20:30–31: One More Round on the Purpose of the Fourth Gospel." *JBL* 124 (2005) 693–714.

Cathcart, Kevin J., and Robert P. Gordon. *The Targum of the Minor Prophets: Translated, with a Critical Introduction, Apparatus, and Notes*. The Aramaic Bible 14. Collegeville, MN: Liturgical, 1989.

Chapman, Stephen B. *The Law and the Prophets: A Study in Old Testament Canon Formation*. FAT 27. Tübingen, Germ.: Mohr Siebeck, 2000.

Childs, Brevard S. *The Book of Exodus: A Critical, Theological Commentary*. OTL. Louisville: Westminster John Knox, 1974.

———. *Introduction to the Old Testament as Scripture*. Philadelphia: Fortress, 1979.

———. *Isaiah: A Commentary. Old Testament Library*. Louisville: Westminster John Knox, 2000.

Chilton, Bruce D. *The Glory of Israel: The Theology and Provenience of the Isaiah Targum*. JSOTSup 23. Sheffield: JSOT, 1983.

———. *The Isaiah Targum: Introduction, Translation, Apparatus and Notes*. The Aramaic Bible 11. Collegeville, MN: Liturgical, 1987.

———. *Judaic Approaches to the Gospels*. Atlanta: Scholars, 1994.

Churgin, Pinkhos. *Tg. Jon. to the Prophets*. Yale Oriental Series 14. 1927. Reprint, Library of Biblical Studies. New York: Ktav, 1983.

Clarke, E. G., ed. *Targum Pseudo-Jonathan of the Pentateuch: Text and Concordance*. Hoboken, NJ: Ktav, 1984.

Cole, Robert L. *Psalms 1 and 2: Gateway to the Psalter*. Sheffield, UK: Sheffield Phoenix, 2013.

Collins, John J. *The Scepter and the Star: Messianism in Light of the Dead Sea Scrolls*. 2nd ed. Grand Rapids, MI: Eerdmans, 2010.

Delitzsch, Franz. *Isaiah*. Translated by James Martin. Keil & Delitzsch Commentary on the Old Testament 7. 1866–91. Reprint, Peabody, MA: Hendrickson, 2001.

Díez Macho, Alejandro, ed. *Neophyti 1: Targum Palestinense MS. de la Biblioteca Vaticana*. 6 vols. Madrid: Consejo Superior de Investigaciones Científicas, 1968–79.

Driver, S. R. *Notes on the Hebrew Text and the Topography of the Books of Samuel with an Introduction on Hebrew Palaeography and the Ancient Versions and Facsimiles of Inscriptions and Maps*. 2nd ed. Oxford: Oxford University Press, 1912.

Edwards, Timothy. *Exegesis in the Targum of the Psalms: The Old, the New, and the Rewritten*. Piscataway, NJ: Gorgias, 2007.

Elgvin, Torleif. *Warrior, King, Servant, Savior: Messianism in the Hebrew Bible and Early Jewish Texts*. Grand Rapids, MI: Eerdmans, 2022.

Elliott, Mark W., ed. *Isaiah 40–66*. ACCS 11. Downers Grove, IL: InterVarsity, 2007.

Evans, Craig. "The Aramaic Psalter and the New Testament: Praising the Lord in History and Prophecy." In *From Prophecy to Testament: The Function of the Old Testament in the New*, edited by Craig A. Evans, 44–91. Peabody, MA: Hendrickson, 2004.

———. *Word and Glory: On the Exegetical and Theological Background of John's Prologue*. JSNTSup 89. Sheffield: JSOT, 1993.

Ferreiro, Alberto, ed. *The Twelve Prophets*. ACCS 14. Downers Grove, IL: InterVarsity, 2003.

Fischer, Georg. *Jeremiah Studies: From Text and Contexts to Theology*. FAT 139. Tübingen, Germ.: Mohr Siebeck, 2020.

Fishbane, Michael. *Biblical Interpretation in Ancient Israel*. Oxford: Clarendon, 1985.

Flesher, Paul V. McCracken, "The Targumim in the Context of Rabbinic Literature." In *Introduction to Rabbinic Literature*, by Jacob Neusner, 611–29. New York: Doubleday, 1994.

Flesher, Paul V. McCracken, and Bruce Chilton. *The Targums: A Critical Introduction*. Waco, TX: Baylor University Press, 2011.

Freedman, H., trans. *Midrash Rabbah*. Vol. 1, *Genesis*. 3rd ed. London: Soncino, 1983.

Gray, George B. *A Critical and Exegetical Commentary on the Book of Isaiah*. New York: Scribner's, 1912.

Grossfeld, Bernard. *Targum Neofiti*. Vol. 1, *An Exegetical Commentary to Genesis: Including Full Rabbinic Parallels*. New York: Sepher Hermon, 2000.

Harrington, Daniel J. "The Apocalypse of Hannah: Tg. Jon. of 1 Samuel 2:1–10." In *Working with No Data: Semitic and Egyptian Studies Presented to Thomas O. Lambdin*, edited by David M. Golomb, 147–52. Winona Lake, IN: Eisenbrauns, 1987.

Harrington, Daniel J., and Anthony J. Saldarini. *Targum Jonathan of the Former Prophets: Introduction, Translation and Notes*. The Aramaic Bible 10. Collegeville, MN: Liturgical, 1987.

Horbury, William. *Jewish Messianism and the Cult of Christ*. London: SCM, 1998.

Kahle, Paul E. *The Cairo Geniza*. 2nd ed. New York: Praeger, 1960.

Kasher, Rimon. "The Interpretation of Scripture in Rabbinic Literature." In *Mikra: Text, Translation, Reading and Interpretation of the Hebrew Bible in Ancient Judaism and Early Christianity*, edited by Martin Jan Mulder and Harry Sysling, 547–94. 1988. Reprint, Peabody, MA: Hendrickson, 2004.

Keil, C. F. *The Books of Samuel*. Translated by James Martin. Keil & Delitzsch Commentary on the Old Testament 2. 1866–91. Reprint, Peabody, MA, 2001.

———. *Ezekiel*. Translated by James Martin. Keil & Delitzsch Commentary on the Old Testament 9. 1866–91. Reprint, Peabody, MA: Hendrickson, 2001.

———. *The Minor Prophets*. Translated by James Martin. Keil & Delitzsch Commentary on the Old Testament 10. 1866–91. Reprint, Peabody, MA: Hendrickson, 2001.

———. *The Pentateuch*. Translated by James Martin. Keil & Delitzsch Commentary on the Old Testament 1. 1866–91. Reprint, Peabody, MA: Hendrickson, 2001.

Klein, Michael L., ed. *The Fragment-Targums of the Pentateuch: According to Their Extant Sources*. 2 vols. AnBib 76. Rome: Biblical Institute Press, 1980.

Lauterbach, Jacob Z. *Mekhilta de-Rabbi Ishmael: A Critical Edition, Based on the Manuscripts and Early Editions, with an English Translation, Introduction, and Notes*. Vol. 2. 2nd ed. Philadelphia: Jewish Publication Society, 2004.

Legrand, Thierry. "À propos d'un messianisme qui divise: Targum Genèse 49.8–12." *AS* 12 (2014) 32–52.

Levey, Samson H. *The Messiah: An Aramaic Interpretation: The Messianic Exegesis of the Targum*. HUCM 2. Cincinnati: Hebrew Union College Press, 1974.

Levine, Étan. "The Targums: Their Interpretive Character and Their Place in Jewish Text Tradition." In *Hebrew Bible/Old Testament: The History of Its Interpretation: From the Beginnings to the Middle Ages (Until 1300): Part 1, Antiquity*, edited by Magne Sæbø, 1:323–31. Göttingen, Germ.: Vandenhoeck & Ruprecht, 1996.

Levison, John. "Prophecy in Ancient Israel: The Case of Ecstatic Elders." *CBQ* 65 (2003) 503–21.

Levy, B. Barry. *Targum Neophyti 1: A Textual Study*. Vol. 2, *Leviticus, Numbers, Deuteronomy*. Studies in Judaism 2. Lanham, MD: University Press of America, 1986.

Longman, Tremper, III. *The Book of Ecclesiastes*. NICOT. Grand Rapids, MI: Eerdmans, 1998.

Lust, Johan. "Iezekiel/Ezechiel/Ezekiel." In *Introduction to the Septuagint*, edited by Siegfried Kreuzer, translated by David A. Brenner and Peter Altmann, 565–82. Waco, TX: Baylor University Press, 2019.

Marsh, William M. *Martin Luther on Reading the Bible as Christian Scripture: The Messiah in Luther's Biblical Hermeneutic and Theology*. Eugene, OR: Pickwick, 2017.

Mays, James L. "The Place of Torah Psalms in the Psalter." *JBL* 106 (1987) 3–12.

McCarter, P. Kyle. *2 Samuel: A New Translation with Introduction and Commentary*. AB 9. New Haven: Yale University Press, 1984.

McConville, J. G. *Deuteronomy*. ApOTC 5. Downers Grove, IL: InterVarsity, 2002.

McKane, William. *A Critical and Exegetical Commentary on Jeremiah*. 2 vols. International Critical Commentary. London: Bloomsbury T. & T. Clark, 1986, 1996.

———. *Selected Christian Hebraists*. Cambridge: Cambridge University Press, 1988.

McKinion, Steven A., ed. *Isaiah 1–39*. ACCS 10. Downers Grove, IL: InterVarsity, 2003.

McNamara, Martin. *The New Testament and the Palestinian Targum to the Pentateuch*. AnBib 27. Rome: Pontifical Biblical Institute, 1966.

———. *Targum and Testament Revisited: Aramaic Paraphrase of the Hebrew Bible: A Light on the New Testament*. 2nd ed. Grand Rapids, MI: Eerdmans, 2010.

———. *Targum Neofiti 1: Genesis*. The Aramaic Bible 1A. Collegeville, MN: Liturgical, 1987.

Peterson, Brian Neil. *John's Use of Ezekiel: Understanding the Unique Perspective of the Fourth Gospel*. Minneapolis: Fortress, 2015.

Petterson, Anthony R. "A New Form-Critical Approach to Zechariah's Crowning of the High Priest Joshua and the Identity of 'Shoot.'" In *The Book of the Twelve & the New Form Criticism*, edited by Mark J. Boda et al., 285–304. Atlanta: SBL, 2015.

Parke-Taylor, Geoffrey H. *The Formation of the Book of Jeremiah: Doublets and Recurring Phrases*. SBLMS 51. Atlanta: SBL, 2000.

Polliack, Meira. "Jewish Arabic Translations." In *Textual History of the Bible: The Hebrew Bible*, edited by Armin Lange and Emanuel Tov, 1A:289–309. Leiden, The Neth.: Brill, 2016.

Rabin, Chaim. "Hebrew and Aramaic in the First Century." In *The Jewish People in the First Century*, edited by S. Safrai and M. Stern, 2:1007–37. CRINT 1. Philadelphia: Fortress, 1976.

Rad, Gerhard von. *Old Testament Theology*. Vol. 2, *The Theology of Israel's Prophetic Traditions*. Translated by D. M. G. Stalker. New York: Harper & Row, 1965.

Reventlow, Henning Graf. *History of Biblical Interpretation*. Vol. 3, *Renaissance, Reformation, Humanism*. Translated by James O. Duke. Atlanta: SBL, 2009.

Roberts, J. J. M. *Nahum, Habakkuk, and Zephaniah*. OTL. Louisville: Westminster John Knox, 1991.

Rosenberg, A. J., trans. *Mikraoth Gedoloth: Ezekiel, Vol. 1*. New York: Judaica, 1991.

———, trans. *Mikraoth Gedoloth: Isaiah, Vol. 1*. New York: Judaica, 1982.

———, trans. *Mikraoth Gedoloth: Isaiah, Vol. 2*. New York: Judaica, 1983.

———, trans. *Mikraoth Gedoloth: Jeremiah, Vol. 2*. New York: Judaica, 1989.

———, trans. *Mikraoth Gedoloth: The Twelve Prophets, Vol. 1*. New York: Judaica, 1986.

———, trans. *Mikraoth Gedoloth: The Twelve Prophets, Vol. 2.* New York: Judaica, 1996.

Rosenthal, Erwin I. J. "Medieval Jewish Exegesis: Its Character and Significance." *JSS* 9 (1964) 264–81.

Sailhamer, John H. "Biblical Theology and the Composition of the Hebrew Bible." In *Biblical Theology: Retrospect and Prospect,* edited by Scott J. Hafemann, 25–37. Downers Grove, IL: InterVarsity, 2002.

———. *The Books of the Bible.* Grand Rapids, MI: Zondervan, 1998.

———. "Hosea 11:1 and Matthew 2:15." *WTJ* 63 (2001) 87–96.

———. *Introduction to Old Testament Theology: A Canonical Approach.* Grand Rapids, MI: Zondervan, 1995.

———. *The Meaning of the Pentateuch: Revelation, Composition and Interpretation.* Downers Grove, IL: InterVarsity, 2009.

———. *NIV Compact Bible Commentary.* Grand Rapids, MI: Zondervan, 1994.

———. *The Pentateuch as Narrative: A Biblical-Theological Commentary.* Grand Rapids, MI: Zondervan, 1992.

Samely, Alexander. *The Interpretation of Speech in the Pentateuchal Targums: A Study of Method and Presentation in Targumic Exegesis.* TSAJ 27. Tübingen, Germ.: Mohr Siebeck, 1992.

Schiffman, Lawrence. *Reclaiming the Dead Sea Scrolls: the History of Judaism, the Background of Christianity, the Lost Library of Qumran.* New York: Doubleday, 1995.

Screnock, John. "A New Approach to Using the Old Greek in Hebrew Bible Textual Criticism." *Textus* 27 (2018) 229–57.

Seeligmann, Isac Leo. *Gesammelte Studien zur Hebräischen Bibel.* Forschungen zum Alten Testament 41. Tübingen, Germ.: Mohr Siebeck, 2004.

———. *The Septuagint Version of Isaiah and Cognate Studies.* FAT 40. Tübingen, Germ.: Mohr Siebeck, 2004.

Seitz, Christopher R. *The Goodly Fellowship of the Prophets: The Achievement of Association in Canon Formation.* Grand Rapids, MI: Baker, 2009.

Shepherd, Michael B. *A Commentary on the Book of Jeremiah.* KEL. Grand Rapids, MI: Kregel Academic, 2023.

———. *A Commentary on the Book of the Twelve: The Minor Prophets.* KEL. Grand Rapids, MI: Kregel Academic, 2018.

———. *Daniel in the Context of the Hebrew Bible.* StBib Lit 123. New York: Lang, 2009.

———. "Daniel 7:13 and the New Testament Son of Man." *WTJ* 68 (2006) 99–111.

———. "Is the Septuagint the Christian Bible?" *TJ* 41 (2020) 149–64.

———. "Semitic Wordplay behind the Greek of the New Testament." In *New Testament Philology: Essays in Honor of David Alan Black,* edited by Melton Bennett Winstead, 52–68. Eugene, OR: Pickwick, 2018.

———. "Targums." In *Dictionary of Jesus and the Gospels,* edited by Joel B. Green et al., 931–34. 2nd ed. Downers Grove, IL: InterVarsity, 2013.

———. "Targums as Guides to Hebrew Syntax." *Themelios* 47 (2022) 49–59.

———. "Targums, the New Testament, and Biblical Theology of the Messiah." *JETS* 51 (2008) 45–58.

———. *The Text in the Middle.* StBibLit 162. New York: Lang, 2014.

———. *The Textual World of the Bible.* StBibLit 156. New York: Lang, 2013.

Smolar, Leivy, and Moses Aberbach. *Studies in Targum Jonathan to the Prophets.* Library of Biblical Studies. New York: Ktav, 1983.

Sperber, Alexander, ed. *The Bible in Aramaic: Based on Old Manuscripts and Printed Texts.* 5 vols. Leiden, The Neth.: Brill, 1959–68.

Stec, David M. *The Targum of Psalms: Translated, with a Critical Introduction, Apparatus, and Notes.* The Aramaic Bible 16. Collegeville, MN: Liturgical, 1987.

Steinberg, Julius, and Timothy J. Stone. "The Historical Formation of the Writings in Antiquity." In *The Shape of the Writings*, edited by Julius Steinberg and Timothy J. Stone, 1–58. Siphrut: Literature and Theology of the Hebrew Scriptures 16. Winona Lake, IN: Eisenbrauns, 2015.

Steiner, Richard C. "Four Inner-Biblical Interpretations of Genesis 49:10: On the Lexical and Syntactic Ambiguities of עַד as Reflected in the Prophecies of Nathan, Ahijah, Ezekiel, and Zechariah." *JBL* 132 (2013) 33–60.

Stevenson, Kenneth, and Michael Glerup, eds. *Ezekiel, Daniel.* ACCS 13. Downers Grove, IL: InterVarsity, 2007.

Strack, Hermann L., and Paul Billerbeck. *A Commentary on the New Testament from the Talmud and Midrash.* Vol. 2. Edited and translated by Jacob N. Cerone. Bellingham, WA: Lexham Academic, 2022.

Syrén, Roger. *The Blessings in the Targums: A Study on the Targumic Interpretations of Genesis 49 and Deuteronomy 33.* Acta Akademiae Aboensis Humaniora 64.1. Abo, Finl.: Abo Akademi, 1986.

Tal, Abraham. "Is There a Raison d'Être for an Aramaic Targum in a Hebrew-Speaking Society?" *REJ* 160 (2001) 357–78.

Toorn, Karel van der. *Scribal Culture and the Making of the Hebrew Bible.* Cambridge, MA: Harvard University Press, 2007.

Tov, Emanuel. *The Greek and Hebrew Bible: Collected Essays on the Septuagint.* Atlanta: SBL, 2006.

———. *Scribal Practices and Approaches Reflected in the Texts Found in the Judean Desert.* STDJ 54. Atlanta: SBL, 2009.

———. *Textual Criticism of the Hebrew Bible.* 3rd ed. Minneapolis: Fortress, 2012.

Ulrich, Eugene. "The Absence of 'Sectarian Variants' in the Jewish Scriptural Scrolls Found at Qumran." In *The Bible as Book: The Hebrew Bible and the Judaean Desert Discoveries*, edited by Edward D. Herbert and Emanuel Tov, 179–95. New Castle, DE: Oak Knoll, 2002.

———. *The Dead Sea Scrolls and the Origins of the Bible.* Grand Rapids, MI: Eerdmans, 1999.

VanderKam, James, and Peter Flint. *The Meaning of the Dead Sea Scrolls: Their Significance for Understanding the Bible, Judaism, Jesus, and Christianity.* San Francisco: HarperSanFrancisco, 2002.

Waltke, Bruce K. "Agur's Apologia for Verbal, Plenary Inspiration: An Exegesis of Proverbs 30:1–6." In *The Challenge of Bible Translation: Communicating God's Word to the World*, edited by Glen G. Scorgie et al., 303–20. Grand Rapids, MI: Zondervan, 2003.

White, Emanuel. *A Critical Edition of the Targum of Psalms: A Computer Generated Text of Books I and II.* PhD diss., McGill University, Montreal, 1988.

Wright, N. T. *The New Testament and the People of God.* Minneapolis: Fortress, 1992.